Deborah Keп

Deborah Kerr

A Biography

MICHELANGELO CAPUA

McFarland & Company, Inc., Publishers

Jefferson, North Carolina, and London

LIBRARY OF CONGRESS CATALOGUING-IN-PUBLICATION DATA

Capua, Michelangelo, 1966–
   Deborah Kerr : a biography / Michelangelo Capua.
     p.   cm.
   Includes bibliographical references and index.

   ISBN 978-0-7864-5882-0
   softcover : 50# alkaline paper ∞

   1. Kerr, Deborah, 1921–2007.   2. Actors — Great Britain —
Biography.   I. Title.
PN2598.K627C37   2010
791.430'28092 — dc22   2010031960
[B]

British Library cataloguing data are available

Cover image: Deborah Kerr, 1953 (Photofest)

Manufactured in the United States of America

*McFarland & Company, Inc., Publishers
  Box 611, Jefferson, North Carolina 28640
  www.mcfarlandpub.com*

For
Stuart T. Williams

Table of Contents

Preface

"The English Rose," "The Ladylike" — that's how Deborah Kerr was branded by the columnists throughout her entire career. The Scottish actress once said, "That 'lady' image gets my goat! All you have to have is decent manners to be considered a Lady. You can be a terrible person — do really awful things to people — and still be thought as a lady. On the other hand I know lots of women who aren't very 'proper' but are truly ladies in their kindness and generosity."

Kerr was a dedicated actress blessed with a natural beauty that faded little over the years. She projected a cool reserve and an aura of serene perfection which often hid passion and insecurity beneath the surface. These qualities often led her to be cast as nuns, widows, nurses, governesses and women who had suffered or chosen to sacrifice themselves to others. Of her several screen governesses, the best known and most popular was Mrs. Anna Leonowens in the musical *The King and I*. However, one of the most successful roles she ever portrayed was outside her usual typecast: the sexually frustrated army wife in Fred Zinnemann's *From Here to Eternity*, which contains one of the most iconic scenes in screen history — the surfside embrace and kiss with Burt Lancaster. Kerr also holds the sad record for the most Academy Award nominations without winning, before she was presented with an honorary Oscar in 1994 for being "an artist of impeccable beauty, discipline and elegance."

Among all the actors I researched, I have never encountered an artist or a person like Deborah. Unbelievably, not a colleague, friend, relative, or journalist ever mentioned or said anything unpleasant about her character. This does not mean that Kerr was a saint, but it confirms what a genuine, compassionate, gracious human being she was on and off the

screen. Indeed, her natural modesty often appeared. In her words, "I don't
know what I'm doing acting! I think I'm too well adjusted a human being.
Not that all the actors are crazy, mind you. But there's a bravura about
them that I feel I lack…. There's not an off-beat angle to my personality
that the press-agent can publicize, poor man!" Those words were the reason
she was never tempted to write an autobiography as she further explained,
"All the same rags-to-riches, or I slept-with-so-and-so. Damned if I'm
going to say that. All successful people these days seem neurotic. Perhaps
we should stop being sorry for them and start being sorry for being so
confounded normal."

I have benefited from the help of many consultants and institutions,
and for the assistance and support of friends without whom the completion
of this project would have been impossible. I would like to thank Beatrice
Nadalutti; Yaakov Perry; Walter Federico Salazar; the fantastic staff of the
British Film Institute in London (in particular the Library Service manager
Mr. Sean Delaney); the staff of Bobst Library, New York University; the
staff of New York Public Library for the Performing Arts at Lincoln Center;
the Museum of Television and Radio of New York; the staff of the British
Library's Humanity Reading Room, St. Pancras, London; and Jerry
Ohlinger's Movie Material Store, New York.

Finally I offer my great great gratitude to my editor Stuart T. Williams
for his invaluable help and patience.

1

A Lonely Childhood

We lived in the country and at home my only playmate was my brother, Edmund, four years younger than I.
— Deborah Kerr

In spring 1914 Arthur Kerr Trimmer and his wife, Mary Jane Dodgin, took their two sons, 21-year-old Arthur Charles (Jack) and Edmund Howard (Ted), (both graduates in civil engineering from Durham University in England), to visit their friends, the Smales, in Lydney, Gloucestershire. Arthur Kerr Trimmer had met Charles Blackwell Smale years earlier during one of Smale's long walks in the countryside. Smale was, in fact, a fanatical walker. The two men shared a passion for the outdoors, along with many other activities, instantly making them good friends. The Smales had one son, John Arthur, and two pretty daughters — 21-year-old Colleen (Col) and 18-year-old Phyllis Jane. The two Smale girls fell in love with the Trimmer boys and, a few months later, became engaged. Col had recently broken her engagement to organist and famous composer Herbert Howells, who had left her for another woman. Many years later, Howells' daughter, actress Ursula Howells, told the following story.

"When I was filming a lot at Ealing Studios, there were a lot of publicity shots and they asked me to come along and choose which one I wanted. It was absolutely extraordinary because they did a shoot of Deborah Kerr on the same day, and they muddled the two of us. It was only because I thought 'I haven't got blue eyes' that I recognized what happened! Of course, we are not really alike, but photographically it was extraordinary. I often wondered who had done what with whom!"[1]

When World War I broke out, John Arthur joined the Royal Naval Air Service. Jack and Ted Trimmer were drafted and sent with the East Lancashire Regiment to Gallipoli in Turkey. Ted eventually lost his life to a sniper, while Jack was wounded and sent home. Ted's death was a profound shock for the Trimmers and for Phyllis Jane Smale, who was ready to marry him once the war ended. On July 1, 1916, Jack Trimmer returned to battle in France where he was shot through the kneecap in the Battle of Somme, in the Villers Bretoneux region of Picardy. The British troops suffered over 57,000 casualties, with nearly 20,000 dead — one of the bloodiest days in British military history. Jack's leg was amputated in a delicate emergency operation performed at the British base hospital in Étaples, outside Calais. The brave Scottish soldier's life was forever changed. A few weeks later back in England, his handicap did not stop him from marrying Colleen, who had anxiously awaited his return.

The ceremony was held on August 21, 1919, at St. Mary's Parish Church in Lydney, followed by a modest reception at the Smale home. Immediately after the wedding, Jack returned to a hospital in Roehampton to learn how to walk with a prosthetic leg. Col was at his side, giving him the courage to face those difficult days. Upon Jack's discharge from the hospital, the couple traveled to the Trimmer home in Helensburgh, Scotland, where Jack later found a job as an engineer in a construction company owned by a friend of Arthur Kerr Trimmer. In January 1921, Col became pregnant and gave birth on September 30 in a private nursing home in Hillhead, Glasgow, to a healthy, lively girl whom she named Deborah Jane. Deborah was named after her paternal great-aunt; the name Jane was in honor of Col's sister, the baby's godmother.

Deborah spent the first two years of her life at her paternal grandparents' home in Helensburgh. Like Col, she was shy and quiet. She immediately took to heart her parents' lessons to be well-mannered, disciplined and sensitive to others. In 1923, Jack, with wife and daughter, joined the rest of the Trimmer family in the small village of Alfold, Surrey. Deborah's grandfather had moved there a few weeks earlier to be closer to his three sisters. Two years later, on May 31, 1925, Col and Jack welcomed the birth of their son, Edmund Charles "Teddy." The birth of Deborah's brother was one of her first childhood memories as it brought about the traumatic loss of her parents' exclusive attention. Nevertheless, her jealousy for her little brother quickly disappeared and Edmund soon became Deborah's favorite playmate.

"When I was small, I was known as 'farthing face,'" Deborah once recalled. "My childhood was lonely. We lived in the country and at home my only playmate was my brother, Edmund, four years younger than I."

Deborah was a shy, imaginative child. She soon found that she could act out her feelings, thanks to her natural flaire for drama. At age five, she impressed her family when she suddenly did a funny impersonation of a male servant. Her brother, Edmund, remembered that Deborah was mostly satisfied when she held people's attention, dancing, singing and often dressing him up in Col's clothes, making him play the part of a girl or of a sophisticated Indian prince. When Deborah's paternal grandfather died in September 1926, Jack decided to move into the house with Deborah's paternal grandmother, Jane, who was living alone. Often Deborah's maternal grandmother, Anne, would visit her grandchildren, and both women — with their Victorian education — made life for the grandchildren miserable. Deborah remembered how her grandmother, Anne, would order her to lie on the floor for hours to straighten her back — absolute torture for Deborah's sensitive personality.

Deborah took her first ballet classes at age five. She danced in the end-of-the-year recital at the Guildford Town Hall in Sussex. As she remembered, "I was a very solemn little thing, I never smiled much, and after the dance my teacher said, 'Go on, take a bow,' I went back and did a boy's bow. And there was a roar of laughter. I never forgot it. I cried for days and I still feel awful when I remember it!"[2]

At age seven, she was enrolled in St. Martha's Kindergarten in Bramley. Since the school was so far from her home, she became a weekly boarder. She stayed at St. Martha's until 1932 when she left to attend Northumberland House Boarding School in Bristol, where her aunt Phyllis Jane Smale taught drama and elocution, after having performed one season in London with Maurice Browne.

Despite being an oversensitive child, Deborah loved being the center of the attention. She took part in all performing art activities organized at school, including a stage production of *The Mad Hatter's Tea Party* and one of *Robin Hood*, directed by her aunt, Phyllis Jane. Her greatest wish was to become famous. She avidly read movie magazines, dreaming about the Hollywood stars who seemed to possess a certain beauty she thought she would never have.

She remembered those six years at boarding school as a hellish nightmare. "At eight, I went to boarding school and I had some horrible experiences there which disfigured my childhood. For my ninth or tenth birthday, my parents gave me a beautiful box of Winsor-Newton paints. It was the first possession I ever really loved.

"I opened my desk one day to find each tube of paint squeezed out and the colors splattered across the box. The palette was smashed and glued together again haphazardly. Each of my brushes was broken in half. I could hear a few other girls whispering, 'Bet you she cries.' 'Bet you she does, too.'

"I was bullied unmercifully at school. Once I dared to head my class and bullying became almost unbearable. After that I made sure my grades were never better than third highest. Perhaps it was my own fault that I wasn't tough enough to hide my tears when a bag of water was thrown over the top of my cubicle or when the strings of my new tennis racket were cut.

"If I ever cried to mother about some childish mishap, she — being a patient woman — would hear me out.... But if my misery were all out of proportion to the mishap, she would always say: 'Never make heavy weather of things.'"[3] Deborah remembered her mother as a "red-haired angel who tirelessly administered to the family's needs."[4]

Several times during her years at Northumberland, Deborah begged her father to let her leave the school. "Pater," she said in one of her holidays at home, "if you will do me one favor, I will be your dutiful child there-inafter endlessly. Let me leave that place."[5] Although Jack did not have any serious objection, Deborah remained in that boarding school until 1937. She spent her summer vacations with her grandmother Anne, who would take her and Edmund to the Mouth of Severn's seashore. Not even on holiday would the stern old lady stop drilling her granddaughter in self-control and obedience.

At fourteen she had her first crush. The object of her affection was a handsome Welsh curate she met at confirmation classes, although the man was never aware of her feelings for him. The day of her confirmation at a small reception given by her mother, Deborah was allowed to drink her first glass of sherry, which instantly made her tipsy, causing general hilarity among the guests.

On August 26, 1937, Deborah faced the most devastating news when she learned that her father, age 43, died of tuberculosis after two decades of failing health. Although she had always been closer to her mother, Deborah never felt more alone. "I knew him and yet I didn't know him" she said later.[6] "It was accepted with a terrible feeling of fate, that I would either dance or act." Her father, a frustrated writer, had wanted her to write. "I was a prolific writer when I was a little girl," she revealed many years later, although she never met her father's literary ambitions for her.[7] Deborah formed a tighter bond with her aunt, Phyllis Jane. Phyllis Jane become a great source of support and encouraged her to pursue her natural aptitude for acting, which she was already showing at school. "I didn't have an opportunity to see many of the arts when I was a girl," Deborah recalled. But I remember my mother taking me to see a production of *Romeo and Juliet* in which Sir Laurence Olivier and Sir John Gielgud alternated every other week, playing Romeo and Tybalt [*sic* Mercutio]. Dame Edith Evans and Dame Peggy Ashcroft were also in the play: seeing that production was embedded in my mind forever."[8]

Deborah began to work harder at improving her grades and was finally able to make a couple of good friends despite the bullying episodes.

At home the death of Jack Trimmer left Col with very little money in the face of her husband's unfinished business. Eventually, with financial help coming from a wealthy uncle, Col was able to sort out all the family affairs and paid off creditors. Afterwards, she decided to leave her mother-in-law's home and move closer to her family in Weston, Sussex.

A turning point in Deborah's life came in the fall of 1937 when her aunt, Phyllis Jane, working as a radio actress for the Bristol's Broadcasting Service, partnered with old friend Cuthbert Hicks to form the Hicks-Smale Drama School in Durdham Park, Bristol. Deborah was asked to be part of it as a full-time student. She lived at home in Weston with her mother, brother and grandmother, commuting 20 miles a day. In addition to drama, she studied ballet, elocution and deportment lessons. Aunt Phyllis Jane also introduced her to radio work, in which she read a few children's stories for the BBC — an experience she greatly enjoyed. Her real stage debut happened in that same year when she appeared as Harlequin in a mime production, directed by Phyllis Jane. *Harlequin and Columbine* was performed at the Bristol's Assembly Hall and later at the Knightstone Pavilion in Weston-Super-Mare. A young man in the audience, Roger Eland, was so impressed by Deborah's performance that he recommended her for the coming year's list of ballet students with Ninette de Valois, a retired Irish dancer. Valois had established the Royal Ballet and was now in charge of the ballet school at Sadler's Wells in London. Deborah was accepted and won a scholarship.

"Are you mad, my dear?" family friends asked Mrs. Trimmer. "Allowing her to go to London alone?!"

"We shan't worry about Deborah," was her mother's resolute reply. "She's got her head screwed on right."[9]

After a few weeks at Sadler's Wells, Deborah realized that studying to be a professional dancer was not exactly what she expected: "I was in the back row of swans and that sort of thing. But I was much too tall

[5'7"] and I hadn't started serious dancing early enough, and I discovered I liked the acting part of the ballet. I was always acting, and always acting my head off, always overdoing it. It was quietly borne in upon me that I'd never make a Fonteyn."[10] She was paid "ten bob a night" (ten shillings).

Nevertheless, it was at the Sadler's Wells Theatre in March 1938 that Deborah made her first stage appearance in London as a member of the corps-de-ballet in *Prometheus* under the direction of Ninette de Valois.

After completing the first year, she finally decided to quit. One of Deborah's new friends, young actress Freda Bamford (who was married to the son of Robert Atkins, the producer-director of the Open Air Theatre at Regent's Park in London), arranged an audition with her future father-in-law, which she successfully passed. Atkins had become known for producing all of Shakespeare's plays in chronological order; he first gave her a small role as a lady-in-waiting in a production of *Much Ado About Nothing* which opened on June 3, 1939, followed the succeeding week by another small part as the Page to Pericles, in *Pericles*. From then on, she appeared in a different play every week for several months. She played an attendant to Hippolyta in *A Midsummer Night's Dream*, then an attendant to Olivia in *Twelfth Night*, after she failed to be cast as Viola. Dissatisfied with her audition, Atkins dismissed her by saying, "Darling, act on stage, not in life!"

About that outdoor experience Deborah commented, "It was noisy, yes. It required a subtlety of acting much like a parade. I was admirably fitted for it."[11] "That demonstrates the marvelous optimism of the British," she joked on another occasion, "having an open-air theater. It was always pelting rain and we were always having to move inside."[12]

In Regent's Park Deborah played a tiny part in James Bridie's comedy *Tobias and the Angel*. However, when World War II broke out, Col summoned her home. As Deborah would later recall: "We all thought we'd be bombed out of existence in London. I went to work in an RAF canteen, but finally got tired of stagnating there and announced to my mother that I wanted to go back to London to look for work as an actress."[13] This time Col decided to follow her daughter to London to help her find a decent accommodation, which they eventually found at the YWCA for thirty shillings a week. After looking for a job in one of the few theaters remaining open after the declaration of war and knocking at the door of all the casting agencies, Deborah heard that John Gliddon was looking for her. Gliddon was the owner of one of the most important artist agencies in London, and was always scouting for new talent. He had been an actor himself, but had found little success. As a journalist, he had written about the entertainment world, but eventually decided to become an agent. He had come to represent many actors who later became stars — the most famous being Vivien Leigh. Gliddon had been tipped off about Deborah by one of his talent scouts who saw her in *Tobias and the Angel*. After that earlier performance, she had suddenly returned to Sussex, and Gliddon had been unable to reach her. When they finally met at Gliddon's Regent Street agency, he offered her a five-year-contract. Col signed on behalf of her minor daughter on November 1, 1939.

Immediately Gliddon sent her to a casting call for a small part in Michael Powell's *Spy in Black*. Deborah was not cast, but shortly after was offered the role of a nightclub cigarette girl in another of Powell's films, *Contraband*, starring Valerie Hobson and Conrad Veidt. The film was intended to be a quick follow-up to the commercially successful *Spy in Black*. For a two-day job at Denham Studios outside London, she was paid ten guineas. She perfectly delivered her two lines of dialogue with Conrad Veidt while wearing a sexy mini-skirt she received compliments of Powell himself, who remembered her as "all lovely liquid eyes and nice long legs." Regardless, her scene ended up on the cutting-room floor.

She was persuaded by Sonia Carol, a Gliddon employee, to lighten her hair, since it was believed that casting agents preferred blondes. Deborah became a strawberry blonde and posed for a new series of publicity shots. One day, Carol took her to lunch at the Mayfair Hotel. Sitting at an adjoining table was Hungarian film producer-director Gabriel Pascal. There are two stories about that meeting, either of which could be true. One, reported by Deborah to Eric Braun, has it that Pascal stared at Deborah for a while, and later approached her table to speak to Carol, who was his old acquaintance. The flamboyant director asked, "And who is this beautiful young lady?" adding, "Sweet virgin, are you an actress?" When he was told so, he immediately replied, "You should wear your hair down around your shoulders. Pinned up that way you look like a tart!" Deborah promptly unpinned her red-gold hair, while Pascal asked Carol where he could get in touch with her.[14]

The other version told by Pascal's wife, Valerie, in her husband's biography, moves the setting to Savoy Grill, the fashionable restaurant of the elegant Savoy Hotel, where Pascal was having lunch with his friend Richard Norton. Pascal told Norton that he wanted a pure, innocent girl with a spiritual face to play a young Salvation Army worker in his next film. "Difficult," Norton sighed. Pascal scanned the dining room and his eyes rested on a girl having lunch at a nearby table with an older woman. "Look Dicky," Pascal said, "look at that face." He got up and went up to them, placing his hands on the girl's shoulder in a familiar manner. "Are you a virgin?" the producer inquired without preliminaries, and before blushing Deborah could answer, Pascal introduced himself and explained his mission. "I have a feeling you can act. Why don't you come out in the lobby after and recite for me something, anything." Deborah and her friend left their table and rushed in the ladies' room, where they rehearsed the only monologue she knew from the Spanish play *Cradle Song*. Later in a quiet corner of the lobby when she began reciting it for Pascal, he stopped her almost immediately. "Do you know The Lord's Prayer?" He asked. She nodded, and her recital of it brought tears to the producer's eyes. "You are the girl," he said simply.[15]

In Braun's version instead, she was summoned a week later to Pascal's suite at the Dorchester Hotel where he was casting his next film *Major Barbara,* based on a popular play by George Bernard Shaw. "I didn't even have enough money for cab fare," Deborah remembered. Keeping a vivid memory of that day she added, "The room was filled with awe-inspiring men, among them David Lean and Vincent Korda. Pascal lounged in a chair and made me stand in the middle of the room. His first words were, 'Take off your shoes, you are too tall.' Obediently, I took them off, hoping that I hadn't got a hole in my stockings. Pascal then said, 'Now, sweet virgin, ACT!'" She plunged into a scene from *Cradle Song* but Pascal interrupted, demanding that she recite The Lord's Prayer. "I launched forth nervously, hoping I could remember it[....]"[16] "How bizarre it was. This room full of chaps smoking enormous cigars and drinking martinis and this young girl reciting the Lord's Prayer. Turning to me, he said, 'You'll be my Jenny Hill.'"[17] A few days later Deborah was invited to do a screen-test. The test was a disappointment for Pascal and for her. Through Gliddon's intervention, she was given another chance. She was then filmed by Pascal's director of photography, the "Master of Light" Ronald Neame. This time the outcome was perfect, and she was officially cast in the part.

2

Stage and Screen Debuts

You are going to be a star.

— Gabriel Pascal

In the spring of 1940, before *Major Barbara* went into production, Gliddon got Deborah an engagement at the Playhouse Theatre in Oxford. There, local students saw her in three infinitesimal roles in the plays *Dear Brutus*, *The Two Bouquets* and *The Playhouse Revue*. It was a way for Deborah to gain some more acting experience before starring in Pascal's film.

Following some location shooting in Devon, *Major Barbara's* principal photography began at Denham Studios outside London on June 17, 1940. To prepare for her role, Deborah volunteered incognito at the Salvation Army. Years later she revealed in an interview that this was an experience which helped her tremendously in shaping the character of the shy but sincere Jenny Hill.

Playwright George Bernard Shaw so approved of Gabriel Pascal's handling of *Pygmalion*, a critical and box office hit of 1938, that he insisted he would only be involved in the production of *Major Barbara* if Pascal were director. Shaw's 1905 play told the story of Barbara Undershaft, a Salvation Army officer who disapproved of capitalism (despite the fact that her father is a wealthy munitions maker) and her romantic association with pragmatic professor Adolphus Cusins, who joins the Army's band just to be near her. The picture had an excellent cast of experienced stage performers. "A wealth of talent," as Deborah called her co-stars, including Wendy Hiller in the title role, Rex Harrison, Robert Newton, Robert Morley, Emlyn Williams, Sybil Thorndike, Marie Lohr and Donald Calthrop.[1]

Major Barbara was Pascal's first film as director, and on the set, according to dialogue director Harold French, it was David Lean, nominally the editor, who really made the picture. The flamboyant and temperamental Pascal would greet the cast each morning with the cry, "You are ruining my picture — you are crucifying me!"[2] Deborah was not spared his temper tantrums; during one rehearsal he called her "a constipated virgin."

Once, David Lean took her aside to console and assure her, "You are going to be a star, you do realize that?"[3] Pascal also fired and then reinstated several of the actors, including Marie Lohr. Wendy Hiller, who had previously worked with him on *Pygmalion*, was called in more than once to calm him down. The director also had a falling out with Robert Morley about a little detail in how the actor should portray his character. The argument became so intense that, until the end of the picture, Pascal gave direction to Morley via David Lean. Adding to these difficulties were the drinking habits of Robert Newton and Donald Calthrop, both of whom had trouble remembering lines. Calthrop, in fact, died of a heart attack a couple of weeks before the end of the shooting, leaving his remaining scenes to be shot with a double and dubbed by an impersonator.

Originally scheduled to be completed in ten weeks, *Major Barbara* took six months and cost more than double its original budget. It was shot during the Blitz, with bombs exploding constantly around the studio (Pascal claimed that 125 bombs fell during the shooting), seriously disrupting the production. Pascal didn't let the war get in the way of his picture. The cast and crew didn't run to shelters every time they heard a warning. Instead, the studio placed some spotters on the roof, protected by sandbags, watching for German airplanes. After the original shooting schedule had been completed, the director insisted on filming additional scenes and retakes. Sixteen new sequences were added for the film, though only six were included in the final cut. Shaw also recorded a "visual prologue" for the American version. The film fell so far behind schedule that producer J. Arthur Rank made a personal visit to Denham and asked Pascal and his staff for an explanation. The director obviously blamed the war and Ronald Neame, the director of photography; Pascal maintained that Neame was very good but extremely slow and threatened to replace him. Lean rescued the DP by indicating that if Neame were fired, he would personally walk off the picture. Pascal had to back down.[4] Harold French revealed to Rank that the director was too indecisive, ordering extra takes and interfering in everything. At the end of the week French was fired by Pascal. In response, the cast would not resume work unless he returned to the set.

In Gabriel Pascal's *Major Barbara* (1941).

So that the picture could be completed, Pascal brought French back, which cost an estimated £250,000.

Despite the tense atmosphere with bombs raining down on the studio, 18-year-old Deborah lit up the set with her radiant freshness and naïveté. She was impressed by Rex Harrison's acting skills (he had been cast after Leslie Howard had turned down the part), especially his perfect timing — a great natural gift she described as "so superb it hurts."[5] She also loved Sybil Thorndike, remembering her as "a positive hurricane of enthusiasm, carrying all along with her."[6]

Major Barbara premièred on March 20, 1941, in Nassau, Bahamas, the island where Pascal had dreams of creating a film production studio. The picture opened in London the following month to mixed reviews and failed to make a profit. It proved more popular in England than in the U.S. In spite of its lukewarm success, Deborah remarked years later (in a preface of a book), "*Major Barbara* produced two top light cameramen and four top directors, all of whom went on to enrich the industry in a remarkable and enduring way."[7]

In September 1941, Pascal wrote a letter to Shaw from Ottawa, in which he told about a press luncheon he had held in London before his departure. At the luncheon, Pascal announced his plan to continue his production with eight of Bernard Shaw's stories and one picture with the Canadian background. However, he indicated that many of the stars of *Major Barbara*, all present at the conference, declared themselves uninterested. One of them was Deborah, who publicly affirmed her refusal to cross the ocean.[8] On the other hand, she was worried whether or not she would be able to continue acting. Pascal, who had an exclusive contract with her, was not reluctant to lend her to other film studios.

A few months later, she got top billing in *Love on the Dole*. The picture was based on Walter Greenwood's bestselling novel about the difficulties of a Lancashire family in the Depression. In May 1940, British National Films acquired the rights to Ronald Gow's 1934 play version, which had been a hit, making Wendy Hiller (in the role of Sally Hardcastle), a star on stage. Attempts to make a film version were blocked by the British Board of Film Censors (BBFC) which raised a ban upon prospective scripts declaring *Love on the Dole* "a very sordid story in sordid surroundings."[9] Finally, in early September 1941, a screen adaptation was finally approved by BBFC. The assigned director was John Baxter, who went up to the north of England, along with Greenwood, scouting for talent and taking background shots. Many actresses auditioned for the part of Sally, including musical star Jessie Matthews.

However, it was Baxter's intention to cast an unknown in the lead as he later explained, "*Love on the Dole* was the sort of subject that would have been artistically unbalanced by big names. A star of her magnitude, billed over the title, would have created the wrong sort of interest."[10] Deborah, encouraged by the Gliddon agency, showed up for a screentest. After her test, the photographer Arthur Gant said to Baxter: "She'll get it." "Why?" the director asked. "She's a girl," said Gant. That simple statement summed up what Baxter wanted for the part.[11]

Playing Sally Hardcastle was not an easy task for Deborah. The story was of a Lancashire girl who decides to prostitute herself to save her family from social deprivation and to compensate herself for lost opportunities resulting from the death of her fiancé. The war and the bombing of London were at their height. Yet every night the cast had to either trail back from the Boreham Studios in Elstree into London to be near their homes or sleep in the nearby subways. Often they would show up on the set tired and dirty; however, nobody complained, and the picture was shot on schedule. Baxter loved realism in his scenes, as Deborah recalled, "My first kissing chore [in films] smelled, literally as well as dramatically. Clifford

Evans [who played the role of Sally's fiancé] had to kiss me among garbage cans outside my slum home. Our director was a fiend of realism and those cans stank to high heaven. In addition to the smell, I was young and shy. When I saw the rushes, my self-consciousness showed and my nose was twitching."[12]

Love on the Dole premièred in London in April 1941. All the critics raved about Deborah's and Clifford Evans's absorbing performances that seemed to have responded perfectly to the masterful guidance of Baxter's direction. *Variety* reported, "Miss Kerr [was] satisfactorily hard as Sally," while the *Evening News* reviewer described her portrait of Sally as "one of the most gripping performances" he had ever seen.

The film scored such a success that British National Films, who already had Evans under contract, teamed Deborah and Evans yet again in *Penn of Pennsylvania*. The director was 33-year-old Lance Comfort who had been formerly an associate director on *Love on the Dole*. *Penn of Pennsylvania* gave Comfort his first chance to make a complete picture after a 16-year apprenticeship.

The idea of making a film on William Penn, the Englishman who founded the "Quaker State" of Pennsylvania, was the brainchild of young producer Richard Vernon. After listening to a radio speech by Franklin D. Roosevelt, Vernon was struck by the similarity of the views expressed by the American president and those held by Penn. The next morning he talked the directors of British National Films into giving him the chance to make a screen version of Penn's life. Screenwriter Anatole De Grunwald, who also scripted *Major Barbara*, worked at top speed to submit a complete screenplay in time for the film to go into immediate production on February 10, 1941, at Elstree Studios.

Deborah played the role of Gulielma Maria Springett, the first wife of William Penn. Although she was billed along with Evans, her part was considerably smaller as most of the action centered around Penn's character. It was a very touching performance although some critics defined it as "subdued."

Penn of Pennsylvania received universally bad reviews. Some critics described it as a parade of stereotypical historical characters without vitality. Comfort seemed to have used an historical setting for propaganda purposes. When the film opened in New York in December 1943 (which was later released for the American market under the title of *The Courageous Mr. Penn*), the *New York Times* panned it stating that the cast had "an annoying habit of speaking down their throats, which makes it difficult for the spectator at times to figure out just what they are saying.... *Penn* definitely is not one of England's better film efforts."[13] Fortunately for Deborah and for Comfort, production on *Hatter's Castle*, their next film together, was well underway before *Penn of Pennsylvania* was released.

Deborah was still living at the YWCA when she was notified by Gliddon that Comfort had cast her in *Hatter's Castle* to replace Margaret Lockwood, who was three months pregnant. Lockwood had been tied to that project for years but the starting date had been postponed to 1941 due to the war and BBFC's objections to some scenes it considered "inappropriate."

Hatter's Castle was based on A.J. Cronin's novel about a family dominated by a tyrannical father, whose young daughter, Mary, falls desperately in love with the family doctor. The film was produced by Paramount in cooperation with their British headquarters. During the filming U.S.A. Paramount chief, David Rose, visited the set along with producer Isadore Goldsmith. The duo was most interested in the American audience's reaction to the picture.

"It was rumored that the American ear was not receptive to any sort of British accent," remembered James Mason, who played Dr. Renwick. The cast was ordered to not speak with any accent. Mason also recalled that the American producer encountered a few problems with Robert Newton, who played the part of the paranoid hatter. The actor had prepared for his role and committed many of his lines to memory, lines written with a Scottish lilt to them, and it was too much to ask him to shake off an accent that had been on his mind already for several weeks. He finally promised to tone it down only to have some sneak let on that Newton was cheating, reactivating the skirmish.[14]

Deborah, like Newton, was still under contract to Gabriel Pascal, and was hired only after Pascal gave his permission. He specially requested that, after their names in the opening credits, it was indicated: *Mr. Newton and Miss Kerr appear by arrangement with Gabriel Pascal.*

Deborah suggested to the director that he cast her 15-year-old brother, Edmund, in the role of Mary's brother. Col Trimmer, after visiting the set, refused to give her consent fearing he would lose too many days at school. While the film was in production, a huge publicity campaign was mounted around its lavish setting. Art director James Carter partially reconstructed the Tay Bridge disaster of 1879 (which collapsed during a violent storm, killing 75 people crossing it in a train). Carter built a flawless period reconstruction of the station and the bridge with a life-size replica of a North British Railway's Company locomotive, and used a large tank and six wind machines producing huge waves to recreate the Tay flood.

The film's stylish black and white photography was the work of the skilled cinematographer Mutz Greenbaum (under the pseudonym of Max Green to avoid German association due to the war).

Hatter's Castle premièred in November 1941 and was released in England two months later during the same week as *Penn of Pennsylvania*. Its reception was generally good with particular praise for Robert Newton and Deborah. The *Sunday Express* wrote, "There's not a foot in this film which isn't interesting ... full of good acting," while the *Daily Mail* called it "one of the best films ever made." Despite the positive reviews, Paramount did not release it in the States until 1948, which was cleverly timed to benefit Deborah's and Mason's increased popularity in America.

In the spring of 1941, Deborah took a room in the elegant neighborhood of Mayfair at the English-Speaking Union, the international charity founded in 1918 to promote international understanding and friendship through the use of the English language. At the ESU she met a Norwegian lady who became her official dialect coach in her next film, *The Day Will Dawn*, in which she played (with a convincing accent) the part of Kari Alstad, the daughter of an old Norwegian skipper.

The picture, directed by Harold French (Deborah's dialog director on *Major Barbara*), was shot at a studio in Denham where Oslo and other Norwegian landscapes were constructed on a lot. The distinguished cast included Hugh Williams and Ralph Richardson, although the latter did not share any scenes with Deborah. The fictional story, co-written by playwright Terence Rattigan and journalist Frank Owen, was set against the background of real events. The story combined a thriller narrative with a romantic subplot involving a British foreign correspondent (Williams) sent to report on U-boat attacks against Norwegian shipping. When he reports his suspicions to the local police chief, thanks to the help of young local Kari, with whom he falls in love. Unfortunately, he is unaware of the chief's secret Nazi sympathies and is betrayed into German hands. As a climax to the picture and to make it more realistic, French included actual newsreel footage of war events.

One afternoon during a pause in the shooting, French and Deborah went to visit Rex Harrison and his German actress wife, Lilli Palmer, at their rented cottage in Denham near the film studios. Palmer, who was pregnant at the time, and Harrison recalled their visit in their autobiographies. This account is from Palmer's memoir:

"One cloudy afternoon we were sitting in the living room with two friends, the director Harold French and Deborah Kerr. Everyone had a drink in his hand.... The all clear had just sounded when Rex, who was standing by the window, suddenly shouted, 'Get down!' I got down as fast as my size permitted; the others were already flat on the floor. Rex had watched a single plane break through the clouds and then — unforgettable sight — had seen the bomb leave the plane. There was a tremendous explosion, then silence, then an extraordinary soft crumbling and grinding sound. The walls of our house were slowly collapsing and falling in on us.

Deborah in an early publicity shot.

The bomb had landed in the garden about fifty feet from our front door. After the grinding, there was silence once again, while we tried to free ourselves from the thick layer of rubble and plaster and broken tiles on top of us. Deborah was first to sit up, and she dug me out. We blinked at each other with some difficulty, because our eyelids were caked with plaster dust. She scratched the debris off my head, but when I tried to do the same for her, I found that the gin had spilled into her hair and, mixing with the cement, had framed her head with a thick white crust like plaster of Paris. Rex and Harold were pinned down under beams, but the house was so jerrybuilt that it had collapsed without injuring us."[15] Fortunately no one received more than superficial injuries: Harrison escaped with a cut across the forehead and Palmer with only a cut to her wrist, while Harold French and Deborah were unhurt but badly shaken.

The Day Will Dawn was released in England in June 1942 and the following November as The Avengers in the States. It was praised more for its tribute to the Norwegian people and their resistance movement in fighting the Nazi invaders than for the originality of the plot, which some critics felt was too slowly paced for an action film. The *Observer* oddly commented, "Little Miss Deborah Kerr, a modest and intelligent young actress who is right out of her depth here, plays a Norwegian skipper's daughter in a style that suggests Garbo after a prolonged session with *How Green Was My Valley.*"[16]

3

A Time of Love and War

I learnt from Deborah what love is.

— Michael Powell

On an afternoon break from shooting *The Day Will Dawn*, Deborah met director Michael Powell at the studio cafeteria. Powell was there for the pre–production of his new film. He saw her sitting by herself, sipping a cup of tea, and went to say hello. She had received her first screen role in *Contraband* from him. Powell recounted the plot of the picture he was about to make, *The Life and Death of Colonel Blimp*. While they were chatting he wondered if Deborah could have been the right choice to play the three major female characters to be portrayed by a single actress.

He had probably forgotten that he had seen her in Gliddon's office earlier that month and dismissed her for being too young for that part. Nevertheless he said nothing about his reconsideration to her or to anybody else.

The Life and Death of Colonel Blimp was a lavish Technicolor epic, covering a period of 40 years of British history. Its subject was the career of an officer in the British Army, Colonel Clive Candy, from the Boer War up to the Second World War. The story also showed the contrast between the old generation of career officers and the new men who had risen through the ranks during the war. The title came from the character of "Colonel Blimp" created by cartoonist David Low for the *London Evening Standard*. Blimp was a pompous, reactionary, upper-class figure representing World War II criticism of "The Establishment." The picture marked one of the first productions from The Archers, a film company established under an agreement by the producer-director-writer team of Michael Powell and Hungarian-born Emeric Pressburger with J. Arthur Rank. Powell and Pressburger had previously collaborated on a pair of fine films, *49th Parallel* and *One of Our Aircraft Is Missing.*

Pressburger carefully researched the period of the film, incorporating not only the major military engagements of the time, but also the small details of that era. In particular he studied the advancement of women throughout the 40 years spanned by the story. In agreement with Powell, he decided to have one actress play three female characters: a governess in 1902, a nurse in 1918 and an ATS driver in 1942.

Casting the leads was a complicated task. In fact, the only initial choice for one of the two lead roles who remained was Anton Walbrook.

Laurence Olivier, who was first cast as Colonel Clive Candy, had to be replaced by Roger Livesey when the Ministry of Information refused to release Olivier from the military forces. However, Livesey proved to be an inspired second choice, thanks to his handsome looks, husky voice and extraordinary acting skills.

A few weeks before the production started, female lead Wendy Hiller (who was married to playwright Ron Gow), backed out having discovered she was pregnant. Possible replacement Anne Neagle could not be released since she was engaged on another film. Suddenly Powell remembered Deborah and told Pressburger about her. Although she was only 20 years old, he thought she had the right qualities for the parts and, with the help of make-up, could be perfectly transformed into the three characters. Pressburger agreed and Powell invited her to his office in Chester Square to offer her the roles.

"We looked at the bulky script together" wrote the director in his autobiography, "and I watched the subtle transformations that passed over her face as I made suggestions about the script. Again I felt that mysterious affinity, as between an artist and his model, which is one of the most inexplicable of the sensual sensations. I made up my mind. I said that frankly we had no time to lose. So long as her agent agreed to our terms, she had the part. She stopped breathing and looked at me. She has told me since that I was already thinking of something else. I said absently: 'All right then, see you at the studio,' and she took her leave. I remember standing at the lattice window watching Deborah walk away up to Belgrave Square and noticing how straight her back was and how high she held her head."[1]

Filming began ten days later on July 8, 1942, but the picture was immediately obstructed by not only the government's refusal to supply military equipment but also by the shortage of young men available to

With Roger Livesey in *The Life and Death of Colonel Blimp* (1943).

play as extras. When only 50 men were available, mannequins had to be used throughout a scene that requested 250 German soldiers. Arthur Rank, who was more conscious of the previous Powell-Pressburger box office hits than the political resentment toward the film, provided the duo with their largest budget yet, recruiting the best men in the industry. Among those recruited were art director Alfred Junge and cinematographer George Périnal, with whom Powell had worked on *The Thief of Bagdad*. Shooting *The Life and Death of Colonel Blimp* lasted twelve weeks with a final cost totaling £188,000. Great harmony reigned throughout the production. Powell revealed that he was not the only director, "There were four directors. I learnt from Anton [Walbrook] what an artist is. I learnt from Roger [Livesey] what a man is. I learnt from Deborah what love is."[2]

Powell, in fact, was falling slowly in love with Deborah. "I knew that we had made a star," he wrote, "Roger and Anton shared my opinion and showed her they did. We were four happy colleagues."[3]

Powell proudly recalled producer Alexander Korda and American director William Wyler giving him a thumbs-up sign on a surprise visit on the set while he was shooting a romantic scene between Deborah and Livesey. Both men approved his choice of casting an unknown leading lady. The director also remembered that, on September 30, 1942, it was Deborah's 21st birthday and his 37th birthday. The crew threw a surprise party in Deborah's honor at the studio. Later that evening, Powell took her out to dinner at a Spanish restaurant near Piccadilly and proposed to her, despite his long-time relationship with Frankie May Reidy. Deborah was ecstatic. Powell's prejudices against mixing his profession with his private life vanished when he had rationalized that she was the ideal woman for whom he had always been searching.

Powell and Pressburger had portrayed German soldiers in a sympathetic light before, but the friendly character of proud Prussian officer Theo Kretschmar-Schuldorff, along with Blimp's inability to grasp the nature of modern warfare, made the duo very powerful enemies. The news of the film production reached Winston Churchill who, along with the War Office and the Ministry of Information, did everything possible to stop the film.

The Prime Minister sent a private memo to the Minister of Information, Brendan Bracken: "Pray propose to me the measure necessary to stop this foolish production before it gets any further. I am not prepared to allow propaganda detrimental to the morale of the Army."[4]

Hence, the British government in the wake of the film's release tried to ban it. Moreover Bracken prompted the production of a film which would portray the army in a way the government wanted to audiences at home and abroad. A year later *The Way Ahead* was produced as a response to the Powell-Pressburger film in order "to set the record straight" about the army.[5]

J. Arthur Rank, who was producing *The Life and Death of Colonel Blimp*, stood absolutely firm behind Powell and Pressburger despite the government opposition. He insisted that the film had to be made exactly as they wanted and released in his cinemas, the Odeon chain, and showed in England. It was even advertised with the slogan, "See the Banned Film." The critics were confused as how to take the 163-minute film in which Powell curiously mixed sentiment with satire. The *Daily Mail* dismissed it "as disastrously bad propaganda in the time of war" but it was the performances that received unanimous praise. Nevertheless, Churchill was able to temporarily ban the film exportation, denying its visa. It took nearly two years for *Blimp* to reach the American screens on March 29, 1945, and even then with a 20-minute shorter print without its flashback scenes. Reviews in the States also were mixed. However, the *New York Times* called Deborah "a lovely and talented actress [who] plays three different ladies in the general's life with remarkable dexterity."[6] The *New York Post* enthusiastically wrote, "In the midst of many excellent performances ... Deborah Kerr handles her three roles in a positively endearing manner."[7] In 1983 when the film was finally restored in its original director-cut, the re-released version of *Blimp* was hailed by critics as a lost masterpiece.

In the spring of 1943 the romance between Deborah and Michael Powell was almost over. She was offered the starring role as Ellie Dunn in the H.M. Tennant's production revival of George Bernard Shaw's *Heartbreak House* at the Cambridge Theatre in the West End. The play opened on March 18, 1943, and received good notices. Deborah played opposite veteran actors Robert Donat and Edith Evans. She had forbidden Powell to visit her backstage, since she was not sure about her feelings for him. In spite of her orders he appeared backstage one night to congratulate her. Once again they fell into each other arms, resuming their relationship.

"We looked for a house outside London, in the country," remembered Powell. "She ordered the wedding dress from one of the dressmakers in the wardrobe department at Denham Studios. We were the most unworldly sweethearts. We were so glad to find each other again, that we thought life was made up of kisses. We didn't plan our lives together. We didn't talk about our careers. Her performance in *Colonel Blimp*, coupled with the West End reviews of the play, put her on the top."[8]

Finally the couple found a house at Bratton Fleming in North Devon, but they did not live there long since Gabriel Pascal, with whom Deborah was still under contractual obligation, decided to sell half of her contract to MGM and organized a trip to the States on her behalf. Powell discovered the truth after he called Tennant's agency to discuss the terms for her part in his next film, *A Canterbury Tale*, in which he wanted Deborah to star. He was told the news of Deborah's future plans and her unavailability. Powell rang her and later met her in Hyde Park under the statue of Achilles, their favorite meeting point. She confirmed what the agency had told him about her future projects, which was to make a film with Alexander Korda, co-produced by MGM, and she was waiting on a call from Hollywood. Powell was enraged over this plan and offered to marry her immediately before devising a way to free her from her contract. But from the look in her eyes, the director realized immediately what Deborah wanted was to pursue her career in Hollywood. She cried and pleaded while Powell swore and raved. They broke up that same day. Deborah signed her contract with MGM eventually, while Powell married his previous girlfriend, Frankie Reidy, a few months later.

Heartbreak House was a hit. After only four weeks in the West End, however, Robert Donat was forced to withdraw from the cast, due to illness. Deborah commented about her co-star years later, "I shall always remember Robert Donat with great affection and gratitude for much he taught me and helped me in my first appearance on stage in *Heartbreak House*. On a humorous note I shall never forget how he introduced me to gin and passion-fruit juice — where he obtained both during war time I *don't* know! I have never drunk it since! He was a superb actor whose career was sadly curtailed by his constant ill-health, and very sweet, loyal and good friend."[9]

The truth was that Donat was in love with her. When the play went on tour in Glasgow, he wrote in his diary about his feelings for her: "*Tell Deborah I love her. (There is no hurry) I don't think it is a rebound. Loving and not 'making.' She doesn't love me but anyway it can wait. I shall go on loving. It's unselfish in so far as I have not wanted even to embarrass her, much less hurt her. I've felt I was too old....*"[10] Donat did not have a simple crush on her; he was determined to divorce his wife even though he had yet to declare himself to Deborah.

In a letter to George Bernard Shaw, Donat wrote, "Deborah Kerr, although sadly lacking in technique, is deeply moving as Ellie, because of her simplicity and sincerity."

Shaw replied that Gabriel Pascal knew that he had fallen for Deborah and if he really loved her, he would agree to play a different part than Deborah's love interest.[11] Deborah eventually left the play, but not until a few months later did she actually fall in love with him, when they met again on the set of *Perfect Strangers*.

About her participation to *Heartbreak House*, she told the press that she had learned more watching Edith Evans than she did from any other experience. "She was a very strong personality, not a very gentle woman, but she was a fantastic actress. She really influenced me enormously. She took great pains with me.... She terrified the life out of me."[12] Deborah mentioned how the actress made her sit on her hands for one entire scene because she gesticulated too much. Also she admitted she found working before a live audience less stimulating than working in a film studio.

"I think the medium of films is thrilling and exciting," she stated. I love the whole technique of the business. The lack of continuity in a screen performance is just one of the factors you must learn and cope with. It means extra concentration on what you're doing and an added sense of the right tempo and the right mood for any given scene. By experience you are able to dovetail something which you have done days or weeks beforehand into what you are doing at the moment. In films a single performance take three months, or however long it may be, instead of three hours of one night, and however much the director, producer, and cameraman may try to help you, it's up to you to keep the whole thing on a consistent plane, so that your different scenes when they are pieced together don't seem scrappy and out of tune with each other. In some ways it seems to me to be very much easier to act on the stage where one scene succeeds another through a complete story. Although that demands a certain concentration too, it is a different kind of concentration and you depend on the impulse of the moment more than a long and accurate memory.... I never even consider an audience while I'm working. Whatever it is I'm supposed to be doing at the moment takes up all my concentration and I'm far too absorbed in the technical side to be bothered about anything else than the part I'm playing. It's a curious mixture, film acting — you mix a certain spontaneity with a certain amount of technique. Half your mind is conscious of what you're doing and where you're looking because you know that perhaps a certain angle will be more effective than if you turn your head round a little bit farther. The other half is concentrated on the emotional side of the performance. That's why I think it would be impossible to work with an audience in front of you. It would be too distracting to that part of you which is concerned with the mechanics of a film."[13]

Thanks to the success of her most recent films Deborah's financial position became more secure, allowing her to buy her first house in Tunbridge Wells, on the Kent-Sussex border. However, not expecting to be so busy with her work, she spent very little time there, and sold it only two years later.

At the beginning of 1943, Alexander Korda's London Films entered in a co-production agreement with MGM in which Korda acted as a producer or executive producer for a series of films. However, only one of those productions ever reached the screen: *Perfect Strangers*. The script preparation took an enormous amount of time. Korda had almost thirty writers under contract and almost all of them had a hand in it at one time or another. Finally it was Clemence Dane who coordinated the disjointed efforts and received the sole credit. Nevertheless, the script was not the only problem Korda faced during pre-production. The producer had difficulty adjusting to the wartime realities of finding a studio to make his picture. Eventually he was able to take up tenancy in Denham Studios. On January 24, 1944, after many delays in getting transport facilities, Wesley Ruggles, one of MGM's most highly paid directors, finally arrived from America. Korda originally planned the picture as a vehicle for Robert Donat and Merle Oberon (Korda's wife), but Lady Korda's part had to be reshaped when she found it impossible to make the trip from Hollywood where she was working. Vivien Leigh was in talks to take over the role. Yet, at that time, a workable script was not ready. Rather than concentrating on producing one, Korda left for Hollywood for a few weeks in an attempt to save his shaky marriage with Oberon. MGM executives were furious since they were left paying for an empty studio and a salary to Donat of £2000 per week. Furthermore Vivien Leigh, who had been cast to replace Oberon, suddenly became unavailable. At Donat's insistence the role was finally given to Deborah who was tied with MGM after Pascal had sold the studio her contract option.

While waiting for Korda to return, Wesley Ruggles passed his time shooting atmosphere shots and filming wardrobe and make-up tests for Donat and Deborah.[14] The first shooting day was April 24, but hardly anything was accomplished since Donat had an asthma attack and was sent to a hospital. When he returned to the set on May 5, he had an argument with Ruggles, who resigned a few days later. Korda took over the direction — it was a wrong move. The producer was bored and impatient since his marriage was still going through a major crisis. He was unhappy and did nothing to hide it, making the cast and crew miserable.

Perfect Strangers (retitled by MGM for its American release as *Vacation from Marriage*) was a human comedy-of-errors. It told the story of a timid bookkeeper and his wife who were separated from each other at the beginning of the war and have their life transformed by the military service. After three years of separation neither husband nor wife looks forward to their reunion, and each is completely unaware of the radical change the other has undergone. It takes only one night together to reconsider their union and to get back together.

Despite all the production problems (including a shortage of materials for sets and costumes, the daily air-raids and a flying bomb that destroyed outdoor sets, smashing windows, and raining glass splinters over Korda's office and the cast dressing-rooms), Deborah enjoyed working under Korda's direction. On the personal side, she finally began a warm relationship with her co-star Robert Donat, who had never stopped courting her and finally left his wife. Nevertheless Donat's behavior was odd. He firmly complained to Korda after he discovered that the Publicity Department was billing Deborah's name with his. He demanded, and received, top billing.

Perfect Strangers was not shot entirely in the studio (where backgrounds of London during the black-outs were recreated with the help of cinematographer Georges Périnal), but also on location in Scotland at Dunoon. Actor Roland Culver played Deborah's character's romantic interest and remembered a curious anecdote while in Scotland:

"I had a scene with Deborah on the downs overlooking Loch Long, and I had considerable toupee trouble as there was a strong breeze blowing. At one point, after spending a couple of hours arranging my hair, Alex thought it might be a good idea if I wore a hat. But the wind must have dropped, I think, as I am sure I finished the scene without a hat. There were many laughs at my expense but I am used to that. Deborah was a dear to work with."[15]

Among the many extras on the set there was 17-year-old Roger Moore, the future James Bond. He played a sailor for two days and had a scene in which he sat in a railway carriage opposite Deborah. Moore harbored a secret crush for her, little knowing that she had only eyes for Donat.[16]

Perfect Strangers premièred in September 1945 at the Empire Cinema in London. It was very well received and turned out to be a remarkable success in England, performing also quite well in America when it opened the following spring. Ironically it won an Academy Award for Best Original Story. To complete his picture, Korda spent over one million pounds, an incredible amount of money for that time. However he was only able to partially recoup his investment since he had to split profits with MGM. Even so, MGM was dissatisfied with the outcome and stopped their collaboration.

In early 1945 Deborah and Donat broke off their relationship. Donat blamed it on his heavy personality, that had bored her. However in a letter to him, Deborah passionately protested that she was not in the least bored by him. Donat later admitted that his attraction to her had been as a rebound from a previous, unhappy affair.[17]

It did not take long for Deborah to replace Donat. She, in fact, met actor Stewart Granger on a blind date. Granger was in his early thirties and was making a name for himself in British movies. Also of Scottish extraction, Granger was a tall, handsome man, who had made his film debut in 1943 with *The Man in Grey* followed by *Fanny by Gaslight* and *Love Story*. It was not so surprising that the two found each other attractive. Each of them reflected back to the other their own attractiveness and success. Still there was one problem: Granger was married to actress Elspeth March. The affair with Deborah was kept very hush-hush because if it had become news, a scandal would have surely ensued. A few weeks later Granger, while shooting *Caesar and Cleopatra* opposite Vivien Leigh, was astounded to learn that everybody on the set knew about it when Leigh, exasperated with his lack of concentration, told him to pay more attention to his work rather than Deborah.[18] In his autobiography (published in 1981), Granger confessed a weakness of the flesh with Deborah, which reportedly occurred in a chauffeured limousine. However there was never an independent corroboration of Granger's claim.[19]

Deborah and Granger had a further opportunity to cement their relationship when they embarked on an Entertainments National Service Association (ENSA) European tour in a production's of Patrick Hamilton's play *Gaslight*. The cast rehearsed at Theatre Royal under the direction of John Fernald. Deborah played the role of Bella Manningham opposite Granger as her husband Paul. The company successfully toured for eight weeks starting in April, in Belgium, Holland and France, entertaining service men. After the show, the cast would often be invited to the local officers' club to entertain. On one of these occasions in Brussels, Deborah was introduced to 26-year-old Battle of Britain pilot and Squadron Leader Anthony C. Bartley. The R.A.F. pilot was so struck by Deborah's beauty and outgoing personality that he decided to watch the show the following night and dine with her and Granger.

Bartley wrote in his journal about that magical encounter that changed his life: "A date was made for that evening, and Jack said that we were dining with our mutual friend, Aubrey Baring. When I arrived at Aubrey's headquarters, a magnificent town house requisitioned from a leading abortionist, Jack [Granger's nickname] was already there, grinning from ear to ear and introduced me to Deborah Kerr. Formalities over, we got down to the cocktails and small talk whilst I appraised this plump and lovely red-headed actress. Before the end of play I managed to get Deborah to myself and suggested that since I had transport at my disposal I could show her the sights of Brussels the following day."[20]

That following day Bartley watched two of *Gaslight*'s remaining performances, shyly courting Deborah, who was a bit reticent since she had just stopped seeing Granger. (In the beginning of the European tour they both had agreed Granger should return to his wife.) Bartley asked her for a date, which she accepted.

"The way she looked when she came to meet me in the hotel lobby, I will always remember" wrote Tony in his journal. "Strawberry complexion, a shy warm smile and a little plumpness accentuated by the Khaki uniform she wore. We wined and dined and talked and danced, and before I dropped her back at the hotel I tried to kiss her, unsuccessfully. The next morning, as arranged, I drove her to the airport to catch her plane, and I asked if I might call her when I was next in London. She scribbled her number and address, and she said she would look forward to it."[21]

Bartley was lucky he was a pilot. Otherwise his romance might have died aborning as he explained a couple of years later in an interview, "It's only a few minutes by Spitfire from Belgium to England; so when Deborah went home I always found some excuse for flying over during my hours off duty. I'd land, check into headquarters, and ring Deborah. We'd have a few minutes or a few hours together, before I had to report back to the battle fronts."[22]

In a letter to his parents, dated April 10, 1945, Tony wrote: "I met an absolute whizz-girl out here the other day. I am afraid it's another actress, but oh boy, what a peach. Maybe, I'll grow up one day."[23]

On her return to London, Deborah had very little time to visit her family since MGM asked her to shoot a few retakes for *Perfect Strangers*. She finally signed a seven-year exclusive contract with Metro with a salary of $250,000 at a guaranteed $3,000 a week working in Hollywood. Regardless, she still owed two films to Pascal to make in England. The first picture was *I See a Dark Stranger*. Deborah was on loan to Individual Films and began to work in the summer of 1945 under the direction of the producer-director-writer team of Frank Launder and Sidney Gilliat, screenwriters of Alfred Hitchcock's hit *The Lady Vanishes*.

Dramatically the war came to an end and Tony flew back to London to celebrate with Deborah. They paraded with the crowds in Piccadilly Circus, laughing and cheering, and then they went to her apartment to drink a bottle of champagne and make love. Within a few days, Deborah had to go to Ireland on location, leaving Tony with the idea of getting married. "Stewart Granger warned me," remembered Tony. "Never marry an actress, old boy. Their careers come before everything, and Deborah's no exception."[24]

I See a Dark Stranger was a comedy-thriller set during World War II, with Deborah playing Bridie Quilty, a proud, naïve Irish girl, who grew

With Trevor Howard on her left opposite Norman Shelley and Raymond Huntley in *I See a Dark Stranger* (1946).

up despising everything British. After leaving her hometown, hoping to join the IRA, she naïvely gets caught up with a Nazi spy. Only the encounter with David Bayne, a British Army officer played by Trevor Howard, makes her realize her mistakes, which she is able to solve with his help.

Much of the film was shot in County Vexford, in Ireland. Although it was the end of the war, it was far from being the end of the privations in Britain. The cast and the crew found themselves in a land of plenty. Launder and Gilliat had agreed that they would take turns directing their films, and with this their first, Launder was in the director's chair. When Deborah reported for make-up tests, Launder looked at her contemplatively and shook his head.

"Not blonde!" he gasped. "It doesn't call for one."

She exclaimed, "Now I can go back to…"

Launder interrupted with an inspiration, "Bright red," he shouted.[25]

Aside from the weather regularly holding up the shooting, one of Launder's biggest worries was the working habits of the 43 Irish actors who frequently took long lunch breaks.

"The Irish," complained the director to *Life* magazine, "do not have a very strong sense of time."[26]

A few scenes were filmed on the Isle of Man, and the cast was taken each morning by car to the set. Along the route a little bridge had to be crossed, where the native driver insisted that everybody had to greet the fairies to forestall disaster. Everybody in the crowded car complied, except Deborah. She refused to say "Good morning" to the fairies, because she thought it was silly. The driver refused to cross the bridge. Clouds gathered and it started to drizzle. The stand-off lasted one hour, while both Launder and Gilliat implored Deborah to bow to the tradition. Finally she mumbled "Good morning" to the fairies — and the sky cleared and all went smoothly.[27]

Trevor Howard, then at the beginning of his career, adored working with Deborah; he loved the fact she was very down-to-earth and extremely easygoing. Sidney Gilliat attributed her sunny disposition and good humor to satisfaction with her role as Bridie Quilty.

The film's interiors were completed at Denham Studios in September 1945 and the picture was released almost a year later, on August 5, 1946. *I See a Dark Stranger* attracted mixed reviews, partially because it was a difficult film to categorize. Some saw it as a thriller, while others saw it as more of a romantic comedy. Either way, it proved to be popular and well received by the public. The film was more succinctly retitled *The Adventuress* when it reached American screens in 1947. A strenuous 16-minute cutting ordered by the American distributor left the picture with some inexplicable gaps in the evolution of the story.

Despite the cuts, Lauder expressed his satisfaction regarding the film years later, "Deborah Kerr won the New York Critics Circle Award for her performance in this film, which ran under the title of *The Adventuress* for more than three months at the large Victoria Theatre in Times Square. It ran for another three months in Boston and achieved long runs in all the principal cities of the States. Its advent coincided, however, with Rank's bold attempt to break into American film distribution, with a large organization and several floors of offices on Broadway, and scores of experienced and enthusiastic specialized staff— but hardly any product.... I was handed some figures in New York which showed that *The Adventuress* had at an early date more than recovered its production cost from the box offices in the States, but alas, after massive deduction from the overweight organization, the meal that resulted was a frugal one."[28]

On the set, some crew members noticed that Deborah had formed a closed attachment with the handsome director of photography, Wilkie

Cooper. However, toward the end of shooting, Deborah announced her engagement to Tony Bartley with plans to get married in November. While in Ireland, she received a telegram from Bartley, who had asked his friend David Niven to write: "Have been posted to the South Pacific Stop Will you marry me." Deborah's answer was: "Yes Stop Where and When."[29] Tony later gave her a three-stone, diamond engagement ring.

In a letter from Palau Island (where he was stationed), Tony gave the news of his proposal of marriage to his parents.

"I am glad all you love Deborah. Spiritually, if not physically, she is closer to me than anyone I've ever known. I love her so terribly much that it frightens me. We have seen so little of each other, and yet I feel I have known her all my life. We want to get married as soon as I get home."[30]

Two months later in a letter addressed to his mother, Tony describes his feelings for Deborah, whom he had missed tremendously, "At heart, I think I am a child who just wants someone to love and care for me, and when I had got to know Deborah I knew she was that person. There has been little passion in our loving of such short duration but maybe that will grow, and it would seem almost absurd to even contemplate marriage, in normal circumstances, but life is not normal. I'm not normal. My total commitment to the war has utterly exhausted me, and maybe matrimony is my final capitulation as the result of this, in which case I'm being more utterly selfish, so God help me. Our two careers which we intend to pursue are in no way complementary, and we are equally ambitious. Maybe Deborah even more than I, but I think I have found my girl who can face this scene. She has had a rough indoctrination to her young life, and beneath her outward gentleness, there lies a toughness which I admire."[31]

On November 26, 1945, with the blessing of the entire crew, Deborah left Denham Studios in the company of Bartley, whose transfer to the South Pacific was postponed only a few days. Tony and Deborah traveled to Swanbourne where she was formally introduced to her future in-laws, Sir Charles and Lady Bartley. Tony's father was a barrister from the Irish High Court; originally from Northern Ireland, who was knighted in 1942 for his able service in India.

Wedding bells rang for the happy couple two days later after they exchanged vows at St. George's Hanover Square in London. Deborah wore a white wool tailored gown created by costume designer Joy Ricardo. She walked down the aisle with her brother, Teddy, and was attended by one bridesmaid — Tony's sister Gillian Bartley. Group Captain "Sailor" Malan, the groom's dear friend, was best man. The Venerable and Honorable

London November 28, 1945. Deborah's wedding with Anthony Bartley. On far right best man, Captain "Sailor" Malan. Others are unidentified.

Stephen Phillimore officiated. A reception was held at Claridge's where an amalgam of friends, many from the R.A.F. and the film industry, toasted the newlyweds. Tony's wedding gift was a silver heart, which Deborah wore at the party.

When Deborah and Tony left the reception, they discovered that their car had a dead battery. They were pushed to a start, leaving Claridge's on their way to their brief honeymoon by a group of fighter pilots. Forty-eight hours later Tony left for the South Pacific, leaving Deborah busily furnishing their home in Mayfield, East Sussex, which she had purchased the previous year. The couple also had an apartment in Claridge's House in London.

Before the wedding, Deborah told Tony about her contract with Louis B. Mayer and his intentions of making her an MGM star in Hollywood. Tony agreed, expressing his willingness to move to Hollywood with her if necessary. Deborah admitted that she would have easily given up her acting career if he was against it.

MGM's call to Hollywood did not come until the end of 1946, before Deborah worked one last time with Michael Powell and Emeric Pressburger in *Black Narcissus*. Pressburger's wife, Wendy, had introduced him to the best-selling novel *Black Narcissus*, written by Rumer Godden. It was an intriguing story of Anglican nuns sent to establish a mission in the remote Himalayas in the Palace of Mopu, which had formerly been a harem. The nuns' attempt to establish a mission ultimately failed, with one of them dying in conflict between the sacred and the profane.

Casting Deborah as Sister Clodagh, the nun in charge of the Convent of St. Faith, was not easy. Powell was, in fact, convinced she was too young for the part. It was Pressburger who convinced his partner to consider his opinion.

"I laughed at the idea," wrote Powell in his autobiography, "I turned it down flat. She was too young, far too young, ten years too young. Emeric was too old a bird to be caught with chaff.

"If she were as old as Garbo, you'd want her to look ten years younger than she is. Deborah is twenty-six and can easily look thirty-six. And she won't mind doing it, either."[32]

Emeric arranged a dinner to discuss the part with her at the Etoile, Powell's favorite restaurant in Charlotte Street. The meeting between Deborah and the director was at first awkward, since the two had not met since their break-up. Finally, when Powell expressed his concern about her young age, Deborah replied, "It's in your hands, Michael. If you say I can do it, I can do it. How old is she?"

"Thirty six."

"I know how to play her. They won't think about the age." A pause. "Who's playing Sister Ruth?"

"Byron; Kathleen Byron."

"Do I know her?"

"I don't think so."

"It's a good part."

"She's good."

"Whoever plays Sister Ruth will steal the picture."

"Are you crazy? Sister Clodagh is the best part you'll have in years!"

"Oh! I thought you said I was too young for it."

"So you are."[33]

Emeric interrupted them, asking Deborah if she thought MGM would loan her out. She did not see any reason why they wouldn't, although she warned him that her salary would not be as cheap as when she played in *Blimp*. In fact Ben Goetz, head of MGM-British, asked Powell for £20,000 to loan Deborah for twelve weeks of work. The director was dismayed since that was the highest salary he had ever paid an actor. Eventually he settled for £16,000. The major role of the general's agent, Mr. Dean, went to David Farrar. The role was originally intended to be play by Roger Livesey and later Robert Donat, but eventually Farrar got the part after Powell noticed him at Elstree Studios and invited him to test for it. Other cast members were Kathleen Byron as Sister Ruth, Judith Furse as Sister Briony, Flora Robson as Sister Philippa, Jenny Laird as Sister Honey, Jean Simmons as Kanchi and Sabu as Dilip Rai. Most of the cast had been seen in previous Powell films.

On May 16, production on *Black Narcissus* was ready to begin. Art director's Alfred Junge built a very elaborate set to recreate a plausible Himalayan background on a backlot at Pinewood Studios. The palace was erected high above other buildings and trees, surrounded by a wall of planks and inclining at an angle of 35 degrees. Over 120,000 feet of tubular steel formed the framework of this monumental piece of landscaping. Timber was affixed to scaffolding and covered with pre-fabricated plaster and cement sheets, painted to resemble the natural rock. Thirty tons of gravel and soil were hauled by rope and pulley to the top of the "mountain" in order to make paths and terraces that were strong enough to take the weight of horses.[34] Sir Giles Loder's estate at Horsham, Sussex, was the location used by the crew to film the exteriors of the Himalayas. The exotic lush garden surrounding the property was evocative of India.

The script was realistic and the production so captured the atmosphere of India that Deborah felt as though she had been there. Every day of shooting became an exciting adventure due to the creative ideas which evolved. Wearing heavy clothes in the middle of a heat wave was probably

With Jean Simmons and David Farrar in *Black Narcissus* (1947).

the only real problem the cast faced during the making of the film. Between takes Deborah knitted or did crosswords.

"Anything more constructive distracts your mind from what you are working on," she revealed in an interview. "Reading starts you thinking about some other character or some other situation and I find that knitting, or doing a crossword doesn't interfere with what's at the back of my mind. I can still be thinking about the character I'm playing; still turning it over in my mind, and I don't want anything which will interfere with the very essential continuity of thought which you must have for films."[35]

Deborah was able to delve into the character of Sister Clodagh. As her daughter Francesca explained years later, "She really understood nuns: the disciplined life, the solitude. They were all things she could relate to, partly because of her childhood and partly because of the discipline of her upbringing."[36]

On the set Deborah was fascinated by the presence of Flora Robson, as she was a lifelong admirer of her work. She constantly observed her way of acting and was interested in hearing everything Robson could tell her of Hollywood, where she was eager to go.[37] Deborah also became good friends with Jean Simmons, a young actress who had been successful as Estella in David Lean's screen adaptation of Dickens's *Great Expectations*, and now playing Kanchi, an Indian woman.

"What an exquisite face, and what a dear, funny person!," was Deborah's comment after meeting Simmons for the first time (they would later work together in two other films). "With her dusky make-up, she looked even more beautiful as the Indian seductress!"[38]

Nevertheless there were bumpy moments on the set, since Powell was a difficult man. Kathleen Byron remembered the director as very abrasive and unpleasant to her and most of the people on the set. This took the form of extreme sarcasm if he was dissatisfied with his performers. Deborah suggested to Byron that when Powell would tell her to do something disagreeable, she would only reply, "Oh, what a wonderful idea!" and then do it the way she originally intended.[39]

Director of photography Jack Cardiff also recounted that Powell could be rude to lesser-known actors saying, "You are not very good, are you? Who's your agent?" He believed this sort of insult would prick them into a better performance."[40]

Cardiff had to take care to create a balance between his own desire to experiment with Technicolor and the difficult supervision of Technicolor's owners who had to make sure that once developed, the proper process was used to maintain the color palette with a flat, even lighting. Anything close to chiaroscuro was forbidden. When the rushes where screened, the supervisors appreciated what Cardiff was trying to achieve and withdrew several objections previously expressed for some scenes where low lighting was used.

Although *Black Narcissus* was completed on schedule on August 22, 1946, it was substantially over budget. Yet, the money spent was apparent on the screen, and the film became a commercial success. The picture was released in Britain on May 26, 1947, and was highly praised for its ravishing beauty, lush studio sets, colorful costumes, stunning color photography and imaginative art direction. Still, the reviewers objected that the story was not very persuasive. Rumer Godden, the author of the novel, was dissatisfied with the film, believing it to be "counterfeit" because of the studio setting.

"I suppose I was so unhappy because I knew what the film could have been," affirmed Godden in an interview.[41]

The following summer the release of *Black Narcissus* in the United States was beset with controversy. The story was considered to be risqué from the start and several key sequences, including the flashbacks of Sister Clodagh's love affair in Ireland before she took her vows, were cut from the American release print. Despite the mutilations the picture was a hit. Michael Powell years later commented, "As predicted by Deborah, Kathleen Byron nearly stole the picture. Nearly … but not quite. Deborah is a modest lady, but she doesn't allow things like that to happen easily. She wrote to me some months later from Hollywood (she was working on a Clark Gable picture, *The Hucksters*), and said: 'There is a new young actress in this picture, who is almost as big a menace to me as Sister Ruth. But not quite. Her name is Ava Gardner.'"[42]

For his work on *Black Narcissus*, Jack Cardiff won both the Golden Globe and the Oscar for Best Cinematography. A second Academy Award was won by Alfred Junge for his astounding production design while Deborah was awarded the New York Critics Circle Award as Best Actress of the year for her outstanding performances in this film and *The Adventuress*.

The popularity of Deborah's last two films in America made Cecil B. DeMille interested in casting her for the lead in the Paramount production of *Unconquered*. Her agent reportedly asked for what DeMille said was too much money. Paulette Goddard got the role eventually.

After watching a special screening of *Black Narcissus*, Louis B. Mayer decided to send immediately for his new star. For Deborah, the Hollywood adventure was about to begin.

4

The Dream Factory

Her name will rhyme with star and not with cur.
— Louis B. Mayer

On the day of their first wedding anniversary, November 28, 1946, Deborah and Tony sailed for New York aboard the *Queen Elizabeth*. Before disembarking Deborah was interviewed by a group of reporters alerted of her arrival by the MGM press office, the first thing she reminded the press was the correct pronunciation of her name with the accent on *Deb* and the last name coming out as *Carr*. After a lunch party at the exclusive restaurant 21, Deborah and Tony spent four lovely days in New York, enjoying every minute. She later confessed how she was impressed by the quantity of food available, something unusual for someone like her coming from post–war England where food was still very scarce.

When they finally arrived in Hollywood, the first order of business for the couple was a meeting with Benny Thau, MGM's top casting man. Thau was very cordial and introduced Deborah to some of the executives and stars passing through his office.

"I was crossed-eyed looking at everybody," commented Deborah.[1]

Then the big moment arrived when Louis B. Mayer was ready to give her an audience. The head of MGM had arranged an intimate lunch on the fourth floor executive dining room in his office building. Understandably nervous, Deborah was put completely at ease by Mayer, who joked that "her name will rhyme with star and not with cur" — a slogan that later was used in many of the articles written in the local press. Mayer was also very interested in Tony's war record and the fact he had shot down 15 German planes. Later they were escorted to the publicity department where

Melvina Pumphrey, Deborah's appointed contact with the press and the public, helped to adjust the Bartleys to their new way of life.

Deborah and Tony took an 18-month lease on producer-writer Casey Robinson's house in a secluded canyon near Pacific Palisades. Deborah was thrilled when she saw that the house included all super-modern appliances, from a washing machine to a refrigerator. She immediately bought a cookbook so she could use the electric stove to cook for Tony. However, those first weeks in Hollywood were so frantic she had very little time to spare for the joy of cooking. A week after her arrival, she was asked by producer Arthur Hornblow, Jr., to take a screen test with Clark Gable for the upcoming picture *The Hucksters*. The truth was that after a disastrous experience with Greer Garson (another British expatriate in Hollywood) in his last film *Adventure*, Gable insisted on first making a screen test with the new leading lady MGM had selected to star opposite him.

The Hucksters was based on Frederic Wakeman's best-selling satirical novel about the ethics and methods of the radio-advertising industry. Metro paid $200,000 for the rights in a pre–publication sale. The book spent nearly a year on the top of the bestselling list and raised a big controversy. Church leaders howled about the affair of Victor Norman, the novel's hero, with a married woman. As a result and on Gable's insistence (he was not impressed at all by the first draft of the script, declaring, "It's filthy and it isn't entertainment"), the story was revised. The character (played by Deborah), was changed into a war widow so that she and Gable could live happily ever after. Before her screentest, Deborah received flowers from Hornblow and from Gable, both wishing her good luck. Deborah was surprised in learning that her husband had previously met her co-star when he was lecturing to American airmen during the war.

Deborah's audition before the cameras was just a formality since Mayer was determined to cast only her in that part. The MGM mogul agreed to the test just to please Gable, even though the actor was still a Metro contract player obliged to obey his orders.

Deborah described that day for the *L.A. Daily News*: "I was very nervous, even though Clark Gable himself did everything in his power to put me at ease. Nevertheless, when the scene was completed I was certain I had failed. I remember I was in my dressing room feeling nice and miserable all by myself. The wardrobe girl happened to walk in. She saw how dejected I was. 'Never mind, dearie.' She said, 'even if you don't get the part, it was worth traveling the 5,000 miles just to get kissed by Mr. Gable.' I couldn't feel nervous after that."[2]

Clark Gable, Ava Gardner, Deborah, Gloria Holden and Adolphe Menjou in *The Hucksters* (1947).

MGM assembled an exceptional supporting cast for the $2.3 million production of *The Hucksters*, including Adolphe Menjou, Sidney Greenstreet and a still-unknown Ava Gardner in the supporting role of a sexy nightclub singer. The making of the picture was rushed by Mayer who wanted to release it the following August, trying to revive Gable's name after the flop of his last film and launching Deborah's in Hollywood.

Metro appointed Jack Conway to direct the picture, a choice some criticized, since he was a belligerent Irishman, who knew very little about New York and its advertising world. Despite being in his late fifties, every week after receiving his salary, Conway donned his boxing outfit and entered the ring, trying to double his money.[3]

On her first day on the set Deborah received six dozen roses in her dressing-room sent by Gable with a note: "Good luck on your opening night from your leading man, Clark Gable." The two hit it off beautifully from the beginning, on and off the set. Between takes he helped her with her interminable crossword puzzles.

"With her ladylike manners, her warmth and grace she managed to charm everybody on the set," a *Time* magazine reporter wrote in a cover story. He quoted Deborah as saying: "I have always wondered what it would be like [in Hollywood]. You come 6,000 miles and then suddenly — bang! crash! wallop!—you've done it. It's like having a tooth out."[4] In an interview with the *L.A. Daily News* she explained, "Hollywood is a place where I expect to spend a great deal of time in the future. I expect to make frequent trips to England because that, after all, is where my roots are. But I am part of the motion picture business and I like the fact that life in Hollywood revolves about the movies. I like movie people and I enjoy being with them."[5]

Nonetheless, Deborah later admitted that she'd gladly have resisted her role in *The Hucksters*. She said of her character: "Kay was most definitely a lady. I wore a halo of decorum and was as exciting as an oyster."

At the box office, *The Hucksters* earned $4.4 million, however the picture was a total failure in the foreign market, which in those days knew nothing about American advertising or commercial broadcasting. The film helped put Gable back into that year's "Top Ten Box office Stars" since his return onscreen after military service. Deborah received many flattering reviews. The *Hollywood Reporter* called her a "charming English star ... a delightful personality in her American debut," while the *New York Herald Tribune* named the Gable-Kerr team-up "ideal," saying she made "an impressive bow on the U.S. screen."

The Bartleys' social life in Hollywood was very hectic. Since Tony was a visitor without a working card he could do nothing but relax and enjoy the mild weather and the evenings out. When columnist Sheilah Graham wrote an article on Deborah for *Photoplay*, she asked Tony if he was interested in becoming an actor himself; he had, in fact, appeared as a pilot in a tiny role in *First of the Few* in 1942 with Leslie Howard. Bartley affirmed his disinterest in acting, having interest only as a film industry executive. Observing Deborah on the set every day he hoped would help him discover the part of the business he liked best and then apply for it.[6]

The Bartleys often entertained their new friends in her new home. Among those entertained were British actor David Niven, who lived only few blocks away and was one of Tony's closest friends and later Deborah's co-star in four films.

Living in Hollywood, driving was essential and Deborah announced her intention of learning to drive on the right side of the road. She gave up the idea when she found herself pregnant in the spring of 1947.

If Winter Comes was Deborah's second picture in Hollywood, which she started immediately after *The Hucksters* was completed. The film was based on A.S.M. Hutchinson's melodramatic novel about the vicious consequences of gossip in a small village in England. It was a remake of a silent movie directed in 1923 by Harry F. Millarde starring Percy Marmont. British director Victor Saville was asked to direct the film. Saville, who had made two of Vivien Leigh's early films, had no particular affinity toward the subject, but the attraction was working with Deborah, as he revealed in his biography: "It was her poise and her utter Englishness that held such appeal to the American audiences.... I qualified as director of *If Winter Comes* because of that same appeal of Deborah — my Englishness —... I was known as the only director who ever came on the stage wearing a tie."[7]

Saville's "Englishness" extended to finding jobs in the picture for several British artistes who were in Hollywood. Among those were Angela Lansbury, Dame May Whitty, Hugh French and Hughie Green. The only two non–British stars were Walter Pidgeon and Janet Leigh. In her autobiography, Leigh revealed that Saville was not aware of her actual heritage until late in the shooting. The studio hired the niece of actor C. Aubrey Smith to tutor in the intonations and inflections so that his accent would sound believably British.[8] Angela Lansbury, then 22 years old, wanted Janet Leigh's touching role of the waif-like village girl, Effie, but was forced by Saville to play Mabel, the 35-year-old bitter wife of 50-year-old Walter Pidgeon. Although Lansbury was very disgruntled, she accepted role.

Deborah was not convinced by the script but, as she said in an interview, "All I can do is put my faith in my employers."[9]

Nevertheless, many years later she publicly

With Angela Lansbury (L) and Janet Leigh (R) in *If Winter Comes* (1947).

expressed her disappointment in being cast in the movie explaining, "If you're paid an enormous amount of money every week under a seven-year contract, you do as you're told — That's the way I was brought up.... I have suffered all my life from too much respect for the boss, I took it for granted that the heads of studios, with all their experience, knew instinctively what was best for me. It took me six years to find out that perhaps they didn't."[10]

She then added, "In the meantime, there was a marvelous offer just around the corner — my best break, acting-wise, to date, to co-star with Spencer Tracy in the film version of the London hit play *Edward, My Son*, to be directed by the great George Cukor."

The shooting of *If Winter Comes* finished in the late summer of 1947, just in time for Deborah to show off her baby bump. MGM shelved the picture until the following summer when it was received with mixed reviews, performing poorly at the box office.

That year the Bartleys purchased their first American home, a Mediterranean-style house in Pacific Palisades overlooking the ocean from a cliff among spacious lawns surrounded by eucalyptus trees. From her new, lush garden Deborah planted rambler roses and red and white camellias. The house originally was the guest house of Edith Rockefeller McCormick's vast estate in Santa Monica, which was never used. The Bartleys had all their furniture shipped from England, and Deborah had only her bedroom repainted since the house was in mint condition.

Years later, when she moved back to Europe, Deborah revealed, "The view over the ocean and the sound of the waves on the beach below remain forever in my memory ... it was a lovely spot. I was sad when I had to sell the house and return to Europe."[11]

On December 27, 1947, Deborah's dream to become a mother was realized when Melanie Jane Bartley was born at the Cedars of Lebanon Hospital in Los Angeles. A nursemaid was hired to take care of the lovely baby, since Deborah was summoned to work a few weeks later, when she quickly regained her perfect shape.

She was asked to test for a film called *Young Bess*, which Metro intended to make. Meanwhile, she was confirmed to star opposite Spencer Tracy in *Edward, My Son*, which was scheduled to be filmed in England the following fall. Deborah was very excited because not only would she have the opportunity to work with one of Hollywood's most respected stars, but it would also enable her to return to England and introduce her family to their new granddaughter. *Edward, My Son*, directed by George

Cukor, was the first film to be made by an American director at an English studio since the war. The picture was adapted by Donald Ogden Stewart from a popular play co-written by British actor Robert Morley and Noel Langley. Morley had starred in a successful version of the play both in London and New York. The story concerns Arnold Boult, an egotistical father who schemes to make his son Edward a success. He ruthlessly commits arson and leads two people to commit suicide. Evelyn Bouth, his wife, tries to stop him but fails, becoming an alcoholic. She later dies when Edward is killed.

Cukor approached Spencer Tracy to accept the role of the obsessed father, which he did with enthusiasm. Although there had been some initial discussion of casting Katharine Hepburn in the female leading role, Deborah won the part. Hepburn accompanied Tracy to England and stayed at Claridge's, while he was hosted by Laurence Olivier and Vivien Leigh at their estate, Notley Abbey. The winter of 1948 was particularly cold and Britain had not yet recovered from the devastation of the war, still lacking gas and coal supplies. Being accustomed to the mild California weather, Tracy felt very uncomfortable at the Oliviers' huge house which was very cold. Moreover, the couple's personal problems made his British stay more miserable.

Deborah and Anthony with baby Melanie, 1948.

Edward, My Son was shot at the new Boreham Wood studio, near Elstree. From the first day on the set Cukor was immediately taken by Deborah, who proved to act with a disarming reality. The director, like Michael Powell years earlier, predicted a bright future for her. Shooting began on time and progressed smoothly with Cukor always ahead of schedule. Deborah and the director worked extensively together on the development of her character, from that of a young woman to an old, miserable alcoholic.

"George had a wonderful way with actors," said Deborah. "He would talk about a particular scene, and then say, 'Now forget everything I've said, and go and do it your own way.' This is very clever psychologically because everything he said had already gone into your head…. George helped me with being aged. He was always encouraging and open to ideas, but I was very young and in awe of him… He was an enchanting man."[12]

The atmosphere onset was very friendly with everybody working very hard. Hepburn made several visits to the set to watch Tracy, who was very impressed to meet and work with British technicians and to discover first-hand that "hands-across-the-sea" was no idle phrase but a vibrant reality.[13]

"I tremendously enjoyed working with Spencer Tracy," revealed Deborah to the *Saturday Evening Post*. "He deliberately tried to play down his part so that Evelyn's role would be sharper, and the director had to coax him to let the audience see more of him."[14]

Cukor urged Tracy to help the less experienced actors. In one scene Deborah had to pour a drink for herself. Tracy stood in the background as she sipped the drink.

"George," he suddenly said, "do you mind if I tell her something?"

"No, of course not, " Cukor said.

"You know, darling," Tracy then told Deborah, "when you're an alcoholic, you don't sip, you just throw the whole thing down."

Deborah later remarked, "Being young and not alcoholic, I didn't know that."[15]

During the shooting Cukor experimented with sustained takes, as Hitchcock had done a year earlier in *Rope*. Cukor also agreed to change Tracy's character from an Englishman into a Canadian to explain the actor's lack of accent and to respect the play's central gimmick that Edward is never seen.

Edward, My Son was completed in 40 days. On October 19, 1948, the first preview of the picture took place with a private screening. It went well except for a problem with the sound. Six months later, in March 1949, the film premièred in London. It was a critical triumph for Deborah, who was widely praised, while Spencer Tracy was panned by the critics as miscast. Deborah was, in fact, perfectly suited to her role. One of the main reasons British and American reviewers disliked Tracy's performance was due to the fact that Robert Morley's definitive stage interpretation of his own dialogue was still very fresh in their minds. Morley also hated the film, except for Deborah's performance. The playwright-actor thought that Tracy was sulky and boring in the part and that the direction was archaic.

"I'll never forget the letter my mother sent me after seeing the film," Deborah revealed years later in an interview. "'You were good,' she wrote, 'but do you have to play that sort of woman?'"[16]

During the making of the picture significant changes took place at MGM. In July 1948, Dore Schary, a former MGM writer who spent three years at RKO, returned to Metro as production head. Louis B. Mayer was uncomfortable with him and left the studio in 1951. Deborah continued working at MGM under Schary until the completion of her contract. In addition, that was the first year of mass-marketed home television sets and many films (including *Edward, My Son*), released in the first half of 1949, fell far below box office expectations. For her extraordinary performance, Deborah was nominated for a 1949 Academy Award for Best Actress in *Edward, My Son*—the first of six nominations she would receive during her career.

Once Schary took charge of MGM, he thought that Deborah needed a change of pace in her career, after her dramatic role in *Edward*. Her part in the light comedy *Please Believe Me* was scheduled to be filmed the following summer under the direction of Norman Taurog. Deborah starred as an English girl who, after inheriting a ranch in the States, is pursued for romantic favors aboard a ship by three men, played by Peter Lawford, Mark Stevens and Robert Walker. Deborah received top billing which upset Walker, who complained to Lawford and Stevens. The matter of billing became a running gag, but the offstage mockery carried over onto film. The cast worked well together, although Walker died in a tragic accident 14 months after the film was released. When it debuted in June 1950, *Please Believe Me* was a box office failure and quickly forgotten.

In mid–July of 1949, MGM cast Deborah in the leading role of Elizabeth Curtis in *King Solomon's Mines*.

"I was invited at the house of Dore Schary," remembered Deborah, "and having read *The African Queen* I thought it an ideal moment to say: 'I read a marvelous book called *The African Queen*; it would make a marvelous film, and I would love to go to Africa!' 'Aha!,' said Mr. Schary. 'That property belongs to Warner Bros. and we already have an African script—*King Solomon's Mines*—and as you say, you would love to go to Africa!' Need I say more? I was on my way to Nairobi before I knew it."[17]

Before leaving Hollywood, Deborah attended a screening of MGM's

Trader Horn, the only black and white feature film with American actors shot in Africa in 1931.

"As I sat in the darkened theatre watching those wild animals," wrote Deborah in a three-part-article about the experiences she had while shooting the film, "I remember thinking that, after all, that was two decades ago. Africa must have become a little more congenial since then. Little did I know."[18]

King Solomon's Mines was the idea of MGM staff producer Sam Zimbalist. For many years he had thought about producing a film based on H. Rider Haggard's 1885 adventure novel. When World

Deborah and Peter Lawford in *Please, Believe Me* (1950).

War II was over he thought the time was right to make the film in Africa and in Technicolor. In October of 1948, Helen Deutsch was appointed as the film's screenwriter, and unit production manager Walter Strohm was sent to Africa to scout feasible locations. It was a very ambitious project that made many MGM executives nervous. The Technicolor cameras were extremely bulky and required constant inspection, cleaning and maintenance. MGM planned to have two units operating simultaneously in Africa; one for principal photography, the other for primary scenic tribal and animal footage with doubles of the principal players.[19]

Opposite Deborah, Zimbalist was interested in casting Stewart Granger, who had emerged as a romantic star of British films in the leading rule of Allan Quartermain, the white hunter. Director Compton Bennett opted for Errol Flynn, with whom he had just worked on *That Forsyte Woman*. Zimbalist overruled and negotiations to have Granger in the picture began. By mid–September Granger arrived in Los Angeles.

"On the flight out to the coast I had a serious worry: the reaction of the leading lady who was to star with me in *King Solomon's Mines*," wrote

Richard Carlson, Deborah and Stewart Granger in *King's Solomon Mines* (1951).

Granger in his autobiography. "The last time I had seen her we had parted unhappily when we both agreed I should return to my wife. She had since married a man I had introduced her to during our European tour of *Gaslight....* What would be her reaction to spending three or four months with me in Africa? I needn't have worried. As soon as the plane stopped, an MGM representative came aboard and arranged for me to leave first, and there on the tarmac were Deborah Kerr and her husband. I was very moved as we hugged each other and Tony slapped me on the back, welcoming me to Hollywood. Thank God. I already had some friends there."[20]

Originally Tony was not meant to go along with Deborah to Africa, but as second unit director Andrew Marton revealed in an interview, "When I heard this I rushed to Zimbalist long before we left and said, 'Sam, you can't do this. You have Stewart Granger playing the lead and you have Deborah Kerr. Now, to send them to Africa together ... you can't do it.' He said, 'Why not? Why couldn't I do it?' I said, 'Well, as far as I know, there was something between those two years ago when she first came to entertain the troops. He was in the war, and they met in one of those USO shows. You can't do this to her. She's a newlywed.' He said,

'Well, let me see what I can do about that.' And that's how the husband came along."[21]

Richard Carlson was cast by Zimbalist as Deborah's character's brother. Along with Deborah and Granger, they were the only cast members brought to Africa. All the doubles were recruited on location except Michaela Denis (wife of travel-documentary filmmaker Armand Denis who was hired as technical advisor) who doubled for Deborah.

The governments of Tanganyika, Uganda, Kenya and the Belgian Congo all cooperated in every possible way to make the movie a success. However, permission to kill any animal was summarily denied. Also, everyone from the filming crew had been warned that no bare breasts of any woman from any tribe would be able to stay in the picture in order to comply with the Production Code Administration.

Cast and crew left for Kenya in October 1949. Deborah, Tony and Granger flew with a flying boat from Southampton. It was a slow and tiring flight with several stops. The trip took three days to the final destination: Machakos, a small village 50 miles from Nairobi.

"Our safari was believed to be the biggest Africa had ever seen," Deborah wrote in *The Star*. "It consisted of 102 people — 50 actors and technicians and 52 Africans to carry supplies, set up camp and handle cooking and laundry. There were seven trucks to carry cameras, sound gear, electric generators, and wardrobe. Two of them had refrigeration units to protect our film from the heat. Another had a bulldozing unit and two more had winches for towing in case equipment became bogged down in the steaming jungle."[22]

Finally, on the morning of October 19 — almost two years and eight months after MGM had begun pre–production — the cameras were ready to roll. For the first sequence 500 natives were required; they were paid about 30 cents a day as extras. Almost immediately the production was faced with several difficulties. Many had to do with Compton Bennett's attitude and direction. The director had made it very clear to Granger that he wanted Errol Flynn in that part and that he was cast only because of Zimbalist. Consequently, there were many arguments, with Granger being particularly outspoken about the director's approach.

"He's extremely good at a number of things," commented Deborah about Granger's behavior, "but getting along with people isn't one of them. For that matter, some of the others who went on our African junket didn't precisely distinguish themselves for tact."

On the other hand, everybody on the set loved Deborah. "She was absolutely marvelous," commented Andrew Marton. Granger once said to her disapprovingly, "Everybody likes you! What do you want to be liked for?"[23]

When told to fire only blank cartridges from his elephant gun during filming, Granger raged like a madman. When he finally calmed down, he admitted, "I have a filthy bad temper. I'm no good at sitting in corners and sucking my thumb if people try to do me in."

Regardless, his macho personality was the key to his sex appeal, as Deborah admitted: "Rightly or wrongly, women sense that there's a bit of a brute in him. A woman's intuition tells her that being a gentleman hasn't watered down his virility, and that he would as soon thwack her on the rear as not." She added, "There are times when I feel my own *derrière* shrink as I pass him."[24]

The filming continued, but not without other mishaps. One of the planes burned after landing at Murchinson Falls; Deborah's double had to be sent to London for plastic surgery after her driver ran their car into a hartebeest; there were also several cases among the crew of amoebic dysentery. Deborah, who was the only one to retain her health and to be untouched by stress (although she came down with a viral influenza when she returned to England) admitted, "I used bottled water, wine or ginger ale, brushing my teeth with a light Belgian wine."[25] Deborah proved to be tougher than any man on the crew: she never complained about the unbelievable heat that once reached 152 degrees, nor did she complain when having to carry her own equipment after the tsetse flies killed off the horses and mules.

"There were times when I wanted to sit and cry, and felt I could not continue for another minute," she explained in an interview. "Somehow we all managed to keep going, but I can truthfully say that I wouldn't dream of trying again."[26]

The sole complaint she filed with the production was at the top of Murchinson Falls, after shooting a scene in which she washes her newly cropped hair (the long hair was a wig) and then lying on a rock to dry. "My own hair was reasonably curly, but I *did* argue vociferously against having it all curled after the bath. But, there was no time to [continue to] argue, so I sported my Toni Home Permanent after cutting my 'hair'!"[27]

Bennett knew that MGM was adamant about the "permanent." She can't go through the rest of the picture with *straight* hair, was the MGM order.

"This scene," said co-director Andrew Marton, "cost me an Academy

Award, because you should have seen the preview cards saying, 'Where did she get the Toni?' Her hair was too elaborate — it was studio curly hair."[28]

By the end of March the shooting in Africa was completed. However, back on Lot Three at the MGM studios in Culver City, work on the film continued along with two sequences shot in Death Valley and at the World Jungle Compound in Thousand Oaks. After explaining in detail what the problems were on location, Bennett was relieved of his duties and Marton was made the sole director for the

With Stewart Granger in *King's Solomon Mines* (1951).

remainder of the shoot. Finally, on April 13 — after six months in production — *King Solomon's Mines* was completed. The final cost was $2 million, $200,000 over budget.

In July the film premièred successfully, first in Los Angeles. and later in New York. It went into general release on November 24, 1950, and was an instant, international hit.

During her African adventure, Deborah was saddened by the tragic news of her grandfather Smale's death at age 87. Only six months later, on April 18, 1950, her mother (who was only 54), was involved in a fatal accident when her car collided with a truck. In the crash Deborah's little terrier, Simon, broke his spine and was later put to sleep. Deborah's stepfather, Tom Purvis, escaped with minor injuries. These events were a devastating shock for Deborah. She did not attend the service, however, and was ready to go again on location — this time to Rome to star in *Quo Vadis.*

5

Hollywood's Most
Elegant Redhead

People always described me as ladylike. If only they knew!!!
— Deborah Kerr

When MGM decided to make the third film adaptation of *Quo Vadis?*, Henryk Sienkiewicz's famous novel set in Rome during the early days of Christianity, the pre–production process spread over several years. The final recommencement of work on the picture saw many important replacements to the original project. Producer Sam Zimbalist replaced Arthur Hornblow, Jr.; director Mervyn LeRoy replaced John Huston, and was undoubtedly Mayer's choice; Dore Schary preferred Anthony Mann, who shot some night scenes for the picture. Stewart Granger was cast as Marcus Vinicius, but he refused to sign a long-term contract and was replaced by Robert Taylor. Deborah took over as Lygia, a Christian slave in love with Vinicius, after Elizabeth Taylor and Jean Simmons were ruled out. Audrey Hepburn made a test in full Roman costume, but she was judged too unknown for the part. Peter Ustinov had been tested for the role of Nero as early 1949 but he was dropped because Zimbalist thought he was too young. However, after Ustinov wired Zimbalist that, historically, he was too old (Nero died at twenty-six; Ustinov was twenty-nine), the producer, amused, changed his mind and cast him.

From the very beginning Schary despised the entire project. He hated epics and dismissed the whole idea of remaking the film, considering it "lumpy."[1]

Mayer decided that *Quo Vadis* (the question mark was dropped from the title) had to be shot in high summer, remembering the disastrous winter in Rome while filming *Ben-Hur* in 1924 when icy rain deluged the city. He appointed Robert Sturges, who had so magnificently photographed *King Solomon's Mines*, as cinematographer.

Shooting began in early spring of 1950. Deborah, along with two-year-old Melanie, left for Italy by boat from New York on April 28. Tony followed her a few weeks later. She was expected on the set at Cinecittà Studios, eight miles outside Rome, a few days later. The Roman studios covered 148 acres, with nine big sound stages all occupied by the production. It was one of the hottest summers Italy ever experienced. Despite the efforts, it was impossible to install air conditioning at Cinecittà. The temperature on the sound stages often exceeded 100 degrees. Between takes, the actors would sometimes strip down and be hosed off. Deborah, when not needed on the set, escaped from the heat of Rome to a mountain hotel two hours away by car.

Throughout the entire making of *Quo Vadis*, director Mervyn LeRoy was very tense, as he revealed in his autobiography: "I knew the enormity of the project. I knew the logistics were such that it could easily go wrong. I knew a picture of that magnitude could, if I erred badly, wreck the studios. There was a lot riding on it, and I had the jitters in a big way."[2]

Quo Vadis was the most expensive picture ever produced at the time. Several ancient buildings were erected, 10,250 costumes were sewn by a thousand seamstresses, 12,000 custom jewels, 2,500 suits of armor and shields, six fighting bulls, a stable of horses, 14 racing chariots and 50 lions were only some of the items used to make the picture as realistic as possible.

Deborah was up at 5 A.M. every day and in bed by 10 P.M. The shooting was very tedious, as she recalled, "The movie was made under terribly difficult conditions, enormous heat and many irritations ... it was almost like making three movies, it went on so long."

Luckily the relationship with her co-star was perfect: Robert Taylor proved to have a wonderful sense of humor. "Bob was good-natured and un-fussy.... I felt that he was a much better actor than he was given credit for."[3]

In addition to the unbearable heat, the strong winds interfered with the sound of the picture. One day, Deborah and Taylor tried a scene together but were stopped several times because of the noisy wind. When it calmed down, LeRoy asked them to do the scene quickly, but Taylor delivered his lines poorly three times. They tried again and again until it went smoothly but, clearly, the episode left them exhausted.

In another scene shot in the arena, Deborah had to be tied to a pole while, a few steps away, 6'7" tall Buddy Baer wrestled with a chloroformed bull. Deborah was terrified. She was very relieved by the fact that it took LeRoy only a few takes to print the sequence.

On May 21, Deborah, Robert Taylor and other members from the cast and the crew were granted a private audience with Pope Pius XII. They presented him with a 16mm sound projector. During the 20-minute meeting the Pope told his guests his memories of a trip to Hollywood he took in 1936.

The cast included several unbilled stars, including Sophia Loren, who played an extra. Elizabeth Taylor was in Rome with her husband Nicky Hilton and, after a fight with him, asked LeRoy to hide her on the set, where she appeared in a mob scene.

In the end, *Quo Vadis* had cost MGM approximately $12 million, making it one of the most expensive films produced up to that time. LeRoy stayed in Rome for 14 months, actually shooting in seven. The film opened simultaneously at the Astor and Capitol theaters in New York on November 8, 1951. It grossed over $12 million at the domestic box office despite a cool reception by the critics. The reviewers mostly focused on the grandiosity of the film and mentioned little about the performances — only Peter Ustinov's portrayal of Nero was universally praised. Regardless, the picture was a colossal box office success all over the world and brought popular recognition to all of its stars, Deborah included.

Deborah completed her work on *Quo Vadis* just before Christmas 1950 and eagerly returned home via London.

With Robert Taylor in a publicity shot for *Quo Vadis* (1952).

Only few months went by before she was back on the set. On loan to Paramount from MGM, she played opposite Alan Ladd and Charles Boyer in *Thunder in the East*. Deborah was cast as Joan Willoughby, intrigued by the challenge to play a blind English girl brought up in the Indian state of Ghandahar. Deborah felt that playing a blind person was one of the most difficult tasks she had to confront as an actress "since it is natural, when talking to someone, to look at them." For verisimilitude in the role, it become necessary for me to focus 'through' the person addressed."

In Rome on the set of *Quo Vadis.*

It was a role that, at first glance, looked promising. But due to the weak plot, it was a great disappointment.

Thunder in the East was based on a novel by Alan Moorehead. It was written for the screen by Jo Swerling based on an adaptation by George Tabori and Frederick Brennan. Director Charles Vidor shot the entire film at Paramount Studios. During the 48-day shooting schedule, Deborah was coached to speak Hindustani by an Indian cinematography student from University of Southern California. She enjoyed working with Alan Ladd, even though off the set she found him rather withdrawn and distant. She loved Charles Boyer, whose French accent she found most seductive. His "liquorice-stick accent was saved from the comical by his ability as an actor," she said years later remembering her French co-star.[4]

Thunder in the East had as its backdrop the violence and turmoil of India in its first year of independence from Britain. In fact, although the plot and the characters were fictitious, the U.S. State Department apparently felt the material was politically inflammatory (the picture was not shown at all in India and Pakistan) and at the Department's request, Paramount withheld the release for two years. The real reason the film was shelved was because nobody knew what to do with this mediocre melo-

With Alan Ladd in *Thunder in the East* (1951).

drama with such unconvincing performances. In addition, the movie went through several working titles before flopping in the theaters as *Thunder in the East*.

In March 1951, the press announced that, in June, Deborah would star in *Ivanhoe*, based on Sir Walter Scott's popular novel. It was to be produced by Pandro S. Berman and directed by Richard Thorpe. When Deborah revealed the following month that she was expecting her second baby, MGM replaced her with Elizabeth Taylor.

On December 18, after five months of complete rest, Deborah gave birth to her second daughter, Francesca Ann, in Los Angeles. Despite the joy of family, Tony was going crazy in Hollywood. Bartley was struggling to find a new identity for himself besides being "Mr. Deborah Kerr." Thanks to Deborah's insistence, MGM had a bill rushed through the House of Representatives to have Tony off the uncertain immigration status of visitor in the U.S. and to receive proper recognition as one of America's greatest allies and heroes, becoming a legal, permanent resident alien. After his trip to Africa for *King Solomon's Mines*, Tony had become interested in the Dark Continent. He later produced, with little success, several documentaries for a television network.

Upon *Ivanhoe*'s completion in England, Thorpe and Berman did not forget about Deborah and offered her a leading role in *The Prisoner of Zenda*. Based on Sir Anthony Hope Hawkins's best-selling book of the same title, it was first adapted into a stage play, which became very popular. In 1922 the Metro Company, forerunners of MGM, made the first silent screen version starring Lewis Stone, Alice Terry and Ramon Novarro. Fifteen years later, their successors were Ronald Colman, Madeleine Carroll and Douglas Fairbanks, Jr., in the David O. Selznick talkie version. On Stewart Granger's suggestion MGM became convinced to produce a new remake of this tale of an Englishman on holiday in Ruritania. The traveler looks exactly like the local king, against whom a terrible plot had been conceived. Dore Schary paid Selznick half a million dollars for the rights to the book and cast Deborah and James Mason along with Granger. The studio decided that the remake would be an exact copy of the Ronald Colman version. On the set Richard Thorpe had installed a moviola which constantly ran the Selznick version to make sure that each shot was perfectly copied. The director, nicknamed "One-Take Thorpe" for his well-known satisfaction with one-take scenes, did not make any effort, with the exception of using Technicolor cameras and minor details, to stray from an exact replica of the 1937 version. Even the music score was an adaptation of the previous film.

Zenda received mixed reviews, and Deborah was hardly noticed by the critics, being relegated to a few brief scenes. Although, she performed her role with great skill, it seemed rather decorative.

One night, while Tony was away on business, Deborah, who was not expected on the *Zenda* set until the following afternoon, went to see Groucho Marx on stage. After the performance, the comedian escorted her to a party. As midnight approached, he learned that she lived in Pacific Palisades. Marx, who was well-known for his frugality, did not intend to waste any gas or any extra time since Deborah's home was far out of his way. He jumped on a chair and addressed the homeward bound of party-goers: "Anyone for Pacific Palisades?" Deborah was surprised by his bizarre behavior and got a ride home by one of the other guests.[5]

Cary Grant wanted to make a movie based on the Alfred Lunt and Lynn Fontanne stage hit *O Mistress Mine* (known in England as *Love in Idleness*) written by Terence Rattigan and with Deborah as his leading lady. Unfortunately, the film rights were unavailable and the project never came to fruition. Nonetheless she co-starred with him in three films; the first was *Dream Wife*, which they made in the spring of 1952.

Academy Award winner (Best Original Screenplay, *The Bachelor and the Bobby-Soxer,* 1947) and later bestselling author Sidney Sheldon, who worked for MGM, became interested in a short story called *Dream Wife,* written by Alfred Levitt. The plot was about the battle of sexes. The central character is Clemson Reade, a bachelor who is engaged to Effie, a beautiful State Department official who is too busy with an oil crisis in the Middle East to have time to marry him. Reade meets a beautiful young princess on a business trip and decides that he would prefer a housewife to a working woman. After he proposes to Princess Tarji, who was born and bred to please her husband, complications begin.

Sheldon had Cary Grant in mind as the leading man, but he knew his schedule was full. When the script was completed he presented the project to Dore Schary, and explained that Grant and Deborah were his dream choices. The screenplay was sent to Grant who accepted five days later on condition that the director would be his choice. Since his preferences were all involved in other movies, Grant proposed Sheldon as director. Schary approved and Sidney Sheldon was appointed as *Dream Wife's*

director. When the news spread, Sheldon received a call from Columbia president Harry Cohn. Cohn warned him that Grant had chosen him to direct the film so that he could use Sheldon's inexperience to his advantage and take charge. Cohn was right and troubles began before the cameras started rolling, as Sheldon recalled in his memoirs: "The night we began to shoot, Deborah Kerr called me. 'Sidney, I just want to tell you that Cary said the two of us should gang up on you. I told him I won't do it.'"

With cinematographer Joseph Ruttenberg on the set of *The Prisoner of Zenda* (1952).

"Thank you, Deborah."[6]

When filming started the next morning, Grant was very bossy. Although Sheldon threatened to quit, he didn't. Every day the star tried to test the novice director, making shooting quite difficult. Grant was physically not well, suffering from a bout of hepatitis, and was thin, drawn, and pale with a yellowish cast to his skin. Regardless, he refused makeup.

A publicity shot for *Dream Wife* (1953) with Cary Grant and "dream wife" Betta St. John.

One day in a scene he had with Deborah, in which the two were to discuss the oil crisis, he spoke the lines with such gravitas, raising and lowering his eyebrows (à la Groucho Marx) that she burst out laughing. Sheldon repeated the takes several times, but each time Deborah laughed. When the director tried to rehearse the sequence without her, he could not stop laughing at the overpowering intensity of Grant's facial expression. Finally, the actor stopped his mannerisms, and the scene was printed.

Despite his problems with Grant, Sheldon loved working with Deborah: "She was enormously talented and she and Cary were wonderful together."

Elvis Presley made an unexpected visit to the set to watch the two stars working. The singer was at the height of his popularity. Deborah, like the rest of the cast, was very impressed by his politeness and modesty.

Dream Wife was filmed in black and white — a "fatal flaw" as Schary admitted. "[It] screamed for the richness of color ... the picture did not work because the central core of the plot was phony. Perhaps if played for farce it might have worked, but it was my fault for not recognizing that possibility long before we put the film in the camera."[7]

The film was a critical and financial disappointment. When it opened in July 1953, the reviewers praised Grant and Deborah, but dismissed the picture almost out of hand. Years later Deborah called *Dream Wife* "a much underrated and amusing little comedy."[8]

After the incredible success of *King Solomon's Mines*, MGM planned another adventure that would have carried Deborah from the African safari to the early American wilderness in *Westward the Women*. According to plans, the studio revealed to the press that Deborah's role would be the head of a group of frontier-bound women headed West under the guidance of a scout, played by Robert Taylor. They were to bring Eastern femininity to pioneer bachelor settlers. The project was to be directed by William Wellman and produced by Dore Schary, but it was aborted for unknown reasons. Instead, Deborah was able to star in the tiny role of Portia in Joseph Mankiewicz's adaptation of William Shakespeare's *Julius Caesar*.

On August 25, 1952, she joined the prestigious cast of *Julius Caesar*. It was Schary's idea to make America's first serious Shakespearean film. (There had been *A Midsummer Night's Dream* made by Warner Bros. in 1935.) John Houseman was to produce and Joseph Mankiewicz to direct. Originally, they all were inclined to play it safe with an all-British-star cast. Houseman argued that the film should be made in England but Schary refused. The first actors cast were indeed British: John Gielgud as Cassius — a part he had just played successfully on stage; and Louis Calhern as Caesar, a choice made by Houseman which had not been unanimously approved, but later no one regretted. For Brutus, Mankiewicz suggested his friend James Mason, who was working full-force in Hollywood. In the small parts of Caesar's and Brutus's wives Schary cast two MGM resident stars: Greer Garson and Deborah. This left one major role to be filled: Marc Antony. Houseman proposed Marlon Brando, who was at the peak of his career after the incredible success of *A Streetcar Named Desire* and *Viva Zapata!* The first general reaction was disbelief. Most people had seen Brando only as Stanley Kowalski and did not think he had the right voice and manner for a Shakespearean character. Nevertheless, Brando refused to do a screentest and sent instead a taped recording of Marc Antony's dramatic entrance into the Senate after Caesar's assassination.

"It was a powerful and flawless recording," Houseman recalled. "Joe was immediately convinced; so was Schary when the tape arrived from New York. But the general skepticism persisted," Houseman wrote in his autobiography.[9]

Although Deborah was appearing in only one scene opposite James

With James Mason in Joseph L. Mankiewicz's *Julius Caesar* (1953).

Mason as the devoted, fanatically loyal Portia, she was invited to join a three-week rehearsal period with the entire cast. It was, in fact, necessary for the leading actors to become word-perfect in their parts. On the first day Deborah elegantly sat at a horseshoe table set up in a corner of an MGM sound stage together with her co-stars to give a cold reading of the script. Brando appeared in a striped sweatshirt with a rolled umbrella. He was the one everybody was dying to hear, and he gave a perfect performance. Deborah's reading was flawless, if not just adequate. The atmosphere on the set was relaxed and the production went smoothly.

Apparently Brando approved of his male co-stars, but dismissed the casting of Deborah and Greer Garson.

"Their names were added just for the box office," he said to Mankiewicz. "I am trying to decide which one to fuck first. If I proposition Deborah Kerr, and I don't think I will, I fear it will not be a match made in heaven. But I hear Garson likes young guys. I think I'd like to fuck Mrs. Miniver. Why not?"[10]

Deborah's relationship with Brando was strictly professional, even though Marlon enjoyed flirting with her every time the two met onset. However, as they did not have any scenes together they did not see much of each other, while Greer Garson did indeed have a short affair with him, as he had predicted.

The fact that Deborah and Garson were working together in the same film prompted the press to invent a rivalry between the two of them — being both English, redheaded MGM stars. But the two actresses had a lot of fun in reading the writers' fabrications. They were bound by a real friendship that would last until Garson's death in 1996.

Julius Caesar opened worldwide in the summer of 1953, and was a smash hit. The film grossed more than $4 million during its first engagement and received four Academy Award nominations, including Best Picture.

Simultaneous to the film's release, Deborah appeared in a magazine commercial for Lux Soap, which featured three photographs — two close-ups, one with a blurb promoting MGM's *Julius Caesar* and another with her painting a winter landscape, one of her favorite hobbies.

Despite its success, *Julius Caesar* did very little to help Deborah's stalling career. She was still being typecast in the same "ladylike" roles in period films like *Young Bess*, in which she appeared next. "All I had to do was to be high-minded, long-suffering, white-gloved and decorative," she recalled years later.

Four years after she had done a screentest for *Young Bess*, the project finally got the green light. Deborah was originally cast to play the title role, but the script presented problems principally because one MGM producer wanted Elizabeth Taylor in the role. So Bess's youth, which spanned the years from 11 to 16 when Taylor was in the script, kept being altered to encompass the 22 to 36 age group when Deborah was to star. The project was shelved. When MGM reconsidered it, the starring roles went to

With Jean Simmons in *Young Bess* (1953).

Stewart Granger and his wife, Jean Simmons, with Simmons winning top billing. Deborah was billed third as Catherine Parr.

Described as "an exceedingly free improvisation on Elizabethan themes and an handsome, Technicolored show window" by *Newsweek*, *Young Bess*, based on a Margaret Irwin novel, tells of the years in the life of Elizabeth I (1533–1603) before she became the imperious monarch. She wins the admiration of her father, Henry VIII (once again played by Charles Laughton, twenty years later after his Oscar victory for playing the same role), and, after his death, she persuades her half-brother, young King Edward (Rex Thompson), to order First Lord Admiral of the Navy Thomas Seymour (Granger) to marry her father's widow, Catherine Parr. But Seymour finds that he loves two women, Elizabeth and Catherine. After the death of Catherine, he confesses his feelings for the young princess. She admits that her love for him is also strong.

As MGM had anticipated, a good deal of publicity was generated by Jean and Stewart joining the ranks of real-life husband-and-wife teams who acted together on screen. Jean was asked about her on-camera romancing with Stewart: "I feel more self-conscious about playing love scenes with him now, with everybody on the set watching, than I did before we were man and wife."[11]

It was not accidental that MGM released *Young Bess* in 1953, the year of Elizabeth II's coronation. The studio tried to profit on the wave of royal enthusiasm and interest in the new queen by making yet another film about her predecessor. Although *Young Bess* was directed by George Sidney, a master of musicals and costume romps, it was only mildly successful. Deborah enjoyed starring once again opposite her close friends, the Grangers, but above all she was happy to appear in a film with Charles Laughton. She always admired him, but never had the chance to work with him.

Deborah began to have some serious doubts about her career: "I had been on MGM's payroll for six years. Critically speaking, after *Thunder in the East* and *Dream Wife*, I was ready to be wheeled away to a fire sale. Even profitwise, I was becoming a hard item to move. Now I was down to play a cameo in *Julius Caesar* and a minor part in *Young Bess*. My 'ineradicable gentility' was an albatross draped around my neck. I wasn't a woman but a 'lady'; anemic, prissy, frigid, given to wear Victorian unmentionables. I yearned to sink my teeth into parts I could chew on!"[12]

Discontented with the roles she was offered, Deborah asked Schary to release her from her contract, so she could accept work from other studios. She knew that the price of her freedom would be $100,000 in salary she would not get. The MGM's chief of production agreed to let her go on the condition that they would have her services for three movies at some future date. Once free, Deborah also severed her professional relationship with MCA, the agency which had represented her during the last six years. She signed with Bert Allenberg, an independent agent who personally represented only a very few artists. Deborah met Allenberg through her friend, director Charles Vidor. That meeting was destined to be a major turning point in her career.

6

A Turning Point to Eternity

That's great for that stuck-up British bitch.

— Joan Crawford

In 1951 president of Columbia Pictures, Harry Cohn, bought the rights to James Jones's controversial best-seller *From Here to Eternity* for $82,000, as part of a strategy to compete with other major studios. Nevertheless there was much skepticism that this more than 800-page-novel could ever be adapted into a film since it featured prostitution, homosexuality, venereal disease, an extra-marital affair and rough language. On the other hand, the book had been such a critical and popular success, winning the National Book Award for 1952 and selling over three million copies. It seemed to be a wonderful opportunity and a great challenge to make it into a picture. After several writers, including Jones, had failed to adapt the novel, Cohn asked Daniel Taradash, who specialized in adapting novels and had spent three years in the military, to work on the script. The skilled screenwriter knew exactly how far he could go and still get the Army's cooperation, especially the use of Schofield Barracks. He was especially skillful at toning down many of the book's controversial points, all the while staying faithful to the spirit of the novel. The screenwriter also pitched his ideas to producer Buddy Adler and suggested Fred Zinnemann as director. Adler accepted to produce the film and Cohn agreed to meet with Zinnemann.

Fred Zinnemann was a well-respected, new director who had been nominated in 1947 for an Academy Award for his moving postwar drama *The Search*. He had also directed Marlon Brando in his first film, *The Men*, in 1950, and had made the Western modern with his minimalist approach

On the set of *From Here to Eternity* (1953).

in *High Noon*. Cohn, however, did not like him, especially after he had directed the box office failure *The Member of the Wedding* for Columbia. Zinnemann and Cohn, in fact, clashed as soon as they met, having different casting opinions for *Eternity*. The president of Columbia became very angry when contradicted, however he agreed to send a copy of the script to Montgomery Clift, whom Zinnemann had proposed for the leading role of Private Prewitt, dismissing Cohn's idea of casting Aldo Ray who had already tested for the part.

After Clift's presence in the picture was confirmed, a stellar cast was aligned. Robert Mitchum was considered for the part which Burt Lancaster ultimately played. Frank Sinatra, Ernest Borgnine and Donna Reed were also selected. Reed, who was under contract to Columbia, was personally cast by Cohn, as he was afraid of losing artistic control if a Columbia player wasn't among the principals.[1] For the critical role of Karen Holmes, the captain's adulterous wife, Cohn wanted Joan Crawford, a movie star enjoying a second comeback. But Adler, Taradah and Zinnemann felt Crawford was wrong for the part. The director was especially displeased to hear she was already selecting a stylish array of costumes for her role, before meeting or consulting with him. Also Crawford was not ready to accept second billing to Lancaster. Whatever the reason, Zinnemann was determined to find a replacement for her. Jennifer Jones and Joan Fontaine were considered before Deborah's name was finally mentioned.

"That's great for that stuck-up British bitch," was Crawford's bitter comment to close friend William Haines on casting Deborah. "It's about time somebody got to fuck her!"[2]

As Zinnemann recalled, "Suddenly the agent Bert Allenberg — a man with the rare talent of reading letters upside down — phoned. He sounded diffident. 'What about Deborah Kerr?' he asked. Dan, Buddy and I thought casting against type a brilliant idea. Up to that point Miss Kerr had played ladies who had what Hollywood calls 'class,' and rather chilly class at that. I thought that, hearing a corporal say at the start of the film that 'she sleeps with every soldier on the post,' the audience would not believe it. They would be curious to see how things would develop, so the casting of Deborah would create an added sense of suspense and excitement."[3] He added, "If you looked at Joan Crawford, you wouldn't find it impossible to believe she sleeps with everybody."[4]

Allenberg had first called Cohn to suggest Deborah, his new client, as Karen. "Why, you stupid son of a bitch," yelled Cohn hanging up. When he met with Adler, Zinnemann and Taradash later that day, he scoffed, "You know what that crazy son of a bitch Allenberg suggested? Deborah Kerr for Karen." The trio looked at each other and said almost simultaneously, "Yes!"[5]

When Allenberg called Deborah to ask if she was interested in playing Karen Holmes, she almost laughed at him, saying she would love to, but that she knew Cohn would never consider her for that part. She was, in

Top: Taking a pause with Montgomery Clift between takes on *From Here to Eternity* (1953). *Bottom:* In Hawaii having lunch with Monty Clift while making *From Here to Eternity* (1953).

fact, right; Cohn hung up on her agent. But two days later Allenberg called her back and said in great disbelief that Cohn had just called him to determine her asking price if she were cast in *Eternity*. Deborah was ecstatic when she was asked to meet with the director who did a screentest of her standing up in a swimsuit and listened to her amazingly flat American accent. He immediately knew she would be perfect for the role. While posing in a swimsuit for wardrobe stills, Deborah was heard to say, "I feel naked without my tiara," a witty reference to the fact that, finally, she was not being typecast in another period character.[6]

"It was astounding getting my part," Deborah recalled.[7]

With her newly dyed blonde hair, as the role required, she reported to the Columbia ranch at the end of February 1953. Shortly thereafter the crew was ready to shoot the exteriors which were filmed at the exact locations described in the novel. Taradash submitted the script to the U.S. Army in order to obtain their cooperation, and they finally agreed after some small changes were made to the script. Some officers were chosen as technical advisors and the Schofield Barracks in Hawaii were made available for the shooting. Cohn set a narrowly scheduled shooting time and a strict budget, making the picture in black and white to contain its cost.

The story took place in a U.S. Army base in Hawaii in 1941, just before the Japanese attack on Pearl Harbor. Private Robert E. Lee Prewitt (Montgomery Clift) had just been transferred from the Music Corps to the Infantry. After he refused to join the boxing team, Capt. Holmes (Philip Ober) made his life hell. Only Sergeant Warden (Burt Lancaster) and Private Angelo Maggio (Frank Sinatra) have sympathy for him. Warden, however, is reluctant to step out of line, since he is having a steamy affair with Holmes's wife Karen (Deborah). Only Maggio bravely takes Prewitt's side in a fight, with fatal consequences.

On March 2 a chartered plane landed at 5:00 A.M. in Honolulu. Frank Sinatra and Monty Clift were so drunk that Burt Lancaster and Deborah had to shake them to wake them up. In Honolulu, they all stayed at the Alexander Young Hotel and often met in the evening for dinner.

Deborah, who had met Lancaster for the first time on the plane recalled, "It was a great help, really, to spend those hours chatting. I'm a bit shy, particularly with a big noise as he was. He was sweetness itself. He couldn't have been more encouraging."[8]

In an interview with *The Times*, she also revealed, "The whole movie was a coming together of parts and personalities that together had magic.

Sinatra's emotional life was linked up with the playing of the thing, and he was a bit on the down. His voice had left him, and he went down on bended knees to get the part. But he was born to play it. And when I watched Monty Clift.... I used to feel that the day when Prewitt is shot, Monty is going to die. I'm going to feel that he's really dead. The intensity of the way that boy lived that whole part was hair-raising. He tortured himself. He suffered so."[9] Deborah was only in one scene with Clift, but she was visibly impressed by Monty's perfectionism. They rehearsed it for two entire days. On the set Deborah worked hard with voice coach Jud Addis to rid her of her British accent.

"There is a chemistry that happened between us," said Deborah about he co-star Burt Lancaster "I was not conscious of it and neither was he. But he had such a good and forceful attitude toward this part — and toward mine." Although they had only six scenes together, one: Scene #106, the beach love scene, became one of the most famous sexy and romantic scenes in film history. It was shot with a crew of 100 on Holocona Cove near the Blowhole Beach in Oahu, Hawaii. "It was a challenging sequence since it had to be timed with the incoming waves so that they would break over the couple at the right instant," recalled Zinnemann.[10]

Deborah commented, "We worked so hard, for a whole day. Burt is a very disciplined and hard-working man, and so is Fred Zinnemann. It was wet and gritty and uncomfortable, but we worked and worked, waiting for the right wave. And it was a scene that couldn't be too much rehearsed in advance, because it wasn't determined how we'd do it until we went to that particular beach in Hawaii, that Fred Zinnemann had chosen. And then we thought, 'Shall we play it up there, or down here?' And as I remember the idea came quite mutually to play it much nearer the water, so that the sea would roll over us as we kissed."[11] Lancaster confirmed that the scene, watched by a group of curious tourists, was not real fun to make: "It was damned uncomfortable in those wet bathing suits with the sand getting in it. Not at all romantic." The Production Code office, which regulated censorship, insisted that four seconds be cut from that sequence, objecting to the presence of the water. It also forbade some publicity shots taken on the beach. Zinnemann revealed that in later years he found out that even more had been snipped out by theater projectionists, as a souvenir. On commenting about that particular scene, Deborah said, "When I see that sequence today ... I am still astounded by how extraordinarily erotic it is. There is a feverishness about the way we undress. And the idea on making love with the surf breaking over us! Thank you very much! It

was quite chilly and uncomfortable, but on the screen it somehow height-
ens the sensuality."[12]

Darwin Porter, in his biography on Merv Griffin, reported that
Griffin, who was invited on the set by Clift, was introduced to Deborah.
She allegedly said to him, "I'm surrounded by men. All of them are a bit
macho for me. I find Burt Lancaster very sexy, but so does everybody else.
What woman in her right mind would say no to him? Or man for that
matter. He's equally attractive to both sexes. As for Monty, I feel very pro-
tective of him. He came on strong to me, but I turned him down. I know
he wants to love women, but sexually, he's attracted only to men." Porter
maintains that later Lancaster confessed to Griffin that he was having an
affair with her, what he called "this thing with Deborah."[13]

Donna Reed, who played the role of a prostitute and shared a long
final scene with Deborah, felt intimidated by her presence. Overcoming
her difference, Reed looked on the scene as an acting duel with Deborah,
one in which there could be no tie. "She was relieved when the scene was
over, and came away feeling she had won," she said to a friend. Deborah,
who liked Reed, was unaware of her feelings. "We seldom met during the
production," she explained in an interview, "and it is true that the cast
tended to concentrate their relationships — mine with Burt Lancaster and
Monty Clift and Frank Sinatra — and probably Donna *did* feel separated
from the whole."[14]

Eternity wrapped in Hawaii around the middle of April, and the company returned to the Columbia ranch to film a few interiors. The picture
was then completed in 41 days with a $2.5 million budget, making it one
of the costliest films of 1953. It premièred at New York's Capitol Theatre
but with no more fanfare than a full-page ad in the *New York Times*. When
it opened nationwide at the end of the summer, *From Here to Eternity*
earned more than $12 million in the first few months of its release. On the
first weekend of its release, theaters in New York had to stay open all night
to accommodate the huge crowds. The New York Critics Association
awarded Zinnemann Best Director of the Year and the picture obtained a
record 13 Oscar nominations (including Deborah as Best Actress), and
won eight. Thanks to her provocative yet withdrawn performance, which
captured the bitterness and yearning of the Karen Holmes role, Deborah
received flattering reviews which allowed her to open her career to a whole
new range of roles.

"Sexy was the word for Karen Holmes" commented Deborah to the
press, "and for the first time in my life I found myself material for cheese-

cake — and it proved something. It proved that I had arrived as an actress who had physical allure. I don't think anyone thought I could until I put on a bathing suit."[15]

Once she completed her scenes, Deborah had time to spend a few days with her daughters before leaving for New York. "As soon I have suitable accommodation in New York," she told the press, "I'll send for the children."[16] First rumors about a crisis with Tony circulated in the press. Deborah called them "pure fabrications" only created by the fact that she and her husband had often been seen apart since her work required her to travel. Deborah was now ready to leave for New York where she was expected to make her Broadway debut. Before her departure she said to the press: "I haven't stepped on a stage in eight years and while I'm quite nervous about my debut on Broadway it is what I've set my heart on.... During the years I was under exclusive contract to MGM I wasn't allowed to accept Broadway play offers. It broke my heart when I couldn't do *Anne of a Thousand Days* but since I am now more or less of a free agent I'm going to realize my ambition — a New York play."[17]

On August 1, 1953, Deborah arrived in New York. A few days later she was invited to be a guest panelist on the popular game show *What's My Line?*, which marked her first appearance on American television. Her reason for being in the Big Apple, however, was to star in Robert Anderson's play *Tea and Sympathy*.

"As soon as Bob Anderson offered me this, I grabbed [it]," she explained to the *New York Times*, "It seemed almost foreordained. Five years ago I'd been East to do a *Theater Guild on the Air* show and Bob was then doing scripts. My radio assignment was *Remember the Day*. It was a schoolteacher role and we discussed an idea of a similar background. Last winter before *Eternity* I was doing another radio show and, as I left, Bob gave me this script and said, 'Here it is.' I knew as soon as I read it that I wanted to attempt this part very much. Immediately I went to Metro and since they didn't have anything in view, they let me go."[18]

Thirty-four-year-old Robert Anderson, who was at the beginning of his career, remembered, "After our initial meeting in New York, I wrote *Tea and Sympathy* after some time had passed: oddly I did not have Deborah in mind when I wrote it. I never have any actor in mind when I write, but when the Playwrights' Company decided to produce the play I told all and sundry that I would like Deborah to play the part. I immediately sent her a script."[19]

Nevertheless Elia Kazan, who was an old friend of Anderson as well as the director of the production, resisted Anderson's choice to cast Deborah in the role of Laura, a prep school housemaster's wife. In the story, Laura befriends a sensitive student, Tom, who is accused by his mates of being gay. Hoping to turn the boy from suicidal despair, Laura, alienated from her husband, offers Tom her physical love. Kazan admitted to have a prejudice against working with movie stars in the theatre. Finally, not finding the right actress and on Anderson's insistence, the director made a trip to Hollywood, where Deborah was shooting *From Here to Eternity*, and met her. Kazan immediately realized she was perfect for that part.

"She was everything good in a woman," he wrote in his autobiography. "Kind, understanding, sensitive, wise, gentle, considerate, helpful, funny, upholding — and very bright.... No one could help falling in love with her. I did and the audience did from their very first look. Bob wrote the play; Deborah made the production."[20]

On stage Deborah was supported by John Kerr (no relation), a young actor who was a hit the previous season in the comedy *Bernadine* and by Leif Erickson, who played the role of her husband.

The rehearsals, which began on August 16, went smooth except for a small incident on the third day, when Deborah had an attack of stage fright and would not come out of her dressing room. Kazan canceled the rehearsal and took Deborah out for a drink, along with Anderson. After a relaxed conversation blaming the playwright for all the problems, the director was able to calm her down. Upon their return to the theater she was ready to go on stage without any more problems. In a few days Deborah became deeply enmeshed in her character.

"Everything Laura was, I am," she said. "There's some part of you in every part you play, but generally a large part of you is left out. In *Tea and Sympathy* it was all there."[21]

In New York Deborah rented a beautiful townhouse with a garden, which belonged to Secretary of State John Foster Dulles. Her daughters finally joined her in New York; Melanie was enrolled at the Dalton School, while Francesca was in the care of a Scottish nanny. Tony did not join the family but went to London and later to Spain to work on two television projects he was producing.

The company had trial runs for a few days in New Haven and a couple weeks in Washington, D.C., before finally opening on Broadway at the Ethel Barrymore Theatre on September 30, 1953, the day of her thirty-second birthday. Before the performance she sent a telegram to Kazan saying, "May you always remember Deborah."

"I thought I would go out of my mind with fear," Deborah said recalling that opening night. "I could hardly drag myself on the stage when the curtain went up. Suddenly I blacked out for a few seconds. I managed to whisper to the stage manager in the wings, 'Get the understudy. I think I am going to faint.' But somehow or other I made it and, at the final curtain I heard a most heart-warming ovation. I'm sure it was my mother's training that stood by me in that hour of terror. For even as I asked for the understudy I could hear Mother saying, very matter of factly, 'Now Deborah, don't make heavy weather out of this.' So I didn't!"

Tea and Sympathy's success was overwhelming. The critics and public alike immediately raved about the play and Deborah's performance. *New York Times*' Brooks Atkinson wrote, "Kerr as Laura is superb, sympathetic without sentimentality, courageous without vindictiveness. It is a perfect blend of beauty, decision, temper and womanliness."[22] *Life magazine* wrote that the play "launched Deborah Kerr as a powerful and sensitive new stage star."[23]

During the long running of the play Deborah revealed, "So many young men would write me letters, and come backstage, and mothers with this terrible fear in their eyes. 'You have a son, don't you,' I'd say to them, I would be able to pick them out without saying a word to me...."[24] Among the piles of mail she received daily, Deborah was moved by one letter in particular sent to her by a young man who stated: "I only wish I'd known someone like you.... Now it is too late."[25]

Deborah's fame was at the top. Apart from the play, she was appearing simultaneously in three movies that had opened at the same time: *Dream Wife, Julius Caesar* and *From Here to Eternity*. Anderson told a funny anecdote about his mother and Deborah's popularity: "My mother had not read *Tea and Sympathy*. Along with not discussing my plays while writing them, I didn't show them to my parents, thinking that they would rather see them than read them. When it was announced that Deborah Kerr had signed for the leading part, Mother said: 'It must be a much better play than I thought it was.'"[26]

Working under Kazan's direction was an extraordinary experience for Deborah who called the director "the next thing to God. He's an angel to his actors. No rank pulling ... no ridicule — and ridicule is our deepest fear.... He made me realize that in some ways my role was literally me. I don't go around saving young men all day, as the heroine does in the play, but I'm full of compassion for stray dogs, lost cats and lame pigeons, and I didn't even know it until Gadge (Kazan's nickname) told me so."[27]

Tea and Sympathy had a record
run of 91 weeks with 720 performances. Deborah played Laura until
the end of May 1954 (later that year
she also went on tour in several
American cities), winning the prestigious Donaldson Award as Best
Actress, along with the Variety
Drama Critics' Poll Award. When
John Kerr left the company a few
weeks earlier than Deborah, he suggested Anthony Perkins as his
replacement. At the audition
Perkins, who idolized Deborah,
arrived at the theater visibly tense.
Deborah took one look at him and
whispered, "Don't be nervous; I
know you are right for the part."[28]
Then she grasped his hand and held
it through the entire reading.
Perkins got the role, but shortly after
he joined the cast, Deborah was

Publicity shot, early '50s.

replaced by Joan Fontaine, with whom he had no chemistry.

Eventually the sacrifice of a year's MGM salary in order to play *Tea
and Sympathy* on Broadway, and later on the road, was paid back with
$125,000 in 12 months.

On March 25, 1954, Deborah was unable to attend the Oscar ceremony, which was held that year at the RKO Pantages Theatre in Hollywood, due to her Broadway engagement. She did go, however, escorted
by Tony, to the Century Theater in New York to assist at a live broadcast
of the event. During the evening she could not hide her disappointment
when Donald O'Connor, the host of the evening, announced Audrey Hepburn as Best Actress in *Roman Holiday*.

A month later she was a special guest at the Art Students League's
Gala Festival, at the Plaza Hotel. The gala's theme was centered around
Greek and Roman mythology. She looked dazzling in a long golden gown
with a high side-front slit and a golden leaf tiara. It was one of her last
public appearances before she sailed for England where she was expected
to play a frustrated wife in *The End of the Affair*.

"In the future parts I choose are going to be about women who are alive," she said emphatically. Real women. They may not be pleasant. They may be wicked. But they will be real people. It's going to be exciting."[29]

Deborah kept her promise by accepting the role of Sarah Miles, the real-life wife of a civil servant (Peter Cushing) who had been involved in a religious conflict over her adulterous affair with a writer (Van Johnson).

The End of the Affair was based on a moving Graham Greene novel set in London during World War II. The picture was directed by blacklisted director Edward Dmytryk and filmed mostly at the Shepperton Studios. The original script was written by Leonore Coffee, but had to be radically revised since its story of an adulterous love affair did not get approval by the British censorship board. On her first day of filming, Deborah was interviewed by several British reporters since she had been away from England for over a year. She expressed her disappointment toward the British censorship, explaining that she had to shoot a kissing scene twice, one chaste, in case the first one would not be approved.

"I don't understand this censorship business," she remarked. "The Lord Chamberlain still won't allow me to act my Broadway role in *Tea and Sympathy* on the British stage presumably because for all its restraint, the topic of perversion is touched upon. So after this picture, I am going back for an American tour of the play in cities where the guardianship of audiences' morals is the strictest in the world."[30]

Deborah was pleased to work with Van Johnson, who was an old friend from her Metro days (Deborah was his daughter's godmother).

"Van is like me," she said. "He, too, had seven lean years in Hollywood — bobby-soxing — and now he is free. It's going to be a very interesting film to make for he plays a 'real man' and I play a 'real woman.'"[31]

Dmytryck enjoyed working with his stars. "Deborah Kerr is a revelation," he wrote in his autobiography. "A superb artist, sensitive and passionate on the screen, she seemed to have no trace of temperament of ego. Like Johnson, she was usually on the set a half hour early, drinking tea with the crew and straining at the leash. Rarely have I seen two people of comparable skill and talent work together so effortlessly and with so little self-indulgence."[32]

The End of the Affair was released in 1955. In Europe some reviewers called it the most adult love story ever made. But in the United States the critical reaction was one of puritanical shock. Despite the controversy, the picture flopped at the box office.

Graham Greene commented, "The film was not a good film, and at

With Van Johnson in *The End of the Affair* (1955), based on Graham Greene's novel.

moments it was acutely painful to see situations that had been so real to be twisted into stock clichés of the screen."[33]

In the middle of September, she left work with Melanie and Francesca for a two-week holiday in Nice, followed by her return to the States where she toured across the country with *Tea and Sympathy* for eleven months. Once again she played to packed houses and received stellar reviews.

Among the offers Deborah received following the success of *From Here to the Eternity* was Alfred Hitchcock's thriller *Dial M for Murder*. She had to turn down the part that was later assigned to Grace Kelly, since she had already lined up *The End of the Affair* and the American tour of *Tea and Sympathy*. Deborah had met Hitchcock in New York years earlier on her way from London to Hollywood, and went to a film première with him at a cinema in Times Square. The usher at the cinema was well known for his very loud, stentorian voice, which echoed across the Square as he called for the stars' cars after the première. He was also known for his thick headedness. And so the MGM publicity boys took him aside before the première, and explained to him that the new British star who would be arriving that night with Alfred Hitchcock was called Deborah Kerr, and that her name was pronounced *Carr*, not *Cur*, as it normally would be in America, and as this was her first public appearance in the States it was very important to get her name right. Therefore, he was to make sure, when she came out of the cinema at the end of the film that he called out *Miss Carr's car!* not *Miss Curr's car!* or *Miss Carr's cur!* or anything stupid like that.

During the film the usher walked up and down outside the cinema. He began shouting out to the drivers of the waiting cars, *Miss Marlene Dietrich's car! ... Mr. Gary Cooper's car! ... Mr. Clark Gable's car!* and so on until Deborah appeared on Alfred Hitchcock's arm. The publicity boys held their breath. The usher bawled out:

Miss Carr's car! The publicity boys breathed again. *And Mr. Hitchcock's cock!*[34]

7

The King and I

The greatest experience in my career.

— Deborah Kerr

Deborah spent the summer of 1955 in the Virgin Islands shooting *The Proud and Profane*. The heat was unbearable and alleviated only for a few hours by the sudden tropical showers. During the ten-week filming a hurricane hit the islands twice. The crew helped the locals to evacuate their tin shacks and brought them back to the hotel where they were staying.

William Perlberg and George Seaton adapted Lucy Herndon Crockett's World War II novel *The Magnificent Bastards*, changing the original title to *The Proud and Profane* since the censorship board objected. A few months earlier Deborah, who had loved the novel, asked her agent if there were any plans to film it. The news came back that Paramount had bought it with William Holden in mind for the male lead and they would be delighted to have her in the other principal role. After reading the script Deborah signed for the film and played sensitive Red Cross worker and war widow Lee Ashley. Ashley had visited New Caledonia during World War II to locate the grave of her lieutenant husband who had died at Guadalcanal, and to learn about his last days. On the island she met and fell in love with Colin Black, a tough and ruthless half-Indian, Marine lieutenant colonel, played by Holden. The handsome star was forced by the producers to dye his hair pitch black, wear a thick black mustache and dark make-up to look the part.

The result was quite grotesque and the screenwriter-director George Seaton regretted it once the film was completed. As he admitted years

With a mustachioed William Holden in *The Proud and Profane* (1956).

later, "It was a successful picture, but I learned another lesson on that, and that is, with Bill Holden, don't put a moustache on him.... It's not his good looks. I don't know if the same thing is true today, but the heavies always wore moustaches. Although he was the heavy, there's no doubt about that, but you had to understand him, you had to feel sorry for him."[1]

On the set, Deborah kept a great professional relationship with her co-star; however, on the screen their chemistry did not convince the critics, who also criticized the unimpressive script.

Years later director George Seaton explained in an interview that it was interesting to work with Deborah because she had always played the same sort of patrician lady. However, "In this role underneath she was a bitch. What I always try do in a film is to have some growth in a character. If the character is the same in the end of the picture as he was in the beginning, I don't think you've got anything. I think a character must learn something about himself, about his relationship with other people, and I think, finally, discovers the truth about himself. In Deborah's case — herself."

Seaton also admitted that working with Deborah was an easy and pleasant experience, describing her as "the most professional, competent actress."[2] On the island, like the entire crew, Deborah lived in a crummy hotel, but never complained about her accommodations. Cruise ships would come in and the passengers would come ashore and eat at the same hotel where the cast was served. Although a unique experience for the tourists, the cast endured the same dinner and listened to the same steel band playing the same song every night.

According to Holden, despite the difficulties, Deborah was "the most no-problem star I have worked with. She has a salty sense of humor which surprises everyone. She's an unusual charming individual."[3]

In one scene, Deborah had to slap him fiercely. She did it so realistically that Seaton printed the first take. "She stung me," Holden recalled with irony, "but I have to admit she didn't rock me like Gloria Swanson did [in *Sunset Blvd.*]."

"He's the darling of all my leading men," said Deborah about Holden. "He's an absolute dreamboat, a gentleman, an actor and a charmer. I can't wait to do another film with Bill."[4]

They became very good friends and years later Holden revealed a funny anecdote in an interview involving Deborah. It concerned his reputation as a ladies' man which he considered ill-deserved: "When I was still under contract to Paramount I lent the key of my dressing-room to a couple of prop men who were pals of mine. Then the time came when I was working away at another studio. So Paramount asked if I'd let Deborah Kerr use the room while she was making a film for them. Of course, I said yes. When I finally returned to Paramount, my two pals said: 'Bill, what are you doing with all that perfume and stuff in your room?' I said: 'Oh it's not mine — Deborah Kerr's been using the room.' Then they both looked sick. 'But we've been having parties in there and taking girls and leaving rude messages on the mirror: *Holden — You missed a good one.*' Well, we all became hysterical. Some time later, when I brought up the matter with Deborah, she said: 'I did rather wonder what sort of double life you were leading....."[5]

The Proud and Profane was one of many films Paramount shot in VistaVision. When it was released in Europe many local Paramount executives discussed eliminating Holden's moustache from the film's billboards because it spoiled his beloved clean-cut image. Ultimately, the posters were untouched. The picture was poorly received by audiences since many reviewers found it a trite melodrama filled with too many distracting subplots. Holden and Deborah never worked together again.

During her stay in the Virgin Islands, Deborah was named winner of the Sarah Siddons Award as Chicago's outstanding actress of the 1954–55 season for her performance in *Tea and Sympathy*. The honor is chosen by ballot from members of the Sarah Siddons Society, an organization of drama devotees, who had previously awarded Helen Hayes and Beatrice Lillie. Being English, Deborah was particularly proud to collect the marble and bronze statuette of Siddon, England's immortal actress of the 18th century. She received the award in a ceremony held the following March at the Ambassador East Hotel in Chicago, where she traveled in the company of Melanie and Francesca.

Deborah finished shooting *The Proud and Profane* on a Friday night and reported the following Monday morning for the pre–production work in *The King and I* at 20th Century–Fox's studios. She was very excited to play the lead in one of the most successful musicals in Broadway history. She was not intimidated by the assessment against the late Gertrude Lawrence, who had created the role on stage. If there had been only Lawrence in the part of Mrs. Anna, she later explained in an interview, she might have been less courageous in accepting the challenge. But, because there were five more following Lawrence, she figured she could do as well as any of them.

"Mrs. Anna is an absolutely heavenly part for an actress," Deborah said. "One of the loveliest ever written. The story has a fairy tale quality yet it is based on reality. The relationship between the English governess and the King is so fantastic and beautiful, so full of changing moods, I feel lucky to get the role."[6]

It all began in 1950 when composer Richard Rodgers and lyricist Oscar Hammerstein II received a call from Fanny Holtzmann, a lawyer representing the actress Gertrude Lawrence, asking if they would be interested in writing and producing a musical adaptation of Margaret Landon's best-selling novel *Anna and the King of Siam*.

The book had been already made into a successful film in 1946 starring Rex Harrison and Irene Dunne. The story was based on the real life adventures of a Victorian English governess Anna Leonowens who went to the court of the king of Siam in the 1862 to teach English to the king's many children. The clash between Eastern and Western cultures is personified in the king and Anna, who, ultimately, find some values in common without falling in love with each other.

Gertrude Lawrence, who became a star after playing in Noël Coward's *Private Lives*, had acquired the rights of Landon's novel for the stage adaptation after literary agent Helen Strauss first brought the idea to her attention. Lawrence was convinced that the character of Anna was the perfect role for her to play in a musical.

Lawrence originally wanted Cole Porter to write the score, but the composer was not available. A chance encounter between Lawrence's lawyer and Dorothy Hammerstein led to an offer to Rodgers and Hammerstein, who were the most successful creative team in American musical theater history at the time. Their musicals *Oklahoma!*, *Carousel* and *South Pacific* were all Broadway hits.

"At first," Rodgers recalled in his autobiography, "our feelings were decidedly mixed.... We had never before written a musical specifically with one actor or actress in mind, and we were concerned that such an arrangement might not give us the freedom to write what we wanted the way we wanted. What also bothered us was that while we both admired Gertrude tremendously, we felt that her vocal range was minimal and that she had never been able to overcome an unfortunate tendency to sing flat."[7]

After a private viewing of the original film *Anna and the King of Siam* in a screening room at 20th Century–Fox, the duo decided to go ahead with the project. They were eager to go to work, but they informed Lawrence that they could not promise a production before the spring of 1951. Hammerstein immediately asked his friend Josh Logan, who skillfully directed *South Pacific* on Broadway, to collaborate with him. Since Logan showed little interest in the project, Hammerstein approached John Van Druten, who agreed to stage the musical despite never before directing a show that he had not written.

In November 1950 the agent Leland Hayward, who was involved in producing the musical, wrote to Rodgers and Hammerstein from Paris that he had discussed the project with choreographer Jerome Robbins and that he was eager to create the perfect sequences for that show.[8]

Meanwhile, in New York the duo hired costume designer Irene Sharaff, who started her research without delay, examining hundreds of pictures from the Royal Archives in Bangkok. She sketched her first costumes based on the fashion in Siam in the mid–1800s and later ordered many yards of Thai silks and brocades to make her first prototypes.

Deborah as a Red Cross worker in *The Proud and Profane* (1956).

Slowly, *The King and I* was taking shape as a sumptuous and expensive production. The $360,000 budget was an incredible amount of money for a musical at the time.

By Christmas, Rodgers had written about six songs and expected to write another dozen by the following spring.

Casting the musical was the most difficult task, especially the problematic role of the king. Since Rex Harrison had skillfully played the king in the film version, it seemed to the authors that he was the first and best choice for the musical, despite the actor's lack of any musical background. When Harrison received a call from the production, he was already involved in another project, but accepted to audition the part out of deference for the two writers.

"That was the last thing I wanted to do. Go and sing for Rodgers and Hammerstein," remembered the actor. "So I said: 'Yes, all right. What theatre do you want me to go to?' And they told me what theatre, Her Majesty's I think, and there they were sitting in the stalls, and I can't even think what I sang. Anyway I sang something and they said, 'Oh, very nice. That's very nice Rex. Thank you.'—'We'll let you know later,' sort of thing!—Well, thank God, of course, I never heard a word, because if by any mischance they had liked what I did, which they obviously didn't, and offered me *The King and I*, I might have been tempted to do it, and what a mess that would have been. I mean, I might have missed an even greater opportunity, and a much more suitable triumph, of Higgins in *My Fair Lady* than ever an Oriental potentate could be."[9]

Among many actors who were considered for the part were José Ferrer, Ezio Pinza, Macdonald Carey, Noël Coward and Alfred Drake. The latter had become a star since appearing in *Oklahoma!* and asked for a salary too high for the production to match.

Discouraged after the unfruitful meeting with Drake, Rodgers and Hammerstein went directly to the Majestic Theatre, where the casting director John Fearnly was holding auditions for the part of the king. In his autobiography, Rodgers recalls, "The first candidate who walked from the wings was a bald, muscular fellow with a bony, Oriental face. He was dressed casually and carried a guitar. His name, we were told, was Yul Brynner, which meant nothing to us. He scowled in our direction, sat down on the stage and crossed his legs, tailor-fashion, then plunked one whacking chord on his guitar and began to howl in a strange language that no one could understand. He looked savage, he sounded savage, and there was no denying that he projected a feeling of controlled ferocity. When he read for us, we were again impressed by his authority and conviction. Oscar and I looked at each other and nodded. It was no more than half an hour after we had left Drake, and now, out of nowhere, we had our king."[10] The truth was that actress Mary Martin, after reading the script, suggested Brynner to the casting director, thinking he was just perfect for that role.[11] He eventually got the part and signed a contract for seven months.

During the rehearsals in Boston, Brynner shaved his head close. The effect on audiences was an immediate success. He covered his skull with the same furniture polish he applied to his body to look brownish yellow. Instantly, his shaved head became his trademark.

On March 29, 1951, *The King and I* opened on Broadway at the St. James Theatre. One reviewer enthusiastically wrote, "Musicals and leading men will never be the same after last night.... Probably the best show of the decade."[12] *The King and I* was a sensational, unexpected success, winning the most prestigious awards of that season.

During the first year's run of *The King and I*, Gertrude Lawrence was plagued by poor health. She had been suffering for some time from cancer that had been misdiagnosed as hepatitis. She took off six weeks in the summer of 1952, resting in her house in Cape Cod. She suddenly died on September 7, 1952. She was buried in the ball gown that she wore in *The King and I*. Constance Carpenter substituted for her and later other fine actresses performed the role of Anna.

The King and I ran on Broadway for more than three years with 1,246 performances, followed by a year-and-a-half tour across America. In addition there were 926 performances with a different cast at the Drury Lane Theater in London.

The extraordinary success led 20th Century–Fox to consider producing a film based on the musical *The King and I*. Yul Brynner wanted to direct it and offered the part of the king to Marlon Brando, the only actor he considered right for that role. After Brando turned it down, Brynner decided to perform the role himself once again elaborating on his Broadway performance.

Charles Brackett, the film's producer, asked Ernest Lehman if he was interested in writing a script based on the play. Lehman, who wrote screenplays for big hits like *Sabrina* and *Sweet Smell of Success*, had not seen the play. He traveled from Los Angeles to New York to watch the show and then accepted the job. The screenwriter was one of the few people to get along with Brynner, who proved difficult to work with on the set. His short temper and petulance were faults that often affected his work and his private life. Nevertheless, this inner anger had helped him show the rage present in the character of Ramses II and in the king of Siam.

Vivien Leigh was first considered for the part of Mrs. Anna, but she was uninsurable since she suffered from manic-depressive attacks. One of Deborah's closest friends, singer Dinah Shore, waged a heavy campaign for that role, but the studio did not find her convincing enough and preferred to cast Deborah, who had not seen Gertrude Lawrence in the original play. However, she saw Valerie Hobson in the part on the London stage and was immediately enchanted by the role. Fox appointed Walter Lang as the film director, and he later admitted: "I had always wanted Deborah in that part after Gertie Lawrence died. I had known her so long, and knew she had dignity and great ability."[13]

Likewise, Brynner particularly wanted Deborah to do the part in the film, having met her briefly when he went to see her in *Tea and Sympathy* on Broadway.

"It was Yul who was the solid inspiration behind the movie," Deborah said. "He knew and loved every line of the story and every note of the music, and it came out so well due to his insistence that this and that had to be done the way *he* wanted. He could be difficult, but only because he knew he was right."[14]

Brynner was indeed not very easy to work with. He so detested 20th Century–Fox that he nicknamed the company *16th Century Fuck* for the changes they insisted on making in the film. For example, the studio insisted on putting in a scene where he would fight an elephant, believing that would have explained why the king dies. Brynner was so outraged that he called a special meeting with Fox executives and explained why the king dies: the monarch dies of broken heart because he cannot fulfill his desire to modernize his country in a way that is better for his son. He hopes his son, under the tutelage of Mrs. Anna, can do the job for him. Moreover, he dies because of his unrequited love for Anna. Although the executive laughed at his explanations, Brynner fought like a tiger and won the studio over.

During the filming, the actor became so exasperated with producer Charlie Brackett that he told him in a burst of rage, "You don't know but you died several years ago."[15]

Brynner's frustration was caused by his perception that the film looked like something made ten years earlier. According to him, neither the producer nor director Walter Lang had truly understood the real spirit of the story, considering it more a fairy tale, making all the set designs look exasperatedly fake.

Actress Rita Moreno, who played Tuptim in the film, remembers never seeing Walter Lang actually directing Brynner beyond instructions concerning the correct angle for the best shot.[16]

Brynner would often deeply offend the director when he would not agree with his ideas. Brynner considered Lang's presence totally unnecessary since he could direct the movie himself. Sometimes the star's outbursts of uncontrolled rage were so intense that he required oxygen to calm him down. Deborah remembered Brynner's habit and explained, "When it came to filming the famous polka, I tried [the oxygen] too. I felt completely drunk.... Obviously, I don't need that."[17]

In preparation for her musical numbers, Deborah trained her voice for a few weeks with coach Rhea Shelters, however after hearing a test recording of her voice, Deborah admitted to the studio, "I'm sorry, I'm just not good enough!"[18] It was not a total surprise since she was not a singer and she could not handle the lead-ins to most of the Rodgers and Hammerstein songs in the films. After a nationwide search, singer Jean Bradley was signed to dub Deborah's songs. While in Milan, playing another role, Bradley suddenly took ill and died, leaving 20th Century–Fox in a bind. Finally in August 1955 they called 25-year-old mezzo soprano Marni Nixon, who accepted the challenge not only to imitate Deborah's exact sound, but also serve the dramatic thrust of each musical scene. Every note Nixon sang had to reflect the character of Mrs. Anna, as portrayed by Deborah. She had to serve Deborah's dramatic intent and mimic her mild English accent. Nixon succeeded perfectly. On her first meeting with Deborah, the singer remembered being very nervous, but Deborah "immediately put me at ease by commenting on the beauty of my hair and the similarity to hers in color," as Nixon recalled. "Her voice and demeanor reeked of British charm and were warm and welcoming.... She told me about her daughter and her now-estranged husband Anthony Bartley, who was a Squadron Leader for the Royal Air Force. In the course of working together, we discovered that our ancestors were from the same part of Scotland, the Isle of MacIntyre. I felt an uncanny kinship with her and was amazed to realize that it wasn't just a theatrical camaraderie, but a real tribal connection coming from her pure, clean spirit."[19] The rehearsals went smoothly; first they performed the songs at the piano and then blocked the scenes. Then when they were both ready to record the songs they were led into two glass-enclosed recording booths surrounded by the magnificent Fox orchestra. Deborah would point to Nixon and she would sing. Then Nixon would point to her and she would ... talk sing. The result was fantastic.

"Marni was so brilliant at adapting her voice to mine," Deborah was reported to say. "I could never be entirely sure whether it was she helping me on high notes — with the help of the experts of sound mixers, of course — or whether I myself was responsible for the sounds which came out in the completed version."[20] In another interview she added, "The dubbing was so perfect I almost convinced myself that I sang *all* the numbers."

"Fortunately ... I had my Deborah Kerr," said Brynner years later. "She was heaven. She was the perfect Mrs. Anna. She understood Mrs. Anna completely. She understood the relationship between the two. And this is really what made the picture work."

On her co-star, Deborah said, "Yul helped me so much, taught me so much. He rehearsed with me — not to tell me how to play the role, but to show how others had done it, so I could play it better in my own way.... He was so wonderful. I'll be forever his slave.... I don't think he can be compared to anybody. He has an extraordinary sort of unexpected attraction. He's not *particularly* tall, he has rather strong Mongol features and he's bald. And they say this man is attractive? Well, he is. Somehow he's very, very handsome, a most unusual personality, a mixture of opposites: and on top of that he sort of has oodles of sex appeal."[21]

There were rumors of a romance between Deborah and Brynner, who was a ladies' man. Yet, as Nixon recalled, those rumors were never confirmed. On that account in her autobiography the singer mentioned a funny episode. Once, after the vocal rehearsals, Nixon asked Deborah to have lunch with her in the commissary. Deborah turned her down with a conspiratorial wink, asking if they could do it some other time since she had a date with "a very sexy person." Nixon thought perhaps Tony was coming to visit. Then suddenly the huge ground-to-ceiling doors of the rehearsal stage opened and a Cadillac convertible appeared with the top down and the license plate read Y-U-L. The car stopped and Brynner, in all his glory, emerged. He wore tight-fitting black pants, a black leather sleeveless jacket with no shirt, enhancing his muscular arms, and black leather boots with silver stirrups. Around his neck was a necklace with an icon hanging from it. Preceding him were two German Shepherd dogs straining at the leash which he held in one hand. In the other hand was a very long, professional, hand-tooled leather whip. He lifted the whip high above his head and snapped it in the air. After releasing the dogs, with a broadest smile, he stretched out his arms and in his trademark "King of Siam" voice proclaimed for everyone with earshot, "I am here!" Nixon dared not look at Deborah, because she thought it was one of the funniest scenes she had ever witnessed. Brynner bowed to Deborah, took her arm, and they left to lunch.[22]

Twentieth Century–Fox hired Irene Sharaff to design the costumes for the film, being aware that her outstanding work done on stage contributed greatly to the play's success. About Sharaff's lavish creations Deborah enthusiastically said, "She outdid herself in costumes. It's the most gorgeous costume design I've seen on almost any picture."

The film version of *The King and I* was created on a bigger scale than the original play, including more opulent costumes, more sumptuous set design and more creative choreography, all of which contributed to make it a classic in film history. According to rumor, one of the greatest single musical numbers in the film, "Small House of Uncle Thomas," was directed by non-credited Vincente Minnelli to help Walter Lang, who did not have any experience directing a musical.[23]

On the set Yul Brynner proved to be masterful not only as monarch, but also as photographer. With his Leica, he shot a series of beautiful candid photographs, many of Deborah, which appeared on the cover and in a spread published by *Life* one month before the film opened.

The King and I was shot with a new (but noisy) Cinemascope camera, the results of which proved to be a magnificent visual experience. However, all the dialogue in the film had to be dubbed after the shooting, bringing less spontaneity to the performances. The picture was completed in seven months. The first six weeks were only rehearsals, followed by six months of filming at 20th Century–Fox studios, and then dubbing and editing. Despite Brynner's tensions with the director and the producers, the cast of the film became one big family. Later Deborah revealed, "It's not like work at all. I only hope that sometime soon I will have the chance to appear in another picture of the light opera type."[24] She called *The King and I* "the greatest experience in my career.... I was delighted to play Mrs. Anna. Yul moved me intensely in all my scenes with him, and I shall always appreciate his unselfishness. He was easy to act with, stimulating and, off set, a million laughs. He is a fascinating man."[25]

To celebrate the end of the production, a Christmas party was organized with gifts for all the children in the cast. *The King and I* opened in June 1956 and met with immediate popular success coupled with critical acclaim. *New York Times* critic Bosley Crowther wrote about Deborah, "Her beauty, her spirit and her English style come as close to approximating those of the late Gertrude Lawrence as could be."[26]

Despite the unbelievable success, Brynner detested the movie, criticizing it severely. "I don't like the film," he revealed years later in an interview. "I say it loud in spite of the fact that I'm very greatly [sic] for the fact that I've got an Oscar for it. I did not like the film when we made it. I did not like the making of it and still get quick [sic] sick when I see it.... The shame of it is that the picture really should have been ten times better, because the play was ten times better. Whenever people say, 'But it's such a marvelous movie...,' I said, 'If you haven't seen it on the stage, you cannot imagine what you are seeing. It is not even ten percent of the power and of the fascination and of the charm and glorious joy that it was on the stage."[27]

On March 22, 1956, three months before the movie opened nationwide, Deborah and Yul Brynner placed their handprints in cement at Grauman's Chinese Theatre. The ceremony, for reasons unknown, took place on a 20th Century–Fox lot containing one of the interior sets for the production. Deborah, in full costume for her role, made her footprints with high heels, signed her name, the date and wrote "AND I." Deborah's square was then carried outside the studio and placed alongside Brynner's, who had written "THE KING," and later moved to the forecourt of the theatre. Deborah remembered that Melanie and Francesca were with her for the ceremony, and although she was delighted at the honor, her daughters were absolutely thrilled at the idea of Mummy plunging her hands into wet cement. They were ready to do it, too![28]

The King and I received nine Oscar nominations, including Best Picture, Best Director, Best Actor and Best Actress. Deborah was ecstatic to receive her third nomination, although she lost out to Ingrid Bergman for her role in *Anastasia*. As soon as she heard of the news of the nominations Deborah sent a telegram to Brynner (who was nominated twice, also for *Anastasia*) saying "A WELL DESERVED DOUBLE VICTORY NOT ONLY ARE YOU A MARVELOUS ACTOR BUT A MARVELOUS DIRECTOR."[29]

8

Bob, Cary & Niv

I've never known anyone like her. She never makes a fuss over any-thing.

—John Kerr

My Dear Vincente —

Bertie told me that there was every chance that you will direct *Tea & Sympathy*, when and if it is made — and I just felt I must drop you a line and tell you how absolutely thrilled I was with the news. I had a very nice talk with Bob Anderson on Saturday Night in Philadelphia — and he has some really quite interesting and unusual ideas about scripting it — and making it a "whole" thing if the Breen office are very difficult about the homosexual angle — impotence is o.k. — but perversion is their bête noir!! But as you will see when you see the play — it really is a play about persecution of the individual, and compassion and pity and love of one human being for another in a crisis. And such can stand alone I think — without the added problem of homosexuality. But above all — it needs a sensitive and compassionate person to make it — and that is why I am so thrilled at the prospect of your doing it. I wish we could do it in color, and incorporate all the atmospheric feeling of spring and "things about to flower" and all the romantic and artistic nonsense!! Anyway — this may all be premature — there are hurdles I know — but in case they are all leaped —

I want you to know how very excited I am —

With affection

Deborah[1]

Through this letter written in 1956 from Toronto, where she was touring with *Tea and Sympathy*, Deborah established her first contact with director Vincente Minnelli, who had been chosen by MGM producer Pandro Berman to direct the picture based on the successful play.

As soon as its Broadway triumph was assured, many studios bid to acquire the play's filming rights. Playwright Robert Anderson rejected all

95

the offers until he felt certain the proposed picture would retain all the values of the original play. On July 19, 1954, MGM announced that they won the spirited competition with the astonishing offer of $400,000, of which $300,000 would be withheld until Anderson delivered a filmable script. However, the film production was delayed for over two years. MGM had to convince the Motion Picture Association of America (MPAA), the Production Code Administration (PCA) and the Catholic Legion of Decency that the picture would clearly punish the sexual transgression of the married woman and eliminate any reference to homosexuality. Dore Schary was delighted with Anderson's first draft in which he had toned down many sexual references present in the play, which did not satisfy either the Catholic Legion of Decency or Geoffrey Shurlock, assistant to PCA director Joseph Breen.

Between January and August 1955, a series of screenplay rewrites were undertaken by Anderson and MGM. However, no matter how they attempted to rewrite it, the two associations always found it morally unacceptable. In addition, the Loew's theater chain, one of the largest in the country, refused to book the film without the sanction of the Production Code.

At one point Shary remembered, "[The Legion] had taken the position that the Deborah Kerr character had to die after being divorced. (This was, in effect, her punishment for having given the young student a healthy sexual experience.)"[2] After the word "queer" (used several times in the play) disappeared from the film script along with Laura's recognition of her husband's latent homosexuality, PCA was finally satisfied. However, trouble continued after the film was completed.

Once the green light was given to the project, prior to Deborah's confirmation into her role, actress Jennifer Jones waged a heavy campaign to play the lead. However, Bert Allemberg, Deborah's agent, was able to successfully secure the film role for his client. When Jones learned the news one afternoon at a tea party she responded by jumping fully clothed into the swimming pool of her host.

Minnelli decided to reunite the same cast from the original stage production, including John Kerr as the sensitive Tom, and Leif Erickson as Deborah's husband. The film had to be delayed several days since John Kerr was busy with a previous engagement. Finally in the spring of 1956 the cameras started rolling. It was a seven-week schedule and, apart from a few days of location work on a local beach and at a country club, the picture was shot at the MGM studios.

As the stars had performed the play together several hundred times, Minnelli felt that the cast would not need much coaching. This was a choice he later regretted, realizing that the cast should have brought a new, fresher approach more suitable to the film, rather than a mechanical repetition of what they had done on stage.

Minnelli loved working with Deborah. Over time he came to deeply appreciate her, particularly after she performed a long and difficult scene in one take. "After such an exhausting emotional ordeal most stars would have rushed to their dressing rooms in a state of collapse," commented the director. "But Deborah, coming off the set, said 'Now I'll make tea.'"

John Kerr, who had shared the stage on Broadway with Deborah for months, declared to the press, "I've never known anyone like her. She never makes a fuss over anything."

The sole problem Minnelli faced during the shooting was John Kerr's refusal to play a scene in which his character decided to prove his masculinity by trying to have sex with a prostitute. A sequence which was only mentioned in the original play, Kerr thought it was unnecessary in the film. Thanks to Anderson's intervention and Minnelli's infinite patience, they eventually convinced him that the scene was needed to explain Tom's later attempt to commit suicide.[3]

For Deborah, those six weeks went along like a breeze. "We knew the lines and the content of the play has not been changed as much as you might imagine it," she said in an interview with the *Los Angeles Times*. "The changes are mainly those that would be normally made in a screen version. Emotions that have to be conveyed broadly across the footlights are cut down to the suggestion of a smile, a tear or the rising of an eyelid. I think I can truthfully say that all the essential values are preserved in the film."[4]

Six weeks after Minnelli wrapped *Tea and Sympathy*, the picture was ready for the usual sneak preview ritual. Once again the censors stepped into shield the public from corruption, demanding a six-line cut in the love scene that the studio finally reduced to four. The Legion of Decency complained instead about the film's sins of omission. Unless the end stressed the boy's guilt as well, *Tea and Sympathy* would receive a "Condemned" rating which, even with the production Code seal, would scare off big theater chains. Schary had no choice to submit to the censors' requests and Deborah, who was on holiday in England visiting her family, had to return to Hollywood, where she had to record (spoken on voice over) a new version of the letter Laura writes explaining that adultery was

With John Kerr in a scene of Vincente Minnelli's *Tea and Sympathy* (1957).

wrong. Finally in September 1956, *Tea and Sympathy* opened nationwide, receiving mixed reviews. Some did not appreciate the "watered down" version and called it, "A *Tea and Sympathy* diluted with milk." The public reaction was also lukewarm; however the picture did decent business at the box-office, earning domestically $2,184,558 against a budget of $1,818,688.

Ironically, the reaction of the French was the complete opposite when the play was performed in Paris starring Ingrid Bergman in Deborah's role.

The show had difficulty in getting produced because everybody saw no story, no conflict, as Minnelli recalled. "So the boy thinks he's an homosexual," a practical French producer told Bob Anderson, "and the wife of the headmaster gives herself to him to prove he's not. But what's the problem?"[5]

For over three years Deborah had campaigned to play the lead in a film based on a novel called *Heaven Knows, Mr. Allison*, written by Charles Shaw. After many attempts, producer Buddy Adler bought the story for her. Originally the screen rights had been purchased in 1952 by producer Eugene Frenke for director William Wyler. The World War II story of an Irish Roman Catholic nun stranded with a U.S. marine on a South Pacific island held by the Japanese was difficult to handle, since church authorities stated that they would ban such a film. Wyler altered the ending of the story by revealing that the girl was not a nun but had disguised herself as one for protection from the Japanese. The director received the church's endorsement. However, he got involved in other projects, shelving the film. It was director John Huston, who had been offered a three-picture contract with 20th Century–Fox, who revived the project. Adler cast Deborah in the role of Sister Angela, leaving the director free to choose the male lead. Huston wanted Marlon Brando, who turned the offer down, to the director's great disappointment. Fox insisted to Huston that he cast Robert Mitchum, who had just signed a two-picture deal. The director was uncertain in hiring him, put off by stories of the actor being difficult. Eventually he decided to give him a chance. Mitchum was not pleased to be second choice and when he found out that the picture was planned to be entirely shot on location on the island of Tobago, he flatly refused to take the part. Yet, when his agent reminded him of his shaky financial situation, Mitchum reconsidered the offer and accepted the role.

In August 1956, an advance team landed on the island of Tobago in the Caribbean. "I picked Tobago for two reasons," explained Huston. "I needed a place that was a dead ringer for the South Sea Island, but I needed nearer. And it had to be a spot where I could spend pounds sterling. This is what we call a 'British quota' picture."[6]

Almost all the rooms in the hotels on the island were booked for the 80 English crew members. A fleet of taxis and trucks was requested to take the filmmakers from the hotels to the beach where the film was shot. Native laborers were hired to build a small village with a tiny church which later was destroyed for a scene.

In September Deborah arrived on the island, uncertain of what it would be like working with Mitchum, who had a "bad boy" reputation and was the only other actor in the entire movie except for the extras.

"I wondered about what it would really be like to work with Bob, and if I was really going to be able to cope with, as I called him then, a weed-smoking character. He was the first of the hippies, really and truly," she revealed years later. "When I arrived on that beautiful island Bob was already there. I remember we met for the first time that evening. And the two of us just sat on the edge of the sea with our toes in the water, generally talking about life. I realized immediately that, far from being like his image of a lazy kind of a character who didn't seem to care about anything, he was in fact extremely intelligent, and cared about so many things. He was such a surprise."[7]

According to his account, Mitchum was expecting Deborah to be a stiff English lady, but he was pleasantly surprised to discover that she was far from that image. "I was impressed by her chaste and genteel demeanor, an attitude eminently suited to the saintly character she portrayed, made touchingly mortal by a few freckles," said Mitchum. "She is warmly human and sympathetic, and possessed of a humor that ranges from the subtle to the downright wicked."[8] *Heaven Knows, Mr. Allison* was a fairly happy experience for Deborah, even though it turned out to be one of the most physically challenging films of her career. The heat was one of the main problems. Tobago's climate averaged, at that time of the year, 90-degree temperatures. "Talk about mad dogs and Englishmen going out in the midday sun," she gasped. "I go out in it with a scratchy nun's habit on. All Bob is wearing is that underbrush on his chin and a pair of trousers."[9] Huston had to hire two members of the crew for the purpose of holding her nun's habit up between takes and, in Mitchum's own words, "cooling her ass with a fan."

In one scene Deborah had to run through a swamp. "It was horrible," she recalled. "There were leeches all over, the stench, I was covered in alligator excrescence [*sic*] from head to foot. The shot was over, John said, 'Fine, cut. We don't need to do it again?' And I went up to him — he was in his white pants and white shirt — and I flung my arms around his neck, pressed my body against his, and all this filth went all over his jacket, shirt and slacks."[10] Huston remembered that episode commenting, "Deborah had to lie down in this mess and she did it without a word of complaint. It was only years later that I discovered this had been such an ordeal for her that it almost unnerved her totally. She had said nothing when we shot the scene, but she had dreams of this swamp for weeks afterward."[11]

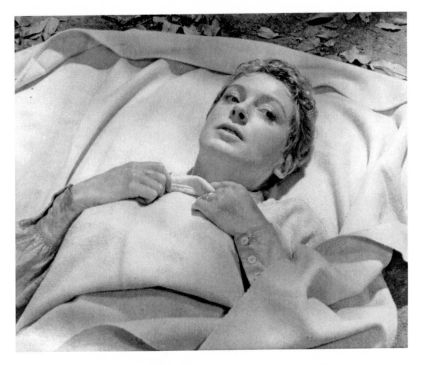

As Sister Angela in John Huston's *Heaven Knows, Mr. Allison* (1957).

Laura Nightingale, a wardrobe girl on the set, remembered one day when Deborah told Mitchum that she hurt her feet on the rocky ground: "He just kneeled down, unlaced her white sneakers, removed them and massaged her feet. It was lovely the way he did it. No show, no affection, just all feeling. Then he put her sneakers back on and said kind of brusquely, 'Gotta keep you alive for my next scene.'"[12] Deborah was so touched her eyes were full of tears.

During those four months spent on location Mitchum genuinely and platonically loved Deborah for her innate gentility and her inner beauty. They formed a friendship that would last the rest of their lives; they made another three films together. Mitchum later confessed that Deborah was the "only leading lady I didn't go to bed with." Above all, he loved her sense of humor. One time she was rowing in open water during the tortoise-chasing scene. "Row faster, Deborah," Huston kept shouting as her hands became blistered. When the oar broke she leaned back and shouted, "That'll tell you how fucking fast I'm rowing!" Huston was amused, and Mitchum, who was swimming nearby, swallowed a gallon of saltwater laughing. There was a small Catholic church on the island and the sisters attached to it were invited to see the rushes. Deborah was always mindful of their presence, striving to maintain an on-camera deportment that would earn their approval. However, that day it happened that some of those local nuns had been visiting the set and they were not amused to see that her composure cracked in that rowing scene.

During the shooting, mosquitoes brought down Mitchum first and then Deborah with dengue fever, which caused them intense joint and muscle pain. Mitchum quickly recovered but Deborah had to be hospitalized for a few days. The press was told that she came down with acute tonsillitis because she filmed in a cave (which was actually a local community center converted into a sound stage, with doors and windows tightly sealed and no air conditioning) under heavy lights, wearing her heavy nun's habit with a cowl around her neck at a temperature that reached 90 degrees in the shade.

Because of the delicate subject matter, the studio decided to have a representative from the American Legion of Decency visit the location, just to make sure that any scene of *Heaven Knows, Mr. Allison* did not offend the audiences. The censor was Jack Vizard (whom the crew often called *Blizzard, Buzzard* or *Grizzard*) about whom Mitchum recalled, "Mr. Huston planned a little surprise. We contrived a scene wherein Sister Angela overcomes the suppression of her base animal urges and, panting and clutching, throws herself on Mr. Allison in a lustful frenzy. With no film in the camera, we 'shot' the scene for our guest, who stood agape and immobilized in shock as John quietly said, 'Cut.' Huston then turned to the stunned Mr. Grizzard and said, 'You should have seen it before we cleaned it up!'"[13]

Huston brought his entire family with him to the island. His younger daughter, Angelica, who was then five, remembered how much she liked being in Deborah's company. She found her very beautiful and called her Mrs. Boogum.

Once the shooting was over Robert Mitchum paid a tribute to Deborah, stating to the press that she "was a much better actress than her opportunities have provided." He also added, "As a receptive artist she is the best receptacle I've ever encountered. Before she becomes a fat gray-haired lady, she should do comedy. She is total in her talent — a brilliant, wonderful gal."[14]

The film was completed just before Christmas at a budget of $2 million. Once it was edited, the Catholic Church endorsed it with its highest audience rating, A-1 classification. After a gala opening in March 1956 at the Roxy Theatre in New York, *Heaven Knows, Mr. Allison* became one of John Huston's biggest moneymakers, despite the cold reviews. Huston explained them away by the expectation for a small sexual part in it, which he never intended to show. Eleven years after playing another nun in *Black Narcissus*, Deborah received her fourth Academy Award nomination for her performance as Sister Angela, but she lost to Joanne Woodward in *The Three Faces of Eve*. (She won, however, her second New York Film Critics' Award.) John Huston and John Lee Mahin were likewise nominated for their screenplay but they lost to Pierre Boulle for *The Bridge on the River Kwai*.

By 1957 Deborah was one of the most in-demand and admired actresses. She was awarded a Gold Medal by *Photoplay* as the most famous actress of the year based on a poll by readers of several popular movie magazines. Her next film, *An Affair to Remember*, finally gave her the opportunity to work close to her family, since it was entirely shot at the 20th Century–Fox studios in Hollywood.

An Affair to Remember was a remake of Leo McCarey's own 1939 film, *Love Affair*, which had starred Charles Boyer and Irene Dunne. McCarey had once been one of Hollywood's top directors, but by the mid–1950s his career stalled after a serious car accident which left him in poor health, addicted to painkillers and alcohol. With *An Affair to Remember*, he attempted a comeback.

"I want to do it," he explained, "because of a lot of people saying it's the best love story they have ever seen — and it's my favorite love story."[15]

McCarey rounded up the original writer, Delmer Daves, to write a new script. However, the new version was quite similar to the original film. McCarey claimed that about a third of the new dialogue had been written but a comparison of the two films later revealed a much smaller percentage.

Producer Jerry Wald told McCarey that he could have financial backing only if he got Cary Grant to play the lead. Grant who was an old and loyal friend of the director, accepted the part, even though it was not a convincing script. Wald hoped to reteam Grant with Ingrid Bergman, attempting to capture some of the onscreen sizzle that rocketed Alfred Hitchcock's *Notorious* to the top of the box office. But Bergman, who was then living in Europe, refused the offer, so the filmmakers quickly turned to Deborah, their second choice for the role.

Once the stars were cast, McCarey seemed enthusiastic for the prospect

Praying with Cary Grant in a scene from *An Affair to Remember* (1957).

of his new production to be filmed in Cinemascope. But not long before shooting started, the director's optimism was challenged when Grant began complaining about the project. The star was furious when he learned that budget cuts had forced the story to be entirely shot on a Fox soundstage and that McCarey had made a few changes to the script. Finally the director agreed to reinstate the original material and production began in the early spring.

In *An Affair to Remember* Cary Grant played Nick Ferrante, a mature artist who is en route from Europe to New York to meet his fiancée. On board the transatlantic liner he meets Terry McKay (played by Deborah), a former nightclub singer with her own past to hide. They fall in love, but they agree to part for six months to make sure of their feelings for each other and then meet again at the top of the Empire State Building. However, unforeseen circumstances change the course of events.

On February 28, 1957, cameras finally began rolling on the set of *An Affair to Remember*. Nevertheless, Cary made a scene, objecting to the buttons on the cabin boy's uniforms, and refused to resume his work until they were corrected. Grant, who was then married to Betsy Drake, was going through a difficult time after Sophia Loren — his co-star in a previous movie — had refused his marriage proposal. He was often nervous and continued making trouble throughout filming. The only person able to calm him down was Deborah. The two got along so well that they even found a way to improvise bits of comedy in their scenes together. The great chemistry between the two showed brilliantly on screen, despite their age difference. Grant was 53, Deborah was 35.

Deborah called Grant "master of the throwaway line," adding, "It was our most successful work together. Cary was not only the king of the 'double take,' but a superb ad-libber as well. He and I ad-libbed a lot on that film and Leo McCarey kept them in the finished film.... It was also in this movie that I saw how Cary had an eye for details in every aspect of the movie being made."[16]

Regarding the film's production, Deborah also revealed a few problems inherent in a smooth lovemaking scene with Grant: "Cary and I danced a few turns, gave each other tender glances, alternated singing a line or two. We had to dance cheek-to-cheek, slowly, dreamily; separate while one or the other sang: remember to turn so that Cary's face would be in the camera when he sang or spoke and vice versa; remembering that both of our faces had to be in camera range for reaction shots.... I'd much sooner learn ten pages of dialogue, and I know Cary would, too!"[17]

Although *An Affair to Remember* was not a musical, Deborah played a nightclub singer with four songs to perform. A representative from 20th Century–Fox asked Marni Nixon to sing them for Deborah, after the perfect experience on *The King and I*. However, Nixon was surprised to find out that Deborah decided this time not to be part of the process. "Oh Marni," she said, "you know me so well by now. Just sing the songs the way you think I would sing them and I'll just do them as you lay down the tracks!"[18] Hence, Deborah did not take part in the song rehearsals and simply adopted Nixon's vocal acting and made it her own on screen. The result was once again so perfect that it was announced that Deborah and Grant would record a full duet version of Harry Warren's title song. Although the album materialized, no duet by the stars was included; Vic Damone instead sang the number which topped the charts.

While filming *An Affair to Remember*, Deborah spent some weekends with Grant and his wife, Betsy Drake, in their Palm Springs home.

"She was very 'in' to hypnotism," Deborah commented about Drake, "and I actually saw and heard her put him fast asleep. He awoke refreshed and full of energy. She also stopped him smoking. I remembering him arriving on the set one morning at about 10 A.M., busily consuming his

With Cary Grant in a scene from *An Affair to Remember* (1957).

lunch and said to me, 'That damned Betsy — she's stopped me smoking, and now I am so hungry I am already eating my lunch !'"[19]

When the picture opened in July 1957, it suffered at the hands of the critics. *The New Yorker* dismissed it as "awfully maudlin," while *Time* commented, "Only sensitive acting from Deborah Kerr and Cary Grant saves this saccharine trifle from suffocating in its sentimental wrappings." Nonetheless, *An Affair to Remember* did very well at the box office, quickly becoming one of the year's biggest hits. Over the course of the years, Deborah received more fan mail on this film than for any other she made.

Just a week after she began working on *An Affair to Remember*, director Otto Preminger offered Deborah the chance to star in his independent production of *Bonjour Tristesse*, based on the best-selling book by French novelist Françoise Sagan. Deborah acknowledged the director's proposal but decided not to make a decision until she had read the script first. "Right now I'm not seriously thinking about anything other than not working in the summer,"[20] she said to the *New York Times*. However, she had already committed to the film version of *Separate Tables*, which was scheduled to be filmed the following October. When the script of *Bonjour Tristesse* was finally completed, Deborah accepted Otto Preminger's offer to star in it.

The Austrian director had bought the rights from producer Ray Ventura, who had acquired them in 1954 from Sagan. Preminger's initial plan was to present it first as a play and later as a movie. He hired S.N. Behrman to adapt the novel into both a play and a screenplay, but later he dropped the idea of a theatrical version and pursued only the film. He scheduled shooting to begin in France at the end of July 1957. The final screenplay was revised and completed by Arthur Laurents, author of such popular scripts as Alfred Hitchcock's *Rope* and Anatole Litvak's *Anastasia*. Laurents did not like the original story but accepted the job only for economic reasons. He also disagreed with Preminger's casting of Deborah, David Niven and Jean Seberg — all foreign artists playing French characters.

As in the Sagan novel, the story is told in retrospect by 17-year-old Cecile (Jean Seberg), who does her best to break up the romance between Raymond, her widower playboy father (Niven) and Anne, an old flame of his (Deborah). Plotting with Elsa (Mylène Demongeot, the only French actor in the cast), Raymond's last younger mistress, Anne's scheme has tragic results.

The picture was shot first in Paris, then on the French Riviera in the small village of Le Lavandou at Villa Point de la Fossette. The villa was an amazing three-story home of Mrs. Helen Gordon Lazareff, editor of *Elle* magazine and wife of French publishing magnate Pierre Lazareff.

Besides lavish scenery of the Riviera, Preminger generously spread Hollywood-style gloss all over the picture, in particular for Deborah's character, who wore gowns by Givenchy, jewels by Cartier and accessories by Hermes — but filmed with bourgeois conservatism.

To keep his stars and crew happy, the director encouraged them to bring their family members along at the production's expense. Deborah had with her Tony, Melanie and Francesca and their nanny. David Niven took his Swedish wife with him, while Mylen Demongeot brought her fiancé. Despite Preminger's good intentions, the general atmosphere on the set was rather tense, due to the director's moodiness and unpleasantness — particularly with Jean Seberg, whom he constantly insulted, regretting his choice to cast her. Deborah sided with the American actress, "It's going to be you up there — your face, your expression and your way of reading the lines, not the director."[21] In their scenes together, Seberg, who deeply admired Deborah, managed to appear relatively relaxed and natural.

"I couldn't stand it," Deborah said about Preminger's despicable behavior, "when he was absolutely ranting and raving at poor little Jean Seberg. I said, 'Please, Otto, do you have to shout at the poor little girl like that? *She* seems to be taking it all right but *I'm* not. I cannot work with this kind of atmosphere. I'm terribly sorry, but I just can't.' The battering she received finished me, but it didn't her. I used to be a bit frightened for Otto. I thought he was going to have a heart attack, with his eyes popping and his face purple. But the next minute, it was gone. Completely gone. And this man who could be a bully on the set, and who could destroy people, would then be a charming, witty companion at dinner who knew the best wines and caviar."[22]

Deborah also regretted not staying in touch with Seberg after the film was completed. "I formed a very deep respect for the quiet strength with which she put up with all the extravagant publicity that had been forced on her by her discovery and the lashing she took from the critics. This strength was also apparent in her coping with Otto.... I think any other woman would have collapsed in tears or just walked out. But she calmly took all the berating and achieved a very interesting and true Sagan-type heroine."[23]

Being very shy, it was not very easy for Deborah to stand up to Preminger. However, she felt in this particular situation that she had to. Like everyone else on the set, the director had great respect for her and after she criticized him, he would back off temporarily.

Bonjour Tristesse was the first of five pictures that Deborah was to make with David Niven, who was an old friend of Tony. While working together he became a firm friend to last the rest of Niven's life. Deborah and Niven shared the same sense of humor and enjoyed each other's company tremendously. Despite some rumors they were never lovers, as Deborah's second husband Peter Viertel revealed many years later, "She didn't see him that way. They were close chums."[24] It was just a true happy friendship.

Geoffrey Horne, who played a small role, recalled, "Otto didn't have to say *anything* to Deborah Kerr: she was wonderful in the role, and she was generous, beautiful and sexy too."[25]

First Vivien Leigh, and later William Holden, both of whom were vacationing nearby, visited the set. Leigh was rumored to appear in Jean Giraudoux's play *Duel of Angels* together with Deborah. They both would have played the same woman, but different parts: one representing the physical woman, her body, the other one the woman's conscience. But Deborah, who was already committed to her next project, was forced to turn down her stage comeback.[26]

Bonjour Tristesse opened on January 15, 1958. The critics' reception was far from warm. Reviewers dismissed it, claiming it lacked true French realism. Ironically, critical redemption arrived two months later when the film was released in France to great acclaim. The Gallic critics especially praised the film's cinematography and Seberg's performance and the picture earned satisfactory results at the local box office.

The final scenes of *Bonjour Tristesse* were shot at Shepperton Studios in London where, as soon as Preminger's film was completed, Deborah and David Niven began work on *Separate Tables*.

Before she started her new film, Deborah refused producer Jerry Wald's offer to star as a pros-

Publicity shot late '50s.

titute in *The Sound and the Fury*, based on William Faulkner's novel. "I don't like that type of role — not yet," was her simple explanation. Wald had sought Deborah and Kirk Douglas for leads in the film; however, the picture came to production only a year later starring Yul Brynner, Joanne Woodward and Margaret Leighton (in the role Deborah turned down).

Separate Tables was adapted from two successful 1954 plays by Terence Rattigan, who collaborated with screenwriter John Gay on making into one story what was two distinct but related acts, both set in the same seaside hotel in England, and centered on four desperately lonely people.

The film rights were bought by Harold Hecht, James Hill and Burt Lancaster, all of whom had formed a production company. The trio hired Laurence Olivier to direct and star in the leading role of Major Pollack along with his then-wife Vivien Leigh. Spencer Tracy was supposed to play John Malcom, a frustrated alcoholic American writer. But Lancaster suddenly changed his mind and decided to take Tracy's part. Following a strong altercation with Lancaster, Olivier quit, feeling unsure of getting what he thought the play needed out of the American actor. (Consequently, Vivien Leigh pulled out as well.) David Niven replaced Olivier as the Major. Delbert Mann was asked to direct the picture, after Carol Reed declined due to existing commitments. Rita Hayworth, who was engaged to James Hill, was cast to play Lancaster's estranged wife. Hayworth's character was transformed into an American to avoid her playing with a fake British accent. Lancaster cast Deborah to be Sybil Railton-Bell, a repressed young woman dominated by her tyrannical mother (played by Gladys Cooper), who falls in love with an older major with a shady past. Wendy Hiller starred as the manager of the Beauregard Hotel in Bournemouth, where the story was set.

The day before the beginning of the three-week rehearsals, Harold Hecht gave a lunch party in a small studio to introduce the cast to one other. "We simply did it as a play," recalled the director, talking about the rehearsal which started as a simple reading around a table and later performed as on stage.[27]

Shot in melancholic black and white, cameras began rolling in November on a Goldwyn sound stage at Shepperton Studios. Deborah was delighted to be portraying what she considered to be one of Rattigan's best characters, and with such a fantastic group of talented actors. Three years earlier the playwright had had lunch with her to discuss her playing the lead in his play *The Deep Blue Sea*, but in the end Deborah's other commitments got in the way. When she finally was offered a chance to star in the screen version of one of Rattigan's most popular plays she immediately accepted.

"The girl I play has lived for many years in a state of negativeness [*sic*]," Deborah told Richard Dyer MacCann, who visited the set to interview her. "I have to be careful when I play the scenes in which she reaches out for something more. I'm sure any kind of bursting forth would not be believable. It has to be very tentative, indistinct. At the end, of course, you're still not quite sure about where her experiences have left her."

The complexity of her part made Deborah feel slightly insecure. "I'm not an actress," she shockingly said in a press release sent by United Artists promoting the film during its production. "I don't know what I'm doing! I think I'm too well adjusted a human being. Not all actors are crazy, mind you. But there's a bravura about them that I feel I lack." This momentary insecurity about her craft made Deborah timidly ask veteran actress Gladys Cooper, for whom she had great respect and admiration, what she thought of the then-fashionable Method school of acting: "I don't understand it, dear; I just go on and I am. That's all there is to acting." Cooper's answer did not enlighten Deborah as much as she had hoped.[28]

On the set, David Niven was christened "mouse face" by Deborah,

With Rita Hayworth (center) and Gladys Cooper (right) in *Separate Tables* (1958).

because of the unhappy look caused by the difficulties of his marriage and the pressure of his serious role. "I think he was a tiny bit scared," Deborah said years later. "I remember him coming to me and saying, 'You know, chum, I don't know whether I can do this. I mean, this is serious stuff, isn't it?' But, of course, he did it superbly."[29]

"She's a dream to work with," Niven wrote about Deborah to the press, "because she's such a giggler. I can sometimes hardly look her in the eye when she giggles at me."[30]

"David and Deborah," said Delbert Mann, "worked gloriously together ... both of them realizing that they were taking wild, wild chances with those two roles. If we had slipped or missed, those relationships would have been laughable with Deborah playing the hysterical woman who is frightened of the word sex and David as the emotionally crippled man hiding behind the façade of the blustering wartime major."[31] About Lancaster's performance Deborah commented, "He was awfully good, Burt. But he wasn't quite the left wing, rumbling angry man that the character was written."[32] This was an observation with which many critics later seemed to concur.

To please both Deborah and Rita Hayworth, United Artists gave top billing to Deborah in half of the advertising campaign and to Hayworth in the other half. Top billing on the actual prints of the film was similarly split.

The *Herald Tribune* spoke for most of the critics in asserting that *Separate Tables* was "one of the year's finest achievements" and "a movie that nobody in his right mind will want to miss." All the members of the cast received their share of praise, above all Deborah, Niven and Hiller.

Separate Tables was successful with audiences when United Artists released it on December 18, 1958. With a $3.7 million gross, the picture climbed to a surprising 25th place among the most popular films of 1959, earning six Academy Award nominations with Niven and Hiller winning for Best Actor and Best Supporting Actress, respectively. Deborah, receiving her fourth nomination, lost to Susan Hayward who won for *I Want to Live*.

On several occasions after his Oscar victory, David Niven paid tribute to Deborah with his witty sense of humor. "I won the Oscar that night," he said, "because two young ladies, Deborah Kerr and Wendy Hiller, cried so well."

9

Peter Viertel:
A Love Affair to Remember

She was modest and almost self-effacing, intelligent and, needless to say, beautiful in a very special way, with her pale skin and reddish blond hair."

— Peter Viertel

For almost 12 years Deborah seemed to have one of Hollywood's happiest marriages. However, off the set she was miserable, frustrated by her listless marital relationship which was slowly disintegrating. Even though Tony had started a new career as a short-film producer for the CBS network, he was still uncomfortable in his own new identity, as a movie star husband. As Francesca Bartley commented years later, "His own fame was diminishing in a sense. I think he felt a little bit of an alien, unfortunately a lot of growing up happened after they in fact married, and I think they just grew apart."[1] Although magazine articles still described their marital bliss, the truth was that the marriage was becoming merely a façade; much of that year Deborah had been away on location, separated from Tony. She was able to channel the pain of her personal life into a dramatic performance in her new film *The Journey*. Despite its mild success, it changed her private life forever.

In the early spring of 1958 Deborah once again left Tony and the girls to fly to Austria. In Vienna, she began to shoot *The Journey* with Yul Brynner. At first, producer Anthony Havelock-Allan wanted Anna Magnani and Brynner as the leading roles. When the Italian actress turned down the offer, Brynner immediately thought of Deborah, recalling the perfect professional relationship they had four years earlier on the set of *The King and I.* He also requested to be directed by Anatole Litvak, with whom had previously worked on *Anastasia*. But Havelock-Allan was not convinced Litvak was the right choice and backed off, leaving the project in Brynner's and Litvak's hands. The two financed the picture after establishing their own production company called *Alby* (a combination of their initials).

The story of *The Journey* was based on a Guy de Maupassant's short story *Boule de Suif,* which had also inspired John Ford's *Stagecoach.* Screenwriter George Tabori, a Hungarian immigrant to Hollywood — inspired by real political events after the Red Army invaded Hungary, generating local resistance — adapted the original theme to the postwar, Austro-Hungarian iron curtain frontier.

The Journey tells of the voyage of 16 international travelers stranded in Hungary after the sudden political changes. Their evacuation is interrupted by Russian militia led by Major Sukov, played by Brynner. Deborah was Lady Diana Ashmore, an elegant British aristocrat who tries to help Jason Robards, in the role of her Hungarian lover, to flee the country. Among the international cast were French actress Anouk Aimée as one of the leaders of the Hungarian resistance, British character actor Robert Morley and Anne Jackson (the wife of actor Eli Wallach, who accompanied her in Vienna).

Shot on location around the hills outside Vienna and at the Hosenhegel studios, the picture caused a great amount of press interest, largely because it was bringing Deborah and Yul Brynner back together on the screen after the international success of *The King and I,* and roused unfounded speculations of a romance.

Suddenly several newspapers accused the film of promoting anti–Soviet propaganda in neutral Austria, while others maintained that it was against the Hungarian resistance. All accusations were pure speculation because nobody involved in the making of the picture (except the cast) knew the contents of the script. Nevertheless, the quarrels kept inflaming the pages of the 11 Viennese daily papers, forcing Litvak to release an official statement declaring his firm intention to continue his work in peace, condemning those who criticized the film without even knowing the context.[2]

Many of the extras in the film who played the Russian military were former soldiers, appearing before the cameras in their own uniforms and wearing Russian medals. They signed up for the picture under false names, all being refugees or defectors from the Red Army during World War II who found sanctuary in Austria. During her stay in Vienna, Deborah threw a party for the cast and the crew. She chartered a riverboat on the

Danube, and more than 100 guests showed up. The evening went off without incident, though there was a report that somebody stepped on the hem of her lace gown, ripping it up the back.

Yul Brynner also gave a party at the Palace Auersperg. Among the guests were a dozen of those former Russian soldiers who played as extras in the picture. After a few drinks, they burst out with some militant Red Army songs that incensed the refugee Hungarians, who also were extras in the film. Things got very tense when a Hungarian dissident in the crowd whispered that the Russians had been paid $1,000 each for three months' work, while Hungarians got only $3.10 a day. Brynner prevented a second Hungarian revolt by stoutly denying the charge and quickly ordering more wine.[3]

While the professional relationship between Deborah and Litvak was idyllic, Brynner and the director did not always get along — especially when the bald actor wanted to enter his Mercedes Benz 300 in a sports car race in Vienna. Litvak refused to allow him to risk his neck and the film. The argument was so heated at one point that some bystanders were afraid it could turn physically violent. Brynner stormed off and refused to work the rest of the day, returning the following morning after he cooled down.

On the set once again, Deborah and Brynner had an equalitarian professional relationship, each trusting in the other completely.

"Deborah is so delightful to act with," said Brynner in an interview with the British press. "With her, one can really do a team job, and not just two solos." "Having made one picture with her, the second was, of course, easier for us. Not only had Deborah an exceptional talent, she furthermore has an exceptional personality on screen, and is an angel off screen."[4]

"I couldn't wish for a better partner," was Deborah's response to a journalist who was writing a profile on her co-star. "Yul Brynner is a handsome man, a striking character, and just enough of a rascal to make it exciting. Of course, he knows it.... He is an actor that never steals a scene but actually makes everyone else look better. He is a genius."[5]

Just a few days before Litvak began shooting, he decided to call his old friend, 37-year-old Peter Viertel, who had written the screenplay for *The Sun Also Rises* and *The African Queen*, to ask if he would consider joining him to do some work on the script. Viertel was not particularly eager to do it but, as he had not yet started to write the novel he intended to, he agreed to go and help him fix a few scenes. Viertel was then introduced to the cast. "Deborah, with her beauty, her simple and direct manner, stood out above all the others," he wrote in his memoir, *Dangerous Friends*, in 1992. "Tola (Litvak's nickname) had told me that she was an exceptional woman, and I soon realized that his glowing description had not been an exaggeration."[6]

After a press conference Litvak hosted a dinner for the crew and actors. Viertel was seated on Deborah's left. "Needless to say, I was delighted with the seating arrangement," admitted Viertel. "Men all over the world had fallen in love with my dinner partner merely after seeing her on the screen. To share her company for an hour or two was even a more telling experience, as she was equally charming in real life. Unlike any of the other celebrated actresses I had met, she was modest and almost self-effacing, intelligent and, needless to say, beautiful in a very special way, with her pale skin and reddish blond hair.... We talked with complete disregard for any of the other people present, and even danced a waltz ... and before the evening had ended I had fallen in love with her."[7]

Litvak, who had noticed Deborah's and Viertel's mutual attraction, dangerously advised Viertel to keep courting her. In the following days while Deborah was busy on the set, the screenwriter visited several antique shops in Vienna where he purchased many gifts for her. Among them he bought a small silver box with an ornate heart on its lid. He left her a romantic note, which was discovered by Tony when he arrived a few days later in Vienna on a short visit. Viertel recalled, "There were unpleasant scenes and confrontations.... It had not been Deborah's intent to change her life, but she was overtaken by the events and before the movie had been completed late in the spring of 1958, we were a couple, happy and plagued by problems at the same time."[8]

The making of *The Journey* dragged out for several extra weeks. Anne Jackson, who was pregnant, used to joke that she would have given birth to the child on the location bus.

One of the two children in the film playing Jackson's children was four-year-old Ron Howard (now the acclaimed director of such features as *The Da Vinci Code* and *Angels & Demons*), making his screen debut.

After a short trip to London during which Deborah tried fruitlessly to come to an agreement with her husband, on May 30th she officially announced from Vienna her separation from Tony after twelve years of marriage. "It is with the deepest regret that I must announce that an estrangement has taken place between my husband and me. I sincerely hope we shall be able to settle our problems amicably."[9] Deborah did not elaborate with the reporters on the reasons behind the split, although the following day a French newspaper carried the story of Deborah's affair with Viertel. The screenwriter immediately denied the news. Yet, on June 3, Tony stated through his attorney that legal steps had been taken to make their two daughters wards of the British Court in order to prevent Deborah from gaining complete custody of Melanie and Francesca, now 11 and 9, and taking them with her out of the country.

A few days later Bartley issued a writ against Viertel, alleging enticement. He said to the press that the move was done to preserve and safeguard his marriage and to protect his children. "These charges are so absurd and ridiculous that no comment is required," was Viertel's reply to the charge that he had enticed Deborah.

The difficult situation caused Deborah great pain as she was not used to that type of publicity about her personal life. Despite the legal complications and a strong sense of guilt, she continued to play her part in *The Journey* with immense moral support from Litvak and Brynner. Deborah's biggest concern was the welfare of her daughters, who were then living with Tony in London where they attended school.

Finally she filed suit for divorce in the Santa Monica branch of Los Angeles Superior Court, accusing Tony of mental cruelty, asking for custody of Melanie and Francesca with visitation rights for the father, attorney fees and cost of the suit.

In seeking her divorce Deborah told a judge that "any ordinary conversation with Mr. Bartley would usually end in an argument. No, [that is] an understatement.... It would end in upbraiding. He upbraided me, using unkind language and caused me a great deal of mental suffering which affected my work.... If it wasn't an argument, it was a case of totally ignoring me."[10]

As soon as the news of her divorce request was disclosed, the press went berserk. Litvak had to ban all visitors from the set to evade questions about the surprise divorce suit. The last days of shooting had to be done on a closed set.

The events drew Deborah and Peter closer together. After the film was completed, they rented a villa in Guéthary — a small village on the border between France and Spain — where they spent the entire month of June relaxing and avoiding reporters. In July Deborah intended to spend the rest of the summer with Melanie and Francesca. However, her attorney, Henry Hyde, suggested that she invite a third party to share the temporary domicile Deborah had with Viertel to avoid further gossip. Marie Daëms, a young French actress who was in the cast of *The Journey*, was invited by the couple to join them. During that time Deborah was introduced to Peter's close friends, Spanish bullfighter Louis Dominguin and his wife, former Italian actress Lucia Bosè.

In the middle of September Deborah returned to Hollywood where she made her last picture for MGM, completing her original contract. *Count Your Blessings* was based on a popular and witty novel by Nancy Mitford. The screenplay was adapted by Karl Tunberg, who had just finished the script of *Ben-Hur*. Directed by John Negulesco, *Count Your Blessings* starred Italian playboy Rossano Brazzi, Maurice Chevalier, and child-star Martin Stephens, who one year later would star in the horror hit *The Village of the Damned*. After a few sequences shot at MGM studios, the bulk of the picture was filmed in Paris and in the wine country around Bordeaux. For Deborah, starring in a comedy was the best medicine, since she was still afflicted by the pending divorce and the separation from her daughters. The atmosphere on the set was very relaxed. The crew celebrated her 32nd birthday on the set and Negulesco offered as a gift a portrait of her she liked, which was used as a part of the set. Much of Deborah's spare time was spent with Chevalier, who acted as her personal tour guide. "The magic of the man was everywhere," commented Deborah after she spent a weekend at La Louque, Chevalier's villa near Cannes.[11]

Count Your Blessings' production was handsomely mounted, beautifully costumed and designed, however the script lost much of its originality in the adaptation, partly because of censorship regulations that were still being enforced. Needless to say, the film bombed at the box office after being universally panned by reviewers.

In October, Deborah was chosen "Star of the Year" by the Theatre Owners of America. She was the first actress to receive the honor in the five-year history of the award, which she received in Miami during a special banquet.

She was able to spend Christmas in London with Melanie and Francesca and continued to visit them every weekend she could before starting to work on her next feature.

On March 13, 1959, shortly before the Oscar nominations were announced (in which she was named for *Separate Tables*), Deborah discussed with columnist Louella Parson her unhappy marital situation: "I will not disregard the California divorce laws which demand a year before the required period is up. I would be extremely grateful if you would clear this up because it has led to a great deal of confusion and trouble in an already confused and troubled situation."

While she was film-
ing *Count Your Blessings*,
Deborah lunched with
columnist Sheilah Gra-
ham, who had written
several pieces since Deb-
orah's arrival in Holly-
wood. They discussed
her future projects and
Deborah mentioned that
her next picture was for
20th Century–Fox, but
she did not know any
details as of yet. A few
weeks later while —
Deborah was in Klosters,
Switzerland, at Peter
Viertel's house — she
read the book Graham
had just published,
Beloved Infidel, a memoir
of her stormy affair with

A funny publicity shot for *Count Your Blessings*
with Rossano Brazzi (right) and Maurice Chevalier
(center, standing) 1959.

novelist F. Scott Fitzgerald, while his wife, Zelda, was in a sanitarium.
Deborah immediately cabled Buddy Adler, who was in charge of production at 20th Century–Fox and had bought the film rights, saying that she
was interested in playing Graham.

Graham, a Cockney-born columnist, moved to America in the early
1930s and was romantically involved with Fitzgerald during the last four
years of his life. In fact, he died in her home shortly before Christmas
1940. Producer Jerry Wald talked her into writing a book, entitled *Beloved
Infidel*, after a poem Fitzgerald wrote about Graham. She was helped by
ghostwriter Gerold Frank and the book was an immediate bestseller. However, when Fox decided to make a film, Graham lost control of the story,
which was entirely changed. When the script was completed, Wald, out
of courtesy to Graham, sent her a copy. She hated it and unsuccessfully
tried to revise it. The first part of the story, which Deborah especially
enjoyed, was completely cut from the script, rendering the personalities
of the two major characters underdeveloped.

Deborah was also disappointed by the script but, as she was still under contract with 20th Century–Fox, she was advised by her agent that it was better for her to make the film rather than face suspension.

Graham disagreed with the casting choices made by Jerry Wald. She thought Deborah was "too controlled, too thin and too ladylike," believing instead that Jean Simmons or Marilyn Monroe would have been more appropriate in playing herself. She also disliked the idea of having Gregory Peck play Fitzgerald. She suggested Richard Basehart, whom she had seen in Fellini's *La Strada*. "Even Bing Crosby would have been better" than Peck, she complained. Fox considered Montgomery Clift and Paul Newman, but in the end, they settled for Peck, who had an agreement with the studio.

Gregory Peck was difficult from the beginning. He detested the script which he thought was a Cinderella story, chronicling the columnist's rise from poverty to riches thanks in part to the once-famous writer. Peck brought to the picture his own writer, however the changes applied to the script were minor. The star wanted to postpone the beginning of the film until the screenplay was satisfactory; however Deborah had signed a contract which involved her presence until the beginning of September. She was, in fact, due to begin shooting *The Sundowners* in England (and later in Australia) under Fred Zinnemann's direction. Since Fox did not want to lose her, principal photography of *Beloved Infidel* began on July 22, 1959, two weeks after Deborah was granted her divorce by the Superior Court of Santa Monica, the divorce would be executed the following year. The community property between Tony and Deborah had been divided in a prior agreement in which she also agreed to waive alimony. However, Melanie and Francesca were still wards of the British courts.

During the shooting Deborah lived in her former house in Pacific Palisades. She was concerned how Peter Viertel would be received by her friends, especially David Niven, who was also very close to Tony. Niven was very welcoming and cordial with the screenwriter and shortly they became very good friends. For the sake of propriety, Viertel stayed in Brentwood in a spare room at the home of Myrtle Tully, Deborah's secretary. Every day at six o' clock he would pick Deborah up and drive her to the studio. A week after Deborah was granted the divorce, Virginia "Jigee" Ray divorced Peter Viertel. Although Peter and Jigee had been married since 1944, they had been amicably separated for many months. Jigee was raising their seven-year-old daughter, Christine, whom Peter would often visit. The child also had met Deborah, whose gentle nature charmed her immediately. Peter was ordered by the court to pay $12,000 a year alimony and $6,000 a year in child support. Six months later, while their final divorce papers were still pending, Jigee accidentally dropped a lighted match on the flammable nylon nightgown she was wearing, resulting in severe burns over 60 percent of her body. After three agonizing weeks in a hospital, she died.

On the set of *Beloved Infidel*, there was much tension, especially between Gregory Peck and Jerry Wald. Deborah was instead very cooperative. As Graham later said, "It is impossible to fight with this charming lady."[12] Wald told a Fox executive that his female lead had to put up with a great deal of "guff, more than many an actress in her position would do."[13] This was in reference to Peck's despicable behavior.

To make sure that he really looked the part of the drunk writer, Peck consumed enough vodka to throw off his inhibitions. Director Henry King, in shock, recalled, "He scared Deborah Kerr half to death. You would think he was a drunken demon. When he gets in to do something, he does it — right to the very limit without hamming it up. Exactly what's on his mind."[14] Peck felt that the rush caused by Deborah's schedule conflict was putting a lot of pressure on him, not allowing him enough time to rehearse, and not enabling him to act at his highest level. Trying to calm him, Deborah revealed, "Before really difficult scenes we try to buck each other's courage up by saying something ridiculous to break the tension. Over the years I've worked up wonderful word games to play between takes."[15] Despite Deborah's tricks, little chemistry appeared onscreen between the two.

The picture's première was held in November 1959 at the Paramount Theater, in New York, as a benefit for the Damon Runyon Fund. *Beloved Infidel* opened its run on November 17. Its total cost amounted to $5 million but it grossed only $3 million over the course of a year. For the first time in her career, Deborah received bad reviews. She was generally considered too genteel as Sheilah Graham. Bosley Crowther, in the *New York Times* called, the film "generally flat and uninteresting.... Deborah Kerr ... is likewise unconvincing and emotionally implausible."[16]

Ultimately nobody was happy with the picture. Graham called it "a complete disaster," complaining that the producer had chosen publicity shots from a scene in which Deborah cries in Peck's arms on the beach of Malibu making subtle allusion to the famous scene in *From Here to Eternity*.

In response to the critics Peck commented, "Deborah Kerr and I both did it to kill off final commitments we had made to Fox."[17] In her own

As columnist Sheilah Graham with Gregory Peck as F. Scott Fitzgerald in *Beloved Infidel* (1959).

defense Deborah added, "The film wasn't all bad, but it became disjointed, between Sheilah's original story, the film script and Greg's own writers, and I was unable to characterize, because half the poor woman's personality was cut out. It was difficult for me to pick up the threads halfway through her life and, for my own self, be genuine. I wasn't able to show where she came from, and what she was, why she became the way she was later on."

Interviewed by Sheilah Graham a few weeks before *Beloved Infidel*'s release, Deborah said, "I've been hoping I wouldn't work so hard in the future. I have two more pictures to do for Fox but I have a wonderful arrangement with the studio. Whenever a role is available that we both like, I'll do it. After *The Sundowners* in Australia with Robert Mitchum, I'll go back to London for *The Grass Is Greener* with Cary Grant. He's going to wait until April for me." As for a return to the stage she explained, "Irene Selznick wanted me to appear in *The Complacent Lover* but with all the films I have to make, I don't think I'll be available."[18]

10

The Sundowners

*Deborah Kerr displayed her vibrant femininity, more exquisite
even in what was left unsaid than in what was said.*
— Peter Ustinov

While filming *Oklahoma!*, director Fred Zinnemann was urged by
Oscar Hammerstein's wife, Dorothy, who was from Tasmania, to make a
picture about Australia. Except for *Overlanders* and *A Town Like Alice* no
one in Hollywood ever made a film down under, despite the existence of
a small local film industry. Finally in 1956 Mrs. Hammerstein sent Renée
Zinnemann a copy of a novel called *The Sundowners*, written by Australian
author John Cleary. After reading it and enjoying it, Renée gave it to her
husband who also loved it.

A "sundowner" is a wanderer whose home is wherever he happens to
be when the sun goes down. In Cleary's story, Paddy and Ida Carmody
and their teenaged son, Sean, are the sundowners, conducting a nomadic
life by taking the job of driving hundreds of sheep across Australia.

"I was drawn to it," explained Zinnemann, "because it showed that
there were these three people who had no money and owned nothing
except the shirts on their backs and this buggy with the old horse. And
nothing could separate them. They were for each other and they were a
family, and that was tighter and closer than anything else. And to me that
was a celebration of family all the way through, with all the troubles they
have.... Having had a pretty good marriage for 58 years, I'm sort of
inclined in that direction."[1]

Zinnemann told Jack Warner he wanted to make a film based on the
book. The president of Warner Bros. liked the idea but attempted to con-

On holiday with daughters Melanie and Francesca, early '60s.

vince the director to shoot it in Arizona to save money. Nevertheless, Zinnemann was firm in asserting that the picture had to be made in Australia. Finally Warner agreed. The first draft of the screenplay was written by a young screenwriter, Aaron Spelling, later a famous television producer. It was not satisfactory and Isobel Lennart was assigned to rewrite it. Earlier in 1959, Zinnemann flew to Australia, along with producer Gerry Blattner, to scout location sites. He spent 12 weeks filming the foothills of the Snowy River Mountains and sequences of jumping sheep and bounding kangaroos. Zinnemann purchased 5,000 sheep for his droving scenes. He also had to use a special schooling of one sheep in order to draw performances from all of them.

Finally, in October, cast and crew arrived in Cooma, New South Wales. Deborah was accompanied by Peter, while Bob Mitchum, her co-star, arrived by himself (his wife, Dorothy, arrived for a ten-day location visit a month later). Originally, Gary Cooper had been cast in Mitchum's role, but he had to refuse on doctor's orders since his poor health kept him from the rigors of the Australian locations. Mitchum admitted to accepting the film only because Deborah would be the leading lady. He genuinely adored her. After the perfect chemistry they had on and off screen in *Heaven Knows, Mr. Allison*, they stayed in touch looking for a vehicle on which to work together again. John Mitchum described his brother Bob's attachment to Deborah as "far beyond anything that could be related to infatuation or flirtation. Deborah to Bob, was an actress of such heights as to defy the imagination."[2]

Zinnemann added a number of excellent Australian actors in the roles of the drover, Paddy, and his wife, Ida. Others hired were young Mickey Anderson, Jr., as their son, Peter Ustinov as a hilarious remittance man, Glynis Johns as a hotel keeper and Dina Merrill as a station owner's wife.

Despite the uncooperative unseasonable weather — intense heat and humidity in one location, bitter cold and rain in another one — which forced the production to shut down for a few days, the atmosphere on the set was very nice, relaxed and cooperative. Deborah, who had loved working with Peter Ustinov on *Quo Vadis*, enjoyed it even more on this film due to "his enormous talent — as well as his unique brand of wit and his amazing sense of fun."[3]

"I shall never forget working with Peter on *The Sundowners*, on a very tough location," she stated in an interview. "We would meet every morning in the rather thrown-together make-up room in Cooma, and the make-up man could hardly manage to make me sit still and 'get my face on' because I was laughing so much at Peter. One morning it would be Beethoven's *Eroica* in which he would imitate *all* the instruments of the orchestra perfectly. The next morning — *Madame Butterfly*! Every day he would be a different person: American-Russian-Chinese-Japanese and so on ad lib! He is possessed of boundless energy. I am filled with admiration for all facets of Peter — the serious side, too — and grateful for the laughter … he has given me and countless others."[4] In fact every evening for dinner Ustinov and Mitchum staged for a free show the crew made up of jokes and witty remarks.

Throughout her long career Deborah never complained in public. One rare exception occurred on the set of *The Sundowners*. As she recalled

The Sundowners (1960) with Robert Mitchum (center) and Peter Ustinov (right) (1960).

years later, "We were on location in Australia in such a heat as you can't imagine. It was a 75-mile drive to the location. One went to make up in a tent that was absolutely boiling. On this particular day, after the long drive and the unpleasant tent, I was 10 or 15 minutes late on the set. Mr. Z, usually so amiable, was stony-faced. He informed me that I'd held up production. 'How dare you!' I told him. 'How dare you!' I did really shout at him and I made sure everyone heard, 'If Ava Gardner were playing this part, you'd be lucky if she were only three hours late!'"[5] Such an outburst was uncharacteristic for Deborah's quiet temper, nonetheless she was able to calm down shortly afterwards and returned to her work as though nothing had happened.

In November the crew moved south to Port Augusta. Everyone stayed at a little hotel, except for Deborah, who found a little house, although she had most of her meals with the cast. Mitchum slept on a rented boat to be away from the fans, who were bothering him, and to get drunk throughout the making of the film.

"Such a pro is Bob," said Deborah in a long foreword she wrote for a biography on Mitchum. "I only remember *one* occasion when Bob did not turn up on time in the morning ... since the setup was a particularly complicated one involving sheep, horses and dogs, our director, Fred Zinnemann — also a very stern 'pro' — was beginning to get quietly angered. He came to me and said, 'Deborah, you've worked with Bob before. Now is this going to go on happening? I'm afraid I am very, very angry.' I told him, 'Please Fred, just ignore it if you can. Just go on as if nothing had happened ... he'll turn up.' And he did. Not a word was exchanged as to why or what. And it never happened again. Nor did I ask what had happened."[6]

On her portrayal of Ida Carmody, Deborah said, "I play a marvelous character with, I hope, tremendous vitality — a kind of glow. She is full of life and humor — bossy too, because her husband would rather sit around and chew the cud. She's a typical female really, no sentimentality at all. I haven't had a part like this before; it's quite new. Oh, I know I've played dowdy people, but the sheer physical roughness of this part is something different. This woman can cope with anything from crisis in the kitchen to a forest fire, with no heroics. She can cook, wash and mend sitting in a tent, and tend horses and drive a wagon. My favorite moment, a moment I find especially lovely is when this woman, who is always battered, dirty and tired, is in a railway siding and sees a girl sitting in a carriage powdering her nose. The two women catch each other's eye, but this grubby, sweaty creature doesn't say a word. Her husband comes, and she still says nothing. Only tears well up in her eyes. I find this terribly touching."[7]

Although the wet weather put the filming a few weeks behind schedule, Zinnemann was able to finish it by Christmas. On December 17, Deborah, Mitchum, Ustinov, and others from the production boarded a Pan Am flight to Los Angeles. Deborah spent her Christmas holidays with Melanie and Francesca before a final week of interior filming in London.

Once the shooting was over, Mitchum was asked by the production if Deborah could have top billing. Even though he was entitled to refuse, he generously replied, "By all means. And you can design a twenty-four-foot sign of me bowing to her if you like." He also admitted, "All I did was feed her some lines. She did the rest. She's really the one who can act."[8]

At its initial engagement in major American cities, *The Sundowners* was quite successful at the box office but its gross faded in the rest of the country. Zinnemann blamed the promotion of the film, which was, according to him, "misleading." The advertising campaign accentuated Deborah's sexuality, trying to reawaken her sexy image in *From Here to Eternity*, and harmed the movie's potential success as the perfect "family film."

Deborah's performance met with universal acclaim. She was named Best Actress of the year by the New York Critics and was nominated for an Academy Award.

On this sixth Oscar nomination, the last in her career, Deborah's time to win was long overdue. However, with her usual graciousness she said to the press, "The Oscar should go to Elizabeth Taylor. Not because of her grave illness (Taylor had just recovered from a very serious illness, which almost took her life) but because her performance on *Butterfield 8* is superb. She deserves the prize as Best Actress. She has been in the running many times and perhaps this will be the lucky time."[9] Taylor did win and Deborah commented on her own defeat saying, "I would love to have won, but I didn't and I'm not bitter. True, sometimes the Oscars are fair, sometimes are not, but I was brought up by a mother who would tell me when I'd say, 'Not fair, Mummy,' 'There is not such a thing as not fair; life itself isn't fair.'"[10]

Stanley Donen's elegant *The Grass Is Greener* provided Deborah with a return to the role of the "cool English lady" that she had fought against since *From Here to Eternity*. This time she did not play a distant, cold beauty but a spirited married woman tempted into an affair with an American businessman. It also gave her a chance to work again with both Cary Grant and Robert Mitchum, and with her dear friend Jean Simmons.

The Grass Is Greener originally premièred on stage in December of 1956 and played to packed houses for more than a year. Cary Grant and director Stanley Donen bought the film rights, hoping to repeat the success of *Indiscreet* by making another movie version of a successful play. Their production company, Grandon Productions, Ltd., financed the project, whose shooting began on April 2, 1960, at Shepperton Studios.

Initially, Kay Kendall and her husband, Rex Harrison, were supposed to act the leading roles of Countess Hilary Rhyall and Victor the Earl of

Rhyall. But she died suddenly at 33 of leukemia before she could start filming. Naturally, Harrison withdrew and Cary Grant, who originally intended to play Charles Decro, an American oil tycoon who falls in love with the Countess, replaced him. Ingrid Bergman campaigned for the leading role, but Deborah personally asked Grant, who decided to cast her in the film as his wife. Donen suggested Robert Mitchum in the role of the American, while the part of Hattie, a wacky friend of the Ryalls,' was assigned to Jean Simmons.

A particularly rainy English spring prevented the use of more outdoor scenes, which were filmed at Osterley Park, home of the Earls of Jersey. Margaret and Hugh Williams, authors of the play and the film script, had to extend the play's temporal settings of eight days to fourteen. They also made the dialogue more accessible to the American audience, removing or changing all slang, jokes and expressions considered too British.

As soon as shooting began, everyone on the set became aware that Cary Grant was not at ease. He was restless over the numerous takes called for by Donen and he showed difficulty with his lines. He was also obsessed by the tiniest detail of the production.

As Deborah remembered, "Cary, whom I loved, was very particular about everything, not just the acting but what everyone looked like. Before we shot a scene, Cary would ask, 'Is anyone wearing red?' Because in that case, they were to be removed from the set. Cary would say, 'The eye always goes to something red.' He wouldn't stand for that."[11]

Actor Moray Watson, who played the role of the butler — the only original cast member from the play — remembered one day when Deborah called him aside and said, "Cary's different. He's just not the man he was when I knew him before. He was fun then, and amusing, and fast, and funny, and professional and always knew his lines, and was cooperative, and there was a total give-and-take. That all seems gone now. It's very sad."[12]

Grant also had peculiar fixations about what Deborah was wearing. "In one scene I was all dressed up in a white satin dress because I was going to London to see Bob Mitchum," said Deborah. "I had on with it a small diamond necklace, only when Cary saw me, he said, 'You can't have those on. We're playing people who are not that well off.'"[13] Deborah replied that those rich families passed their things from generation to generation and even if they didn't have money they did have possessions. Grant complained to Donen who responded with the same argument, saying: "Cary, you're poor but you have this house, you have these paintings on the walls, these acres. Deborah can have her necklace. Besides, she looks good in it." Eventually Deborah removed the necklace. "She was a good sport," remembered the director. However, at the wrap party, Deborah got the costume department to make her a necklace of mushrooms and went to swish it up to Grant. "Good morning, darling," she said to him as he was busy reading a newspaper. He replied to her greeting without looking at her, but then when he looked up his mouth fell open. As Deborah recalled, "Poor Cary didn't think it was the least bit funny."[14]

The cast tried to make the best of a dull screenplay. In the evening they often discussed the fact that the home of the Earls of Jersey was supposedly haunted by a lady who had thrown herself from a window to her death in a wedding gown because her husband had rejected her. The thrilling mystery kept them entertained. Nevertheless Robert Mitchum was not amused, he complained that his role was underwritten, consisting mostly of reactions like "really?" and "oh?" amid long stretches of dialogue from either Grant or Deborah.

Despite the difficult time with her husband, Stewart Granger, and their divorce (asking for custody of her daughter), Jean Simmons enjoyed making that film. "She was quite enchanting and hilariously funny," remembered Deborah years later. "We started talking in Cockney accents and, like two schoolgirls, couldn't stop! What fun we had."[15]

Donen asked Noël Coward, who was also considered for the part of the butler, to compose the film's background score, which consisted of a new theme and adaptations of his most popular airs. When Coward saw a rough cut of the picture on June 19, 1960, he wasn't impressed. "It is too slow and the color is hideous," he wrote in his diary. "These defects, I hope, can be remedied."[16] Sadly they weren't. The owners of Radio City Music Hall in New York, who had planned to use *The Grass Is Greener* as their Christmas film of 1960 changed their mind after they saw the first cut. The same reaction came from the Hollywood press; they found the picture "tedious." The *Hollywood Reporter* called it "the year's most disappointing film." Reviewers blamed the poor script and the lack of chemistry among the stars. Needless to say, *The Grass Is Greener* bombed at the box office.

While she was in Australia shooting *The Sundowners*, Deborah announced she would marry Peter Viertel the following summer. Finally, after months of waiting and changing dates, Deborah and Peter tied the knot on July 23, 1960, in the tiny town hall of Klosters in Switzerland. She had flown from London the day before after telling Melanie and

Francesca all about the celebrations. They could not attend because they were still wards of the court. Peter picked Deborah up at Zurich Airport and drove her to the city where they received papers for the ceremony. Then they drove to Klosters where he had built "Wyhergut" (Good Weir), a new chalet halfway up a mountain overlooking the village that became their home.

The ceremony was full of surprises. Deborah's wedding dress (made by Givenchy) and a gift from Audrey Hepburn and Mel Ferrer got lost in the mail and was delivered only one hour before the ceremony began. The same fate had befallen Deborah's personal documents attesting to her divorce, which had only become final on the previous day. Without those documents, the couple could not have been married. Finally, when everything seemed fine, a flower pot was accidentally knocked from its pedestal at the top of the stairs leading into the Gemeindehaus, the local town hall, and missed some of the guests entering the building with the bride and groom. The witnesses were novelist Irwin Shaw, author of *The Young Lions* and a resident of Klosters, and director Anatole Litvak. After a 20-minute ceremony celebrated by alderman Peter Joos, the newlyweds, together with Peter's daughter, Christine, were driven in a pony cart to the reception in Shaw's chalet. Yul Brynner and his wife Doris were among the guests as were Mel Ferrer (his wife, Audrey Hepburn, was nine months pregnant and unable to travel) and Viertel's mother, Salka.

Deborah and Peter left the next day for Biarritz, France, on a brief honeymoon, as she was due in England in less than a week. Spending time with her daughters, she did not return back to work until late fall. "Tony and I are now very good friends," said Deborah to the press. "For a time we weren't. But now we see each other when I visit the children in England, and things are much better. That's the only way I could have it. Anything else would be so uncivilized. I hope now that the children will soon cease to be wards of the court — although that, of course, is not my decision to make."[17]

In the fall of 1960 Deborah rented a house in Denham, which was about halfway between Elstree Studios and Ascot. "I can make it to the studio in half an hour if I get an early start," Deborah said in an interview on the set of *The Naked Edge*. I try to arrive at about 7:00 A.M., which makes a very long day. About the middle of the afternoon I start to fall apart."[18]

Starring Gary Cooper, Hermione Gingold, Peter Cushing and Michael Wilding, *The Naked Edge* was a psychological thriller, drawn from

Max Ehrlich's highly suspenseful novel *First Train to Babylon*. Cooper accepted it after reading a rough draft. Then the script was sent to Deborah, who was enthusiastic about playing the lead in her first thriller. Moreover, she was thrilled to work with Cooper who was one of her childhood heroes. "I met Gary Cooper when I first went to Hollywood in 1946," recalled Deborah when interviewed for a biography on Cooper. "We met socially, and I became very good friends with him and his beautiful wife, Rocky. They invited me many times to their house, and indeed it was at a party at their new and very modern home that I had the honor to be seated next to President Kennedy, who was then Senator Kennedy.... Coop had a shyness and a quietness that hid his very dry wit. He was truly a 'gentle-man' and I never met anyone who did not have the greatest affection for him."[19]

Cooper was gravely ill and died soon after the film was completed. Before shooting began, producer Walter Seltzer was very worried that the star would not pass the physical examination required by the insurance company, but it did give a green light to the project. However working was very exhausting for Cooper and his health remained shaky. He was obviously in great pain but he never missed a day of work in the nine weeks required to complete the picture. His wife and daughter came with him to London and accompanied him every day, staying at the studio until he left. Cooper's performance required lots of makeup and a wig. He cost the production time and money by faltering over his lines. "He knew he was a very sick man, and we would lunch together almost every day, and he would reminisce and reminisce about his early days in the movies," recalled Deborah. "It was fascinating but, for me, of course rather sad. When he worked he was always humorous and cooperative, and to match his wonderful inborn timing was a joy as well as a lesson. He was a complete 'natural' as an actor."[20]

Directed by Michael Anderson, best known for his direction of *Around the World in 80 Days*, *The Naked Edge* was a story of an American businessman (Cooper) with a British wife, played by Deborah, who thinks her husband is a murderer. Joseph Stefano, who had just achieved widespread acclaim for Hitchcock's *Psycho*, wrote the film's screenplay. The original story was set in the States, but Stefano, at Anderson's suggestion, shifted it to England, centering London. Both supporting actors Peter Cushing and Hermione Gingold enjoyed working with Cooper and Deborah. In her memoir, Gingold called Deborah "the most 'unstarry' star I've ever had the pleasure to work with. She inspires great respect but in a natural and unassuming way.... [Making the film] was great fun. Deborah has a very amusing sense of humor and I found her delightful to play against."[21]

While making the picture, Cooper was nearly killed, however not by his illness, but on location at the Tower of London where Deborah and Gary had movable dressing rooms. Two minutes after Cooper left his own room for a shot, his dressing room exploded due to a faulty heater.

The Naked Edge was completed just before Christmas and it was released in June 1961, a few weeks after Cooper's death. United Artists decided to emphasize the suspense and the connection to *Psycho* rather than the star's premature death. A red light was installed in the theater lobbies, which was turned on for the last fifteen minutes of the movie warning that no one would be admitted during that time. Despite all the gimmicks the film was dismissed by the critics and audiences due to its lack of suspense.

Life in Klosters with Peter was sweet for Deborah. Their beautiful house—filled with the things they both loved: books, fine china, precious antiques and big comfortable sofas and chairs—was often full of guests visiting from all over the world. The only sad moment occurred when she miscarried a baby she was expecting by Peter which had been due around her 40th birthday. However her husband's great love and the presence of Melanie and Francesca (now allowed to visit their mother in Switzerland) helped her through this difficult moment. Nonetheless, the best medicine for Deborah proved to be going back to work.

"It's the most exciting and exacting role I have ever played. The most exciting project I have ever worked on," declared Deborah about her new film *The Innocents*. Jack Clayton, who directed *Room at the Top*, approached her with the script, based on Henry James's 1898 story *The Turn of the Screw*, considered one of the author's most controversial novels. James offered a ghost tale of fascinating ambiguity, which was first written in short-story form, and in succession became a novel, a stage play by William Archibald, a chamber-opera by composer Benjamin Britten, a television play starring Ingrid Bergman in 1961 and finally a film produced and directed by Clayton.

Deborah accepted as soon as she read the script which was based on Archibald's stage version with work by Truman Capote and John Mortimer. Her role was Miss Giddens, a governess who believes two souls were reborn of her young charges, Miles and Flora, two precocious orphans from a wealthy family. "Apart from the fact that I had always wanted to work for Jack Clayton, who was the second assistant director on my first film, *Major Barbara*," Deborah admitted, "I had wanted for years to play the governess role in the Henry James story."

Another reason for Deborah to accept the part was that the picture was planned to be shot entirely on English locations and at the Shepperton Studios, a great opportunity for her to be closer to Melanie and Francesca, who were attending school in England.

The Innocents was set to begin production in early February 1961. Clayton splendidly selected the cast with one major exception: Deborah who was imposed by 20th Century–Fox in the leading role. Yet, the director couldn't have wished for a better actress. They were, in fact, in perfect sync on the set as to how her performance was pitched. As she recalled, "With Jack Clayton's help, plus my own feelings, I tried to tread a very narrow tight-rope between Miss Giddens being internally and sexually tormented woman, and a completely normal human being who found herself beset by evil powers. I think Jack and I both wanted to leave it to the audience, which resulted in the film's strangely disturbing quality."[22]

Clayton found the children, Martin Stephens and Pamela Franklin, only two weeks before he started shooting. The kids never saw the complete script of *The Innocents*—they only learned the next day's lines the night before each day's shooting. Clayton was worried that they could come to psychological harm from reading the story. As a result, both children played their roles through mimicry. Everything that motivated their performances came from Deborah and the director. In further casting choices, Clayton picked Michael Redgrave for a cameo role as the children's uncle. Originally the director asked Cary Grant to play the tiny part. Grant said he would have done it if Clayton could bring back the uncle at the end of the film. "I was torn," the director revealed. "Having Cary in the film would have meant a lot to it, but seeing him at the end would have been impossible. I'm probably the only director who ever said no to Cary Grant."[23]

On February 6, 1961, after a delay due to the film's rights problems, *The Innocents* officially began 12 weeks of principal photography. Cast and crew spent the first several weeks shooting at Sheffield Park near Brighton in a magnificent old Sussex estate, where cinematographer Freddie Francis made artful use of the black and white CinemaScope cameras and careful lightning to capture the lush gardens with three lakes and the Georgian-style mansion and its surroundings. (Francis later revealed that it was just a few weeks before shooting began that Clayton was "shattered" to learn from 20th Century–Fox that he would have to shoot the film in Cine-

With Martin Stephens and Pamela Franklin in *The Innocents* (1961).

maScope, because he wanted an intimate approach with the characters which that film technique did not allow.)

Once the outdoor scenes were completed, the company moved to Shepperton Studios, where Wilfred Shingleton's set occupied several sound-stages. Since she appeared in literally every scene, Deborah was on call every day from 7 AM until 6:30 PM, including weekends. She commented on the ferocious heat of the lights needed for some of the special effects. The close-ups brought the camera so nearly on top of her that she felt herself going crossed-eyed as she and it confronted a distance of inches. In addition, wearing hoops and crinolines prevented her from resting her back for long periods as she set upright on a short wooden stool. "By the time this is over," she patiently commented with her usual irony, "I should make a good advertisement for one of those television commercials about the relief of backache. At least I wouldn't have to act the part!"

The Innocents completed photography in May. At a party thrown to celebrate the end of the shooting came evidence of the tremendous esteem in which Deborah was held by the entire crew. She was presented with a rare volume of *The Turn of the Screw*. Deborah was moved by the gift and in her farewell speech she mentioned she would treasure the book as a memento of one of the finest films in which she ever worked.

Once Clayton finished editing, he screened the finished version with Fox's executives, who generally liked it. Nevertheless studio head Spyros Skouras did not like the controversial ending with the governess kissing the dead child on the lips. For more than two weeks Skouras called the director begging him to change the ending, which he did not do. The picture opened in November 1961 in London, and the following month in New York. On both sides of the Atlantic the reviews were mostly raves. Deborah received one of the best noteworthy reviews of her career.

In May 1962, *The Innocents* was presented at the Cannes Film Festival. However, despite its critical acclaim, the film did only mediocre business at the box office. In recent years it has been rediscovered and is now considered one of the most admired and respected thrillers in film history.

11

Iguana

I'm not very competitive. Being feminine is being pliable. Bending like the willow in the wind.

— Deborah Kerr

At the end of 1961 Deborah accepted an offer to make her television debut in three short plays comprising a 90-minute trilogy, *Three Roads to Rome*, which ABC aired two years later and only in England due to sponsorship problems in the U.S. The taping of the show was done in London a few weeks before Christmas. *Three Roads to Rome* was co-produced in cooperation with Associated Rediffusion, Ltd., of London by Fred Coe and Arthur Penn, whom Deborah had met socially several years earlier in Hollywood and later became an acclaimed director. All the stories, which take place in Rome, were about women in love. Deborah portrayed three different characters ranging in age from late twenties to early sixties. In two of the plays she is as an unmarried English woman and in the third she is an American widow. The trilogy was written by Pulitzer Prize–winning writer Tad Mosel, who adapted them from short stories: Edith Wharton's *Roman Fever*, Martha Gellhorn's *Venus Ascendant* and Aldous Huxley's *Rest Cure*. British actress Celia Johnson played opposite Deborah in *Roman Fever*, a two-character play in which the women spend the entire time reminiscing about their former romances.

"I wanted to find something different for my TV drama debut," said Deborah. "And this enabled me to exploit three facets of myself. But it was absolutely the hardest work I have ever done in my life."[1] In another interview she added; "I found myself confronted by seven cameras: men were crouching on the floor and were sending signals and signs in all directions. Before long I had no more than a quarter of me under control and I was praying I wouldn't forget my lines. One had to know them — or else."[2]

The year 1962 was a sabbatical one for Deborah. According to the press, she was living a "second life." The reporters who went to Switzerland to interview her found a new Deborah, more relaxed, self-confident and, above all, happy. Most of the changes were brought about by Peter, who was giving her a direction she never had before. The sense of loneliness she had felt in the past was gone. She and Peter had many stimulating, intellectual friends.

"I'm really happy now," she said. Before, there was always a nagging thing inside me. I knew things weren't quite right; that one day I'd explode. With Peter I feel fully alive. But I never think: 'Oh if only I'd met him years before. One has to be ready for someone. One matures; one changes. There's a right time for everything. We live a very simple life. We don't have servants. And Peter does all the cooking.... Cary Grant often talks about searching for the truth within himself. Well, I don't think you'll find it in yourself. You find it in someone else. And when you do, you give them everything you've got, everything. That's the secret of happiness, sure. And that's why I'm happy now."[3] In addition Melanie and Francesca, who were then 15 and 11, were spending a lot of time with them. Tony had established a warm and affectionate relationship with them, just as Deborah had with Christina, Viertel's daughter.

Finally in March 1963 Deborah returned to work in England for American producer Ross Hunter in *The Chalk Garden*. Hunter had established his reputation in Hollywood producing a few of Douglas Sirk's melodramas and a series of comedies starring Doris Day. He had contemplated turning Enid Bagnold's 1955 play *The Chalk Garden* into a film for quite a long time. The story tells of a rich old lady, Mrs. St. Maugham, who seeks a governess for her 16-year-old granddaughter, Laurel, who had managed to drive away each and every governess with her impossible behavior. When Miss Madrigal, an applicant with a mysterious past, manages to get the job, Laurel vows to expose her.

Ross's project of making a film finally materialized at the end of 1962. To direct, Hunter hired Ronald Neame and traveled with him across England to scout the locations and to organize the casting. Dame Edith Evans was the first to be chosen in the role of Mrs. St. Maugham, which she had masterfully performed in the original stage production. However, Hunter had it in mind to cast Gladys Cooper for that role. But Evans was able to impose herself with her intimidating persona. Ultimately it proved to be a perfect choice, but Cooper was bitterly disgruntled. Sandra Dee had originally been picked to play Laurel, Mrs. St. Maugham's troubled teenaged-granddaughter, but had to bow out when she became pregnant. Hayley Mills replaced her, working together with her father, John, who was cast as Mrs. St. Maugham's butler. Deborah, who had worked with Neame in *Major Barbara* (he was one of Pascal's assistant directors) was cast as Laurel's governess, Miss Madrigal.

It was Deborah's third role as a governess. "But the films were so different that I don't think it matters," she said to a reporter who asked if she was being typecast. "The irony of it all is that you dream all your life of being able to choose your own roles, and then when you can you're frightened to death at making the choice. But I liked this one, the film has a great deal of depth, a lot of scope."[4] *The Chalk Garden*'s exteriors were shot in Sussex at a period country home in Littlington, as well as locations in Alfriston, Beachy Head and the White Cliffs of Dover. However, the majority of the film was shot at Elstree Studios in Borehamwood.

Neame called Deborah's performance "meticulous." He also recalled "her demeanor towards Edith was one of patience and understanding. She stepped back, making Edith feel like a star, even though Deborah was the far more important film celebrity. I was terribly grateful to her for that gesture. It would have been impossible if my two leading ladies had competed for center stage."[5]

Evans "misbehaved" with Enid Bagnold, the author of the play, who asked the actress if she could visit the set and watch a day's shooting. "She had the nerve to ring me up and say, 'Yes, dear, if you keep quiet in your corner,'" revealed the outraged playwright.[6]

The screenplay was written by John Michael Haynes since Bagnold never wanted to adapt her own works into movies. Sadly something was lost in the adaptation as part of the original dialogue was Americanized and drastically shortened. On its release *The Chalk Garden* received dreadful reviews, particularly in London, where the memory of the play had remained strong. Hunter Ross tried to convey some comfort from the fact that he had secured Radio City Music Hall for the American opening, and although the New York critics were more indulgent, the final result was still a box office disappointment. The only surprises came a few months later when Dame Edith Evan was nominated for an Academy Award for Best Supporting Actress and Deborah received a BAFTA's nomination as Best Actress.

A scene from *The Chalk Garden* (1964) with Hayley Mills.

On the set of *The Chalk Garden* Deborah revealed an interesting side of her personality in an interview (which nowadays would likely upset many feminists) she gave to the *Los Angeles Times*. "I'm not very competitive," she said, explaining how she managed to be so feminine. "Being feminine is being pliable. Bending like the willow with the wind. You stand longer than oaks when there is a storm. I think the big trouble is that women try to tell men what to do. And men can't abide it. Femininity is made of a lot of little things—never talking too loud, being clean and fresh at all times and always letting the man be in the driver's seat. I think every woman longs for someone to assume responsibility and take over. Whenever she tries to boss, the relation of the sexes becomes out of balance."[7]

The press wrongly announced that Deborah's next part, after a brief holiday with Peter in St. Jean de Luz, Spain, would have been in a film adaptation of Penelope Mortimer's novel *The Pumpkin Eaters*. She preferred instead to be part of the all-star cast in John Huston's *The Night of the Iguana*, based on a play by Tennessee Williams, whose rights were acquired by Ray Stark, an agent-turned-producer forming the Seven Arts Productions Company. Stark proposed the picture to John Huston, who loved the idea of making a third film in Mexico, a place he knew very well since shooting *The Treasure of Sierra Madre* in 1948 and *The Unforgiven* in 1959.

The story of *The Night of the Iguana* is about the Reverend T. Lawrence Shannon, an American minister who had been expelled from his church for molesting a girl and who had become a tour guide for American women traveling the coast of Mexico. He gets in trouble once again with a wild teenaged girl, part of a tourist group, and ends up in a crummy hotel run by Maxine, an old friend of his. The guests at the lodge are later joined by an elderly poet and his spinster sketch artist granddaughter, Hanna Jelks. The three women — the hot-eyed willful teenager, the earthy hotel owner and the ethereal artist — can save or destroy the former Episcopal priest in a single night.

Huston favored Marlon Brando to play the ex-minister, but Stark thought Richard Harris, Kirk Douglas or William Holden might be a better choice. They finally agreed to cast Richard Burton, who accepted immediately. The director and producer then met Deborah in London. She willingly took the role of Hanna Jelks, accepting a salary of $250,000. For the role of Maxine, the hotel keeper successfully played on stage by an extraordinary Bette Davis, Huston and Stark had in mind Ava Gardner. They flew to Madrid, where the star was living a wild life, and convinced the actress to accept the role. Even though Gardner agreed, Stark found out that Melina Mercouri, his second choice, was available in case Ava backed out at the last moment. Sue Lyon, fresh from *Lolita* stardom, was enlisted to play Charlotte Goodall, the hot teenager who seduces the priest.

The original play was set in Acapulco, but Huston wanted a more secluded location which could better reflect the anguish of the characters and chose Puerto Vallarta and Mismaloya, which were at that time two primitive villages on the Mexican west coast. Huston convinced Stark to shoot the film in black and white because he believed the location's exotic colors would be distracting, a decision he later regretted.

Before leaving for Mexico, Deborah agreed to keep a journal during the making of the film to be published, for $800, by *Esquire* magazine. She arrived in Puerto Vallarta accompanied by Peter on the 8th of October and it took her five days to adjust herself to the terrible heat and humidity, along with the noises of the village heard around the house which the production had rented for them.

The intricate web of relationships among the cast of *The Night of the Iguana* set something of an odd record. Richard Burton arrived with Elizabeth Taylor who was still married to Eddie Fisher and constantly consulted

Burton's press agent, Michael Wilding (her second husband), who visited the set. Deborah was with Peter, who had a tryst with Ava Gardner years earlier during the making of *The Sun Also Rises* and was also the author of *White Hunter, Black Heart* a novel which negatively depicted John Huston's obsession with big game hunting while making *The African Queen*. Peter was also linked to Gardner and Burton's visiting friend, screenwriter and author Budd Schulberg, having married Schulberg's first wife, Jigee.

Before starting the picture, Huston, amused by those strange connections, gathered all his stars (as well as Elizabeth Taylor) and solemnly presented each of them with a gold-plated derringer. Each gun came with four golden bullets engraved with the names of the other recipients. Deborah commented in her journal, "Not John's name [on the bullets], needless to say. I sensed a certain nervousness in the laughter and the thanks of everyone concerned. It was almost like the start of an Agatha Christie murder novel."[8] Obviously not a single bullet was ever used and all the members of the cast got along famously. They also had nicknames for everybody, as Ava Gardner revealed in her memoir, "We called Deborah Kerr 'Miss Continuation' because her voice never changed from a film into the other."[9]

Huston shot the film in sequence, like a play, which began in the village square of Tepozotlan, then moved to Puerto Vallarta for two weeks, but it was often interrupted by heat, heavy rains and bugs, leaving the troupe with little to do but play gin rummy and get drunk.

The principal hotel set was built on a mountainside which the film unit named the Rock, situated about half an hour away from Puerto Vallarta, reached only by boat. The production hired almost 300 native laborers and 80 burros to construct 25 cottages (for the use of the actors and technicians), a restaurant and a movie set on the edge of the jungle near the location site.

Deborah would arrive on the set by a small boat rented by Peter. Sometimes they would also ride in Ava Gardner's faster boat which she would also use for waterskiing.

Tennessee Williams's unexpected arrival on October 4 along with his boyfriend, Freddy, caught everybody by surprise. The playwright immediately ordered some changes to the script which he personally supervised, including two new scenes which found Huston's greatest approval.

On November 17, two assistant directors, Tom Shaw and Terry Morse, were badly injured when a balcony of the terrace outside the cottage they shared suddenly collapsed. They were both taken to the hospital in Puerto Vallarta and later Shaw, who was severely hurt, had to be flown to Los

Angeles. Peter and Deborah witnessed the terrible accident. Deborah wrote in her diary, "We didn't get to bed until six A.M., and I couldn't get to sleep at all. I kept seeing them both fall like rag dolls again and again all night long, and Tom's terrible groans are still with me."[10]

During the course of filming Burton and Taylor were always together; their relationship attracted many reporters from United States who were looking for a scoop, pestering the other stars on the set with stupid questions about their relationship.

"I am a bit bored with being asked if I think Elizabeth and Richard will be married," Deborah wrote in her journal, "and did I know Sybil [Burton's first wife], and is Ava as difficult as 'they' say and is she on the make for Burton, or is Sue Lyon? My God! What business is it of theirs or mine! I am revolted by the mass of moronic muck that is printed every day everywhere in almost every newspaper and magazine, and more revolted by the people who assure me this is *only* what people want to read, how they have *tried* writing nice, pleasant and interesting pieces about famous personalities, but that it just hasn't *worked*! I just don't believe the majority of people are *really* so filled with envy and jealousy that *all* they want to read about are people's misfortunes and trials and tribulations. Depressing thought. I feel more and more like Hannah in this movie. *Nothing human disgusts me unless it is unkind or violent.* I loathe and detest unkindness and violence and gossip and troublemaking and envy and malice. It does disgust as well as depress me."[11]

On November 22, three days after the accident, the cast heard the news on the radio that President John F. Kennedy had been assassinated. Deborah was on a beach and she met with Ava Gardner who was in a bar. They looked at each other, without speaking, in disbelief. They joined the rest of the crew on the set where everybody was so overwhelmed by the tragic news that a break was called. After observing a minute of silence, Huston made a short moving speech, while Deborah and Ava sobbed unashamedly. It was decided to go on with the daily shooting, to keep everybody's mind distracted.

The picture was completed ahead of schedule. A 12-hour party was thrown at the end of the shooting on November 30. Food and booze was specially catered from California and a 15-piece mariachi band was hired to play local music for the occasion.

During the making of the picture a 15-minute theatrical short entitled *On the Trail of the Iguana* was shot to promote the film before its opening. It dealt with various aspects of the production, with a small intervention by Deborah, who, with her great sense of humor, told a reporter she was bored with the prevalent notion that she was the only cast member about whom no one worried. She amusingly added that "it would serve them right" if she suddenly screamed, threw tantrums and in all other ways become a real diva, which she never did.[12]

Prior to its release *The Night of the Iguana* incurred some questions of its nationality. To Seven Arts and MGM, it was American; however, because of the use of a crew mostly of Mexicans, many believed that the film was Mexican.

Deborah did not attend the June film benefit première at the Philharmonic Hall in Lincoln Center in New York which raised over $100,000 for the Heart Fund.

Upon its nationwide opening on August 6, 1964, *The Night of the Iguana* quickly became one of the year's top grossers, followed by an enormous success in Europe.

Talking with French director Bertrand Tavernier about that Mexican experience, John Huston had particular words for Deborah, "I intensely love Deborah Kerr in this movie. She is an actress I adore. There is something deep in her, something complex which contradicts her appearance and the type of roles she had been too often offered. She could be very sexy, like in Zinnemann's *From Here to Eternity*, and very reserved."[13]

While in Mexico Richard Burton asked Deborah to play Gertrude in an upcoming production of *Hamlet* the following April in New York. He had received a cable from John Gielgud who was the production director saying, "Deborah Kerr first on my list to play Gertrude." Deborah did not sleep that night thinking about that great offer. Regardless, the following morning she told Burton she could not accept it because she could not bear to be separated too long from her daughters.

12

Memorable Years,
Not So Memorable Roles

I absolutely cannot work in disharmony with anyone.
— Deborah Kerr

Peter, Deborah and her daughters spent the summer of 1964 in St. Jean de Luz, Spain, renting the home of former French actress Annabella, Tyrone Power's first wife. Viertel was finishing *Love Lies Bleeding*, a fictional biography based on the life of his famous friend, Spanish matador Miguel Dominguin, whose villa was not far from their house. The Dominguins hosted many international guests which included, Yul Brynner and his wife Doris, Robert Mitchum, and Wes Herschensohn, who wrote a detailed chronicle of that summer in his book *Resurrection in Cannes*.

"Here was Deborah Kerr, pale and exquisite, sensual in her 'ladyness,'" wrote Herschensohn in his book. "She was real and full of humor, being hovered over at every turn in our conversation.... She chatted away charmingly in her personal, instant-intimacy kind of magic way that made one like her and confide impulsively in her."[1] Herschesohn, who was planning to write and direct a film called *The Picasso Summer*, was so charmed by Deborah that he planned to ask her to star if Audrey Hepburn, his first choice, could not do it. The film was made four years later but neither of the two stars were involved in the final project.

In November 1964, Deborah was a guest (along with Peter) on *The Tonight Show* and on *The Dinah Shore Show*. Before the end of the year, Frank Sinatra sent Deborah the script for *Divorce, American Style*, a comedy for which he wanted her in the leading role of his wife. Deborah was hesitant since she had decided to pick only selected roles; however she agreed to do it, after asking advice from David Niven. Niven encouraged her to accept it after talking about the project over the phone with Sinatra.

"I'm terribly excited about it," she said in an interview with the *London Express*. "Dean Martin will play the boyfriend. I have listened to these two at parties and I never pretended to be able to keep up with them and their slick style of humor. But I will have to fit in it with them in the film…. It could be ghastly. If it is, I will blame David Niven."[2]

Before the shooting began, the witty but risqué script by Cy Howard had to be changed since the producers thought that domestic audiences might find it offensive; they also wanted to retain Deborah's wholesome image. So an extensive rewrite was called for. It took four months of story conferences involving Howard, Sinatra, director Jack Donohue and many others. Unfortunately the new script, re-titled *Community Property* later changed into *Marriage on the Rocks,* seemed too old-fashioned, like an unfunny screwball comedy of the thirties. The film, produced by Sinatra Enterprises in conjunction with William Daniels, was almost entirely shot on a soundstage and backlot, while the exteriors of Sinatra and Deborah's house in the picture were the real-life home of Dean Martin.

Sinatra's daughter Nancy was part of the cast in a role originally meant for Mia Farrow. The singer was a little hesitant because of her lack of acting experience. She was, in fact, a little stiff and nervous at the beginning but after Deborah and the director taught her to relax she finally gave a decent performance.

Making *Marriage on the Rocks* was an absolute blast for Deborah. It was her first film in Hollywood after seven years. She was impressed by Dean Martin's healthy attitude toward his profession. She enjoyed laughing at his jokes and behavior. Martin who, like Sinatra, was shorter than Deborah, nicknamed her "the Jolly Green Giant" (a popular brand of peas) after they had to play a scene together in which she wore a very green evening gown with high heels.

The screenplay featured Sinatra as ad executive Dan Edwards, a businessman too busy with his career to pay any attention to his marriage with Valerie (played by Deborah) who falls again for her husband's best friend (Martin) a carefree bachelor she turned down in favor of Dan many years earlier.

Despite the daily changes and improvisation on the set, the film was completed nine days ahead of its 12-day schedule, and nearly a quarter of a million dollars under budget. After a poorly received sneak preview,

Having a laugh with Frank Sinatra in *Marriage on the Rocks* (1965).

Warner Bros. released it, cutting out 14 minutes. However, when it opened nationwide in September 1965, the critics labeled *Marriage on the Rocks* "one of the worst movies ever made," filmed for no apparent reason except to make money which it failed to do, bombing at the box office. A reviewer for *Time* magazine wrote, "[The film's] least comfortable performer is Actress Kerr, whose fans may wonder what a nice girl like Deborah is doing in a play like this. Wasted on farce, she sidles from gag to gag with the faintly startled air of a very proper matron who somehow finds herself pouring tea at a disreputable party."

The following summer, at the request of John Huston, Deborah played the small part of Secret Agent Mimi, masquerading as Lady Fiona McTarry, in *Casino Royale*. It was a plotless spoof of spy films, based very loosely on Ian Fleming's first James Bond novel and involved seven directors and an extraordinary all-star cast. Deborah's scenes were shot on location in Ireland. "I worked for eight days — most of it spent in my dressing room," she remembered. For the comical cameo producer Charles Feldman offered her a "sizeable sum," which she could not refuse. In the picture David Niven played an elderly, retired Sir James Bond. The film was confusing, unfunny and a waste of the talents of William Holden, Peter Sellers,

Orson Welles, Peter O'Toole and a young Woody Allen. *Casino Royale* was a $12 million disaster.

At the beginning of December 1965 while in Klosters, Deborah received a call to replace Kim Novak in a British production of a horror film called *13*. Her role was as the distraught wife of an English lord, played by Niven, who is caught up in a family tradition of devil-worship.

Julie Andrews was first considered for the part however, since the leading man was Deborah's dear friend David Niven, he suggested her to the production as replacement. She accepted with no hesitation, and immediately traveled to London where the film was being shot at Borehamwood Studios.

The picture was 80 percent completed when Kim Novak abruptly left the set. It was allegedly reported by the press that the American star had suffered a back injury (or a broken leg) in a riding accident; however, actor David Hemmings revealed in his autobiography the real story: "I can't recall what Marty [producer Martin Rosohoff] said to upset Kim, or if it justified her reaction, but I have an indelible vision of her stubbing a cigarette in his one good eye, which led to an ugly scene, a failed press conference and Kim being sacked from the movie."[3] The film's insurers had to pay out £600,000 for all Novak's scenes to be re-filmed with Deborah (only a few long shots of Kim Novak were left in the final version).

The director Lee Thompson recalled an atmosphere of tension within the production unit, "It was fraught with intrigues between the cast. Sharon Tate, I remember, was the ex-girlfriend of Rosohoff, so there were fireworks between her and the producer on the set. She went to live with Polanski during the film and Rosohoff was naturally furious about it and there were lots of worries and things going on."[4] (Sharon Tate, who played a sinister witch, was to be murdered by the Charles Mason satanic cult gang four years later.) In addition to all the problems, the main location, the impressive Chateau d'Hautfort in the Dordogne, France (which burned down three years later), had to be revisited in the New Year when the defoliated condition of its environs created continuity problems which became evident in the finished picture.

Niven was very excited to play opposite Deborah once again (in a letter to a friend he had called his previous co-star, Novak, "a horrid lady").The picture seemed to be jinxed. Niven suffered an accident when a low-flying jet upset his horse and he was thrown off. Other members of the location crew were crushed by a car. The troubles continued also in post–production. MGM, the picture's distributor, got cold feet about some unapproved script changes made by the director, afraid that Donald Pleasence's character as a heretic priest would cause protests from Catholic organizations. The studio decided to delay the film's release for eighteen months as well as changing its title to *Eye of the Devil* to help suggest that the fertility cult depicted owed its allegiance to Lucifer rather than Christ. The picture opened at the London Ritz Cinema in early March 1968. Deborah's and Niven's presence, along with such great professionals as Flora Robson, Emlyn Williams, Donald Pleasance and David Hemmings, could not help the film's lethargic pacing and its dull script, which had suffered from several replacements of its writers. "Hilariously bad," was the verdict of the *Times.* MGM

Having fun while shooting *Casino Royale* (1967).

was so embarrassed by the final product that it released *Eye of the Devil* in the States on a double-bill entry. It died instantly at the box office.

"I'm doing about one film a year now," Deborah told Sheilah Graham in a interview. "Sometimes it's not ideal to work, but if you've done it all your life, you just can't drop it. There are some days when I want to give it all up, then somebody comes along with something ... and you get all steamed up. It keeps you young, if it doesn't kill you."[5] Once again lured by David Niven's presence, Deborah made another glaringly disastrous choice, accepting to star in *Prudence and the Pill.* Also in the cast were Robert Coote, Dame Edith Evans and Keith Mitchell. The picture's screenplay dealt with the troubles confronting couples when birth control pills

An intense moment with David Niven in *Eye of the Devil* (1966).

are swapped for aspirins, causing great commotion for an older couple, played by Deborah and Niven.

"In this," said Deborah to the *Evening Standard*, "I play a bit of a bitch. It's time I played a bitch. It's a very good script. Except that I looked up a guide to the Pill carefully and absolutely none of the brands could be remotely mistaken for an aspirin."

On the set the two friends enjoyed working together and were often found giggling like school children. In the middle of the shooting at Pinewood Studios, Deborah suddenly suffered from dizziness and nausea caused by fluid in the inner ear. The labyrinthitis lasted for almost a month and prevented her from going to work, forcing her to stay in bed. During her bed confinement she received a phone call from Vivien Leigh who said, "Darling here we are, both of us in bed! Isn't it ridiculous?" The two actresses, who had not seen each other in a long time had kept a friendship that endured over the years, sharing the same physician, Dr. Michael Linnett. Linnett would only a few days later hasten over to Deborah to personally inform her of Leigh's sudden tragic death, being afraid she would hear of it on the news.

Troubles continued during the making of *Prudence and the Pill*, when

MGM at one point withdrew its financing of the project, and 20th Century–Fox took over the production. Moreover, three-fifths of the way through filming, director Fielder Cook quit because of differences of opinion and the un-credited Ronald Neame finished the picture, using Cook's style.

Deborah called the comedy "a great third act part." Critics disagreed with her opinion finding the farce unfunny and boring. The picture, however, grossed an amazing $4.5 million in its American release. *Prudence and the Pill* was banned from South Africa where censors considered it offensive because of its subject matter and because it depicted love scenes in an offensive way. The film distributors appealed the South African censor board's decision to ban the film from the local theatres. Finally it was agreed that *Prudence and the Pill* could be shown only "to whites" over the age of 21. During the shooting, Deborah took a magnificent suite at the Connaught Hotel, since she no longer owned her house in Mayfair. That had been sold after Melanie and Francesca completed boarding school.

David Hemmings recalled in his memoir a funny joke he played on Deborah with David Niven and his son David Niven, Jr., who were also staying at the Connaught:

"David Jr. went to see her and told her that a reporter from the *Lapland Gazette* was very anxious to interview her. He easily persuaded her to see him, on the grounds that he was a bit thick and it would be a kind thing to do. Naturally, I was the idiot who was going to wear the outfit, confident that Miss Kerr wouldn't recognize me through a screen of a make-shift Nordic face-fungus, despite our brief time together on *Eye of the Devil*. When I was ushered into her suite by a Connaught skivvy, Deborah looked at me with deep suspicion. But although I'd made a movie with her, living next to her for a month or two, she did not apparently associate me with this balmy Lap reporter. I swiftly got into character, waving a spiral bound notebook I'd borrowed from reception at the Connaught and blathering in a terrible bogus Scandinavian accent. Inevitably I pushed it as far as I could, egged on by both Nivens, who were standing behind her, wincing painfully with suppressed laughter. The questions became more absurd, the accent progressively more ridiculous, but it still took her twenty minutes to be sure it was a hoax. 'This is bullshit! Hemmings, why are you playing this extraordinary game?' she demanded haughtily, while the Nivens were pissing themselves."[6]

In the fall of 1967 one project announced for Deborah failed to materialize: *The Lonely Passion of Judith Hearne*. It was planned to be filmed in

Belfast by Irvin Kershner who had just completed *The Luck of Ginger Cof-
fey.* However, for unknown reasons, the picture was aborted, with great
disappointment for Deborah, who was very eager to make it.

"I absolutely cannot work in disharmony with anyone," Deborah
stated, "and consequently I will perhaps wrongly put up with jealousies
and suffer gladly in order to work happily and establish contact — so important is any acting, to me, anyway." Nevertheless, she accepted to star in
John Frankenheim's *The Gypsy Moths* opposite Burt Lancaster in the summer of 1968. It was not an easy assignment for Deborah due to a controversy
which immediately reached the media as to a nude sex scene, performed
by her double. However, the idea made her feel very uncomfortable, spoil-
ing that sense of harmony so important for her work. By July 1968 the
filming of *The Gypsy Moths* was ready to commence. For Deborah it was
an opportunity to work once again opposite Burt Lancaster sixteen years
after *From Here to Eternity,* which gave a lot of buzz to the movie.

James Drought's 1955 novel was the source of William Hanley's script,
in which three rootless sky divers during a Fourth of July layover in a small
Kansas town perform their acrobatic air stunts. Hanley added to the story
more psychological depth through an intimate study of the complex mental
states of the characters and their relationships. Originally the director,
John Frankenheimer, hoped to cast Steve McQueen, then at the peak of
his career, but eventually picked Lancaster with whom he had worked in
four previous films. The other tormented characters were played by Gene
Hackman, fresh from the success of *Bonnie and Clyde,* and John Philip
Law, who injured his hand so severely four days into the shooting that he
had to be replaced by Scott Wilson.

The Gypsy Moths was filmed on location near Wichita, Kansas, and
on a soundstage at MGM Studios. Deborah called Frankenheimer "a fascinating character, but disturbing in many ways, a little bit difficult to
understand his why and wherewithal."[7]

Many on the set described him as very tough and difficult to deal
with. Nevertheless, Deborah was able to give a very convincing performance of a gentle but sexually repressed housewife, even though some found
her nude love scene with Lancaster far too explicit and lacking the same
magical emotion they transmitted in *From Here to Eternity.*

The film opened at Radio City Music Hall on August 28, 1969. Since
the venue drew family audiences, the picture received an "M" (for mature
audiences) rating after a few cuts were made. In particular, the infamous
nude love scene and a striptease by Sheree North were removed from the

print against the director's will. *The Gypsy Moths* was poorly received in New York. Later, when the original cut was restored on its general release in November 1969, the film was not a commercial success. Most reviews were lukewarm, only praising the fantastic aerial stunts. The disappointing box office performance in the States forced the distributors to put the film out in England as a second feature to James Garner's thriller *Marlowe*. The director claimed MGM did nothing to promote it. Years later, Deborah said, "I don't think he [Frankenheimer] himself quite got it. I don't know what he was after."[8] Lancaster shared the same opinion, admitting that the movie was not well done, appearing too pretentious.

Deborah finished *The Gypsy Moths* on a Friday and went to work on Elia Kazan's *The Arrangement* the following Monday. The picture was based on Kazan's bestselling novel and featured Deborah as Kirk Douglas's wife, opposite Faye Dunaway who played his mistress. "She's a woman who's made her husband what he is, but he doesn't *like* what she's made him," said Deborah in explaining her character of a devoted and supportive wife in an interview with the *Los Angeles Times*. "She's done all the right things, said all the right things, and she doesn't understand what's happening to her."[9]

Deborah recalled that when she first discussed her role on the phone with Kazan, the director told her frankly he had not been impressed by her last roles. Based on her past work, he had great confidence she could play the part he wanted to offer. Deborah accepted the challenge admitting that, for Kazan, she would have done "even two lines as the charlady."[10]

The Arrangement was a very thinly disguised autobiography. Kazan wanted Marlon Brando to play Eddie, but after lengthy phone calls, letters and meetings (during which the director asked Brando to lose weight to play his character), the actor eventually withdrew from the role after Martin Luther King's assassination to spend more time involved in social causes. Kazan instead hired Kirk Douglas, who loved the book and was thrilled to star in the film. "If you ask Gadge [Kazan's nickname]," said Deborah, "he'll say that the characters are all fictional, and I don't think that any of us approached the parts as if we were playing actual people, but every so often, as we worked, Gadge would say to me, 'Remember how Molly was in a moment like this, how she would just not bend on this particular point.'"[11]

Deborah's character was loosely based on Kazan's first wife, Molly Day Thatcher (although, he never admitted that the three main characters were based on himself), and on his mistress, Barbara Loden (later his sec-

The Arrangement (1969) with Kirk Douglas.

ond wife). Loden, who was an actress, was very eager to play herself in the film, but Kazan cast Faye Dunaway instead.

"I just love working with Gadge," Deborah stated "I don't have to prepare. I just trust him."[12] While the director said that Deborah "is better than Florence in the book. Her figure is softer, whereas her character in the book is caricatured."[13]

Once again, as in *The Gypsy Moths*, the film benefited partially from the advance word of onscreen nudity and reports which called the film the most sexually daring feature yet to be made by a major studio. This time Deborah's attitude on briefly exposing all her skin was more relaxed: "I always said I would do it if it was really a part of the action, after all, I can't go on pretending forever that I don't have a body. There it was real, because they were in bed together and they had no clothes on."[14]

Unfortunately, *The Arrangement* did not match Kazan's expectations. He spent a huge budget of almost six million dollars, putting on screen what many thought would have been more effective in a modest, economical setting. *The Arrangement* previewed very unsuccessfully in November 1969 in the Strasberg Theatre in New York, with a gala dinner afterward. When it opened few days later domestically it was criticized as a complete mess and dismissed as the director's worst work. In England, however, the reviews were more favorable and Deborah felt that the film in the States was not received well because it was "too near the knuckle in the direct shots it took at the very basis of the American way of life, which came just a little too close to home to be comfortable."

13

Stage Comeback

*[Theater] is like a drug—although it's a nice drug. I think it has
something to do with the power of controlling an audience.*

Deborah Kerr

At the end of December 1971, Deborah returned to the stage, joining
a small group of distinguished names like Joyce Carey, Trevor Howard,
Celia Johnson and Wendy Hiller. They all gathered for a reading of Terence
Rattigan's play *Separate Tables*, which was scheduled to be performed at
the Haymarket Theatre on January 10, 1972, in a special single all-star
Midnight Matinee to honor the playwright's knighthood. It was Deborah's
first stage appearance in 17 years. She had played the same role in the 1958
screen version, for which she received an Oscar nomination. Despite being
a nervous wreck until the curtain rose, it was a refreshing experience. She
then seriously thought of a possible return to the stage. "I've been won-
dering about it," she told the *Evening Standard*, "but it's awfully difficult
to find the right thing. Nobody writes for women any more ... all the
plays are for men. I'd like to do something new. There is no one like Tennessee Williams anymore. I just want a role I feel comfortable in."[1] Her
wish came true only a few days later when playwright Frank Harvey, after
seeing her in *Separate Tables*, sent her the script of his play *The Day After
the Fair* (adapted from a Thomas Hardy short story), offering her the leading role. Deborah accepted. The play opened at the London Lyric Theatre
on October 4, 1972, after several sold-out tryouts at the Theatre Royal in
Brighton. Despite the lukewarm reviews, the play was a great personal
success for Deborah. The public adored her and *The Day After the Fair*
broke every box office record at the Lyric, running until May of 1973.

In the play, Deborah was Edith Harnham, who writes, at her maid's request, love letters to the young girl's beloved, who eventually finds out who the real author is. Thanks to the play's overwhelming success, the producers offered Deborah the opportunity to tour with the play across America, which she accepted, debuting with great acclaim the following September at the Shubert Theatre in Los Angeles. On opening night Deborah received a big floral arrangement of exotic plants and African violets in her dressing room. Delighted with the beauty of the gift, she reached immediately for the card and almost dropped it. It was signed: "With deepest admiration and warm welcome — John Ford." Deborah was stunned since the director had just died two weeks earlier. First she thought of some macabre joke but later she found out that the flowers had been ordered before the director's death.

"John Ford and I had never worked together, but we corresponded," explained Deborah. "Many times I have written him letters after seeing one of his films. And he always replied with something flattering about my work. This was the kind of relationship we had, a mutual admiration society."[2]

To avoid the possibility of getting sick during the tour, Deborah had several flu shots and took Vitamin C every hour to avoid the sniffles. Moreover twice a week, on matinee days, she took Vitamin B-12, to get an extra boost. Ultimately, she never missed a performance.

The audience's enthusiasm for Deborah continued in San Francisco, Denver, Chicago (there the show sold out in advance for the entire run), Boston, Toronto and finally Washington, D.C., where the show closed in the early spring of 1974. Despite the pressure, she decided not to take the play to New York. Since she had devoted almost two years of her life to it, a Broadway run would have meant more months away from home and from her daughters. For her role, she was awarded the Los Angeles Critics' Circle Best Actress of the Year. She also agreed to resume her role in a film version of the play; however, the project never materialized.

Deborah divided her year between her house in Marbella, Spain, and in Klosters where in July she was visited by Edward Albee, the celebrated author of *Who's Afraid of Virginia Woolf?* and *A Delicate Balance*. He offered her a role in his latest play, *Seascape*, which he was also planning to direct. Deborah was not the playwright's first choice; the script had been sent to Dorothy McGuire, who had expressed interest in doing it, and later to Maureen Stapleton, but Albee finally thought that Deborah would have been a more appropriate choice for the leading role.

"I fell in love immediately," said Deborah after reading the play and accepting the role. To complete the cast, Albee picked Barry Nelson and Frank Langella as the two male leads. Before rehearsal time began, Deborah exchanged copious correspondence with the playwright. Talking about her character, Nancy, Deborah wrote Albee, "I am floundering around with Nancy and will be for a while ... although there is so much of me *in* her, that at times I worry that it is not more complex to me!... I want her to be gay and energetic and funny and sad, and, as you say, carrying enough life for both of them."[3]

On October 16, Deborah arrived in New York. After the first day of rehearsal, Albee decided to reduce almost one-third of the dialogue and much of action from the three-act play, much to the amazement of the actors. Albee took *Seascape* on an extended out-of-town tryout before opening on Broadway. The play, which was a witty allegory examining the merits of evolution, opened just before Thanksgiving at the Mechanic Theater in Baltimore. The space was too large and Deborah's voice had difficulty being heard. The reviews were bad and the cast joked that the play was "a turkey special." More rewrites were introduced and the show went back into rehearsal. The storyline improved, although Frank Langella began to upstage his co-stars, upsetting Albee. Albee called him "a selfish, cruel actor," explaining that the actor was so pushy and self serving that "he had Deborah and Maureen [Anderman] in tears, stepping on lines."[4]

On the experience of working with Albee, Deborah said to the press, "He is extraordinary, I admire him so much for being both author and director. And he has the ability to say about something we've done, 'Oh, that's beautiful, just that way.' We all tell each other we can't imagine anyone else directing this play. To put it through another mind — that would be impossible."[5]

During a brief run in Philadelphia, Deborah learned about a theft at her house in Klosters. Among many valuables, two of her own paintings were stolen, leaving her heartbroken since she admitted she could never do them again; however, she was happy that an original Picasso was left hanging on the wall.

Seascape finally opened on Broadway at the Shubert Theater on January 26, 1975. It received mixed reviews but *The Times* critic Clive Barnes called it "a major critical event" and praised not only Deborah but the entire cast. Nonetheless, the show survived only 65 performances, closing earlier than the date originally scheduled. Frank Langella was awarded a Tony as Best Featured Actor while the play unexpectedly won the Pulitzer

Prize for drama. The best compliment was paid to Deborah by Greta Garbo who made one of her rare public appearances just to see her on stage. Later the actress visited Deborah's dressing room to personally congratulate her.

Before the Broadway debut, Deborah returned to Europe where she and Peter attended the funeral in Paris of her old friend, director Anatole Litvak, who had died of stomach cancer. Later she spent the Christmas holidays with her family at home in Switzerland.

It was not until the end of 1975 that the Viertels announced their first collaboration in a play called *Souvenir*, written by Peter and George Axelrod, starring Deborah. It was a romantic comedy in which she played a movie actress who is involved in a love affair with a younger man (played by Tony Musante) and learns how to cope with changing moralities in her career and private life. Since the play's action moved from the mid–1950s to the present, it was a great challenge for Deborah to appear onstage first looking like a woman in her twenties, and later like one in her forties. *Souvenir* was directed by Gerald Freedman and produced by Arthur Cantor. It opened at the Shubert Theatre in Los Angeles on October 14 and was scheduled to tour in four major American cities before reaching Broadway.

During the rehearsals, the costs kept mounting due to an elaborate production and a large cast. Finally *Souvenir* opened in November with solid advance bookings; however, it had to bring down the final curtain three weeks ahead of schedule. Plans for the tour and the New York opening had to be canceled after the losses amounted to more than $225,000. It was a sad, unavoidable choice which the producers had to make. After that disappointing experience, Deborah stayed away from work for several months. In April 1976, she was offered a leading role in Eugene O'Neill's masterpiece *Long Day's Journey into Night* opposite Charlton Heston, who was also one of the producers. She accepted it three months later on the condition that she receive top billing. Heston found Deborah's request irritating but was so determined to have her in the play as his wife, Mary Tyrone, that he agreed to take second billing.

In November Deborah became a grandmother when Francesca had her first child, Joe, with her husband, actor John Shrapnel. She flew to London to see her grandson and to help with presentations at the first Society of West End Theater drama award ceremony. Afterwards she shot a commercial for Yardley soap, for which she was paid $100,000. Later she started to study for her role in *Long Day's Journey into Night*, directed by

Peter Wood. Deborah refused to talk to the press once rehearsals began, devoting her total energy to her part. In an interview with the *Hollywood Reporter* a week before rehearsals were scheduled to begin, she admitted to being excited and scared.

"It's really a fantastic part for an actress," she said. "What's missing in both movies and the theatre today — nobody's writing for women, That's one of the reasons everyone is doing revivals now.... When Robert Fryer came to me and asked me if I'd like to do this play, I thought why, yes of course, why didn't I think of it myself?... I've always thought that *Long Day's Journey into Night* was a fantastic play, but it wasn't until I started studying it myself that I realized how marvelously contemporary it is.... It is fresh now as when it was written.... But this role is also really a killer. I don't see how anyone could do this play in a commercial run for more than two months. It's so draining on everybody."

On stage as Candida, 1977.

Deborah also revealed that on April 2, when *Long Day's Journey* would close, she would immediately begin rehearsals for George Bernard Shaw's *Candida*, which was scheduled to open in London the following summer.

"This will be fun," Deborah said, "going from a woman who has let herself be destroyed to the earth mother of us all. It's a lovely play and one of the few compassionate women that Shaw wrote."[6]

O'Neill's play opened on February 18, 1977, at the Ahmanson Theatre in Los Angeles. Along with Heston, Deborah appeared onstage with Bruce Dern, who took the role of her son.

At the première followed by a party at Bonaventure Hotel Center, Deborah was moved to see how many friends had come to watch her onstage. Among the many stage veterans were Fredric

March's widow, Florence Eldridge, who had played the role of Mary Tyrone several times in her career, and Burt Lancaster, who surprised her with an unannounced visit backstage.

Heston commented in his memoir about Deborah's acting skills. "She found an elegiac quality in the part that worked.... She was resistant to the textual cuts Peter and I felt had to be made, not only to sharpen the impact of the play, but to get the running time under three hours."[7]

Deborah, like the entire production, was very disappointed in the reviews, which were lukewarm.

After a break in Spain to learn the long part of Candida, she returned in June to England with Peter for the première in Leeds, which was followed by the West End opening on June 23 at the Albery Theatre. It was a great success. Among the enthusiastic reviews, the *Daily Mail* wrote, "Deborah Kerr *is* Candida." The play ran for almost nine months.

"It's like a drug—although it's a nice drug," Deborah commented. "I think it has something to do with the power—and I say this most humbly — of controlling an audience. In movies you have no control except that you know what you can give."[8]

Those words probably are the best explanation of Deborah's healthy addiction to the stage. She preferred this time to play in the comedy, *The Last of Mrs. Cheyney* by Frederick Lonsdale, a forgotten English playwright, rather than in Oscar Wilde's *Lady Windermere's Fan*, when producer Roger Stevens asked her to pick an English play. She finally picked *Cheyney* after Peter called her attention to it. She read it and instantly knew that it was the one she wanted to do.

Londsdale's play depicted the stuffy world of British high society in the 1920s. Deborah was charmed by its wit and frivolity and by how the playwright had been able to portray the mentality of the upper classes, but above all she was struck by how her character, a jewel thief, was written to include a soft heart and a sense of decency. Deborah rehearsed in New York in the summer of 1978 with director Frank Dunlop, whose work for the Royal Shakespeare Company she had long admired. As her leading men, the director engaged Monte Markham and Donal Donnelly.

The revival of *The Last of Mrs. Cheyney* finished its five-week run at the Kennedy Center in Washington, D.C., on the day of Deborah's 57th birthday. It then followed a four-month tour in 11 major cities across North America, opening on Broadway the following November. Audiences loved the show, which broke the house record in several cities. Nevertheless, critics found it an unworthy vehicle for a star of Deborah's caliber. She responded with disappointment to the poor press explaining, "I've learned never to be upset. You'd think the critics would appreciate our doing a famous old play that's never seen anymore. It should be regarded as a piece that belongs to its time. Of course, it has a very simple plot, but it's a comedy of manners, and they were meant to be outrageously simple. But it has wit and clever dialogue, and all it needs is a good ensemble playing."

The Last of Mrs. Cheyney's tour ended in San Francisco in March 1979. When she appeared in Pittsburgh, she received a letter from a woman who praised her performance adding, "Please, could you tell me the name of your plastic surgeon? I want to have my daughter's nose made like yours." Deborah wrote back, "I'm so pleased you liked my performance. The name of my plastic surgeon is God."

The unflagging Deborah was happy to return to Klosters for a few weeks prior to accepting an offer from Paul Dainty and the MLC Theatre Royal Co. of Sydney to star the following September in a 12-week Australian tour of *The Day After the Fair*, directed by Frith Banbury. The play opened first at the Comedy Theater in Melbourne and later moved to the Theater Royal in Sydney. The Aussies packed the two theaters and the local press gave her a great welcome, praising her performance. She returned to Europe just in time to be closer to Peter, who was recovering from a gallbladder operation.

"Considering the rubbish that comes through the post to me in the way of scripts nowadays," Deborah said. I'm inclined to think I'm well out of it, though of course I'd love a film if the right one came along. But I don't much want to do 50 lines as a guest star in some disaster movie under a thousand feet of water and there seems to be remarkably little else around. For a while I even began to wish I'd been in *Murder on the Orient Express*, at least until I saw it on television and realized that had been just another lucky escape."[9]

This was one of the reasons she responded positively to Peter Ustinov's call when he asked her to star in his latest play, *Overheard*. Ustinov chose not to act in his own work, helping only with the casting choices and collaborating with the director Clifford Williams. Set in a small, unnamed Balkan country, the action of *Overheard* took place in the British Embassy, where the ambassador and his wife (Ian Carmichael and Deborah) have grown bored with each other. When a dissident poet bursts in seeking asylum, he quickly seduces both the ambassador's wife and his secretary (played by Ustinov's daughter Tamara). "What is so marvelous about *Over-*

heard is that it gives me a chance to play comedy," said Deborah to *The Times*, "and play a really intriguing character; most are written either exclusively for men or exclusively for men and gorgeous 20-year-old blondes. Also, Peter Ustinov and I go back a long way together and he does write the most marvelous, if difficult to learn, dialogue."[10]

Rehearsals started on February 2, 1980, for a March tryout in Billingham, Richmond, Bristol and Brighton, prior to the West End unveiling at the Haymarket Theatre the following May. *Overheard* drew packed audiences keen to see the latest Ustinov play and its two stars who were so well known from their films.

Ustinov's personal judgment of Deborah was that she "was a marvelous actress when she was being soft, but perhaps because she had done so many films she felt constrained to talk much louder than was necessary in the theatre."[11]

The play proved to be very popular both in the provinces and in London, where it ran for six months, despite the mixed reviews. It was a reassuring feeling for Deborah, who particularly enjoyed that experience; she, in fact, accepted Ustinov's offer to appear in the American run of the play, which never happened.

While in London with the show, Deborah was invited to present to both Michael Powell and Emeric Pressburger special BAFTA awards for their long careers in the film industry. In her brief speech she rightly described the recognition as long overdue. Powell was not aware of her presence until she gave him the award at the ceremony. "She looked absolutely wonderful," he later commented. "I fell in love with her all over again right in front of about 12 million viewers. Wonderful girl."[12]

14

A Gentle Fadeout

People always expect me to be the same — pretty — pretty, charming and gentle.

— Deborah Kerr

Once her engagement with *Overheard* was over, Deborah appeared in a BBC production of one of three plays (eventually only two were produced) written by Noël Coward all set in the same New York hotel suite. She starred in *Song at Twilight* opposite Paul Scofield, playing Carlotta Gray — a former lover of an eminent writer whom she confronts and threatens with the disclosure of his secret homosexual past. The play was shown as part of the BBC2 Playhouse series, airing on July 9, 1982.

In February 1982, Deborah was invited to make a brief appearance for the Gala Actor's Fund of America benefit in *The Night of 100 Stars* at Radio City Music Hall. This televised show which would have her reunited her with many Hollywood colleagues was to feature Deborah walking on stage arm in arm with Burt Lancaster in a segment called "famous couples." Nevertheless she had to decline the invitation since she had already committed to star in a CBS Hallmark Hall of Fame TV-movie adaptation of *Witness for the Prosecution*, the Agatha Christie stage play that had previously been made into a 1957 film by Billy Wilder.

"A lovely little character part," as she described her role of Nurse Plimsoll, played by Elsa Lanchester in Wilder's version. "I was thought of primarily for nuns and governesses earlier in my career. Now I'm back in that mood," she told the *Los Angeles Times*.[1]

The all-star cast of this television remake included Ralph Richardson, Beau Bridges, Donald Pleasence, Diana Rigg and Wendy Hiller.

"In *Witness*," explained Deborah to the *Daily News*, "I get a chance to be a comical, contentious, yet curiously vulnerable person. That's why I grabbed it. I absolutely loved doing it."[2]

The film was shot on a three-week schedule with the courtroom set at Twickenham Studios outside London. *Witness for the Prosecution* aired the first week of December 1982, receiving mostly good reviews by the American press.

For two years, Deborah stayed away from work enjoying the pleasure of traveling with Peter and relaxing at home. She appeared in December 1983 in a special tribute organized in her honor by Frédéric Mitterrand at the Olympic–St. Germain Theater in Paris. It was a memorable event in which she was introduced in glowing terms, and clips of her best moments in film were shown throughout the evening. Afterward, she tearfully thanked the audience for the moving experience. She was later mobbed by autograph seekers before continuing the evening at the Brasserie Lipp, where she dined with Peter and a few friends. The previous night she had finished shooting a documentary on the Louvre Museum with Raymond Gérôme for a French television network.

In May she returned to France at the Cannes Film Festival where she was given a special award as a tribute to her career. At the ceremony she looked radiant. She graciously thanked everybody, apologizing for not speaking French.

That same month she returned to a television set to co-star in *Ann and Debbie*, an hour-long drama opposite Claire Bloom. It was the story of two old friends who met for their regular drink to discuss their fading marriages. The film, produced by British Granada Television, was filmed in Manchester and London in only 16 days. "*Terribly* hard work," she commented about its making. "We had to sit down, quite still for about four weeks. *Jolly* hard work."[3] *Ann and Debbie* was shown on television two years later, exclusively in England.

That same year Deborah also played a small but important role in the mini-series *A Woman of Substance*, adapted from Barbara Taylor Bradford's bestselling novel. It was a rags-to-riches saga chronicling the life of Emma Harte, from lowly servant girl to matriarch of an immense department store dynasty. Deborah played an aging Harte (Jenny Seagrove was the young Emma). She enjoyed being part of the mini-series even though the pressure was enormous. She had to do three weeks' work that was ordinarily done in six, getting up at 5:30 A.M. and driving an hour and half to a location outside London where it was bitterly cold. The four-part series premièred on American screens at the end of 1984, and in England on January 2, 1985. *A Woman of Substance* became the highest rated program ever on Channel 4 in the U.K.—peaking at almost 14 million viewers on its third night. Deborah received an Emmy nomination for her role, which she did not get.

"It's classic for me not to win," she commented about her loss, referring also to her six Academy Award nominations. A year later the production company offered her the starring role in *Hold the Dream*, a two-part, four-hour sequel of *A Woman of Substance* in which she would again play Emma Hart at age 80. She immediately agreed, explaining that working in the mini-series gave her a chance to shed the "goody-two-shoes" image with which she had been associated since she first started in Hollywood. This was the same reason why, in the summer of 1984, she decided to make her comeback on the big screen (after a 15-year absence) starring in the independent film *The Assam Garden*. Deborah was, in fact, looking for the right part when producer Nigel Stafford-Clark sent her the screenplay.

"I could hardly believe that she would take on such a demanding part and one that put years on her, rather than glamorizes her," said the young producer.[4]

He was able to arrange a meeting with Deborah in Paris at her favorite restaurant; however, as soon as they started their conversation he immediately knew she was already hooked on the script. Surprisingly, Deborah was pleased at the idea of appearing older in the film. "I wanted to look not in the least like me or the character I've played so many times," she explained. "People always expect me to be the same—pretty—pretty, charming, and gentle.... That is the awful reign that's put on you if you have a certain look. The audience doesn't want to see you in old gum boots and sloppy hair and an old scarf, slopping around the garden."[5]

That was exactly how she looked in the film playing Helen, a lonely elderly woman, whose husband, a former colonial administrator in India, had just died, leaving unfulfilled his ambition to see his Assam Garden included in *Great British Gardens* magazine. She decides to pay him a final tribute by completing the project when she makes the acquaintance of an Indian neighbor, a woman in her sixties whom she promptly recruits as her assistant.

The role was extremely demanding for Deborah who, for six weeks, weeded, cut grass and hauled heavy buckets of water in the English countryside. *The Assam Garden* was an original script written by Elisabeth Bond,

With Madhur Jaffrey in *The Assam Garden* (1986).

whose story is also about the relationship between two women from different social classes with a garden as catalyst. The entire picture was shot in Gloucestershire where a location scout found a house called Priors Mesne. The house had two spectacular gardens laid out by Henry Cook, a former surgeon general in the Indian Army, who had written a book about the gardens in 1903. Deborah was thrilled to be working, for the first time in her career, on a film directed by a woman: Mary McMurray. For McMurray, who had previously collaborated with Granada television primarily on documentaries, this was her first feature experience. Despite weather problems due to a rainy summer and a plague of wasps, the shooting of the film, budgeted at only $1 million, went pretty smoothly. McMurray was very satisfied with Deborah's performance, saying, "I always thought she'd be very good in it, not because of those rather 'English rose' pieces she tends to be associated with, but because of her grittiness."[6]

When Deborah saw the final cut she was moved to tears and confided that the fear of a husband or a partner dying before you, as shown in the film, looms larger as you get older. After being shown in several prestigious film festivals around the globe, *The Assam Garden* opened in England on July 4, 1985, where it had a run of six months at a London West End cinema. A year later when the picture had a limited release in America, the *New York Times* noted, "Miss Kerr gives a nice modulated performance in the somewhat familiar role of a proper English gentlewoman, outwardly confident but filled with misgivings about her ability to carry on."[7]

In 1968 when Robert Mitchum was asked on television about working with Deborah he said, "I haven't worked with her as often as I'd like to." The occasion came 16 years later, on September 26, 1984, when the two were reunited for the first time since 1961 when they made *The Grass Is Greener*. The two stars had kept in touch during the years with Deborah always addressing him in letters as Dear Mr. Allison." Both were very thrilled to star in *Reunion at Fairborough* — a two-hour movie produced by HBO. The film was mainly shot on location in the Home Counties and in Cambridge, with a studio base at Shepperton. Deborah arrived in England from Switzerland, while Mitchum flew in from California.

"When I read the script I didn't know Deborah was going to do it," said Mitchum, who joked with the press that the real reason he agreed to make the film was because his wife wanted to go to London.

Deborah was more forthcoming about why she took the part, saying, "When I read the script I thought it was a very interesting and very romantic story. Terribly touching, very nostalgic and also very topical in that my granddaughter in the story is a very modern young woman who's a protester, being anti–nuclear war and anti–missiles. But yes, I'm sure there will be many thousands of women who will identify with the character I'm playing. Women who fell deeply in love during the war and had a war-time romance which, of course, ended when the war was over. I'm sure, too, many of them ended up as very lonely women indeed."[8]

Reunion at Fairborough was a gentle piece of nostalgia, a story of renewed friendship and rekindled past loves. Mitchum played an old American ex–bomber pilot returning to his wartime haunt in a Surrey village, re-encountering his old flame (Deborah) 40 years later from whom finds out he had a daughter.

"We found ourselves right back to where we used to be," Deborah said in an interview the week the film was shown in England in March 1986. "We would laugh at ridiculous *in* jokes, reminisce about the old days … it just felt wonderfully comfortable to be working with him again.… I suppose it's like a good tennis match. We seem to be able to hit the ball back and forward to each other."[9]

In the spring of 1985, stage director Frith Banbury asked Deborah to star in a revival of Emlyn Williams's play *The Corn Is Green* to mark the eightieth birthday of its author. Deborah jumped at the chance, feeling that the role was perfect for her. *The Corn Is Green* was first produced in 1938, with Williams playing the young Welsh miner who gains a scholarship to Oxford. He becomes an accomplished writer, thanks to the determination of Miss Moffat, an English school teacher. The play had several autobiographical elements, especially in the character of the teacher, who really encouraged Emlyn to study and even paid for him to go to France at age 15 for a whole summer. The original production had Sybil Thorn-

A publicity shot for *Reunion at Fairborough* with Robert Mitchum, 1985.

dike as Miss Moffat, a role which was played on the screen in 1945 by Bette Davis and in a television version in 1979 by Katharine Hepburn. However, Deborah did not see any of her illustrious predecessors playing her part, which she thought could have influenced her performance. The production company scheduled a six-week tour in Britain's provinces at the end of April, followed by another six at the Old Vic Theatre in London. On the opening night, at the Royal Theatre in Bath, Deborah suffered a severe case of stage fright, something she was always able to control in the past. Once on stage she had trouble remembering her lines, and more than a dozen times she had to be prompted. Several members of the audience walked out and some demanded their money back. The story immediately made the newspapers and for the rest of the week there were reporters in the audience waiting to see if the star broke down, collapsed, or quit. Sadly, the following two nights Deborah again fluffed her lines. The rest of the cast rallied around her, ad-libbing on occasion to bring her back into a speech when she forgot a cue. However, when she "went up" dried in a scene where she was alone on stage, the prompt could be heard loud and clear all round the theatre. The producers called off a planned press conference after Deborah read a critique in a local newspaper. "It really was embarrassing to watch Deborah Kerr. She needed so many prompts it was impossible not to believe that there was something seriously wrong."[10]

Hurt by the way the press handled the incident, Deborah responded, "Forty-five years of work behind me and it was the only thing that put me on the front page of newspapers."[11] Nevertheless she received so many letters and cards from caring fans with warm words of support and understanding that she was extremely touched. With strong resilience she decided not to give up, as many had expected.

"I want to carry on working, I never want to retire," Deborah insisted. "Despite my ghastly nerves, which I know are the cause of my problems, I will plough ahead. The play is wonderful and I hope to get it right."[12] Before appearing on the Old Vic's stage on May 22, 1985, Deborah confessed, "I'm facing it with some fear, but Peter is coming to hold my hand. He'll be there pacing up and down at the back. When my husband is in the audience at least I know one person will be clapping. He's the strength of my life."[13] Deborah delivered her lines perfectly; however, critics found the production overshadowed by her insecurity in the role.

"She has a vulnerable air, tremulous refinement wavering into obstinacy where she should show irresistible conviction and ruthless single-mindedness," wrote Martin Hoyle in his review.[14]

Despite all the troubles, in November Deborah was honored, along with Roddy McDowall, with the prestigious American Cinema Award in a sumptuous ceremony at the Beverly Wilshire Hills Hotel in Hollywood. It was one of the largest reunions ever of film stars from Hollywood's golden era. Elizabeth Taylor, Robert Mitchum and Robert Wagner hosted the stage presentation, which included a retrospective of excerpts from more than 40 years of film in which the honored guests performed. Deborah's close friend Dinah Shore reminisced about their long friendship, while Deborah talked about her trip to Hollywood, her first in ten years.

"Even though the streets and the buildings have changed," she remarked in her speech, "the past is still there to greet you. Coming back to a place you used to call home, a town where you once lived and worked, is always an overwhelming experience.... I must confess I'm a little lost and very frightened. When you arrived once again, you can't help thinking of the friends who are no longer around ... the friends you were looking forward to meeting again on past occasions. But that's life, I'm afraid. All we can do is soldier along."

At the tribute $100,000 was raised to build the American Film Cultural Center in Malibu.

The year 1986 marked the 40th anniversary of Deborah's career in film. She was made a Fellow of the British Film Institute, the first actress to win one of the British film industry's highest awards; previous winners included Laurence Olivier and Orson Welles. In October Deborah traveled to London with Peter to attend the ceremony and to promote the miniseries *Hold the Dream*, which aired on British television that same month. Afterwards she flew to Chicago where she was warmly welcomed by the mayor of the city before she appeared at the Chicago International Film Festival, which was hosting a retrospective of her best films, including a special preview of *The Assam Garden*.

The next years in Deborah's life were quiet. She spent much of her time voraciously reading, playing the piano, and enjoying her family, including her three grandchildren. She lived alternately in Switzerland and Spain, where Peter had bought a cottage on a hillside in Marbella. Deborah stayed away from the limelight until the summer of 1993 when she received an unexpected phone call from her business manager, Jess Morgan, in Los Angeles. He told her that the video sales of *An Affair to Remember* had suddenly skyrocketed. It had, in fact, become the hottest video in America. Deborah was baffled by the news since she had made that picture 36 years earlier. Morgan explained to her that writer-director Nora Ephron, who was a fan of the film, had incorporated several scenes of *An Affair* into her unexpected blockbuster summer hit, a poignant love story called *Sleepless in Seattle*, starring Tom Hanks and Meg Ryan. Like Deborah and Cary Grant, Hanks and Ryan did not find each other until the last scene. The success of the new movie sparked the boom in video sales of *An Affair to Remember*. All of the sudden Deborah was rediscovered by younger generations. She was overwhelmed by calls from reporters from all over the world who asked her to comment on what was happening in her life.

"I think I understand what women see in the movie," Deborah said. "There is a sweetness that is appealing and far removed from today's crudities. It makes them realize that the world has lost something delightful. Of course we mustn't be foolish and think we can go back. Sure, we'd like a world of chiffon dresses and pink Champagne but that will not happen. Still, I think it is possible to extract some of the best from the past and bring it forward to the present — going back there and salvaging something kinder for our own times."[15]

In January 1994 another phone call from Los Angeles shook Deborah's quiet retirement. Arthur Hiller, president of the Academy of Motion Picture Arts and Sciences, announced that she had been selected to receive an honorary Oscar. As soon as the story broke in the news, Deborah told the press that she was in a state of shock. She confirmed her intention to attend the ceremony and laughed, saying that she put herself immediately on a diet to get into a new dress. Finally, after receiving five Best Actress nominations (making her the most-nominated non–winner in that category) and one Best Supporting Actress nomination, Deborah received the official recognition she deserved from the industry. Before leaving for Hollywood in March, she learned the sad news of the sudden death of her close friend Dinah Shore, to whom she had spoken recently and planned to visit while in California.

On March 21, the woman the Academy called "an artist of impeccable grace and beauty, a delicate actress whose picture career has always stood for perfection, discipline and elegance," finally appeared on the stage of the Dorothy Chandler Pavillion receiving the Oscar from actress Glenn Close. "Thank you, thank you," she said tearfully. There should be more words for thank you, shouldn't there? I've never been so frightened in all my life but I feel better now because I'm among friends." A very dignified and elegant Deborah made a brief but moving speech acknowledging the work of many of her colleagues and "all the men and women behind the lights" without whom her career would have not been the same. A long standing ovation ended her gracious acceptance.

Before leaving for Klosters, Deborah and Peter got together again with Glenn Close backstage at the Shubert Theatre after watching a performance of the musical *Sunset Blvd.* in which Close was starring.

Slowly, in the last years of her life, Deborah's health became very frail, so much that in 1998 when she was awarded a CBE (Commander of the Order of the British Empire), she was not well enough to go to Buckingham Palace to receive the award from the Queen. Many of her fans rightly complained that the honor had come too late since no other British actress went from England to Hollywood and achieved such worldwide recognition and distinction.

At the beginning of the new century, Deborah stopped giving interviews and answering fans' letters, since she suffered from Parkinson's disease. Her voice had become very weak, she was able to say only yes or no. In 2004, when her beloved brother Teddy, a retired journalist, was murdered in a "road rage" accident in Birmingham at the age of 78, she was devastated and remained wordless and desolate for several hours before asking to be wheeled to her room to weep alone. Unfortunately, her illness reached such an advanced state that she had to be moved back to England, closer to her daughters who provided for her the best care in the strictest privacy.

On October 16, 2007, agent Anne Hutton announced to the world that Deborah had died peacefully in the little village of Botesdale, Suffolk, in eastern England, at age 86. A private function was held the following day and was attended only by the closest members of her family.

As mere coincidence or twist of fate, three weeks later, on November 4, Peter Viertel passed away at a hospital in Marbella as a result of a serious disease which had worsened after his beloved wife's passing.

In one of her last interviews Deborah wisely affirmed, "Interviewers are always aghast when I say I have no fear of age, unlike

Celebrating her honorary Oscar with Glenn Close (1994).

so many women. But I haven't. The years are feared only by the unhappy who have never found themselves.... My life is full as a human being."

Filmography

Contraband

1940. British National. *Directors:* Michael Powell and Emeric Pressburger; *Producer:* John Corfield; *Screenplay:* Brock Williams, based on a story by Emeric Pressburger. *Cast:* Conrad Veidt (Capt. Andersen), Valerie Hobson (Mrs. Sorensen), Hay Petrie (Axel Skold), Joss Ambler (Lt. Cmdr. Ashton), Raymond Lovell (Van Dyane), Deborah Kerr (Nightclub cigarette girl, subsequently cut).

Major Barbara

1941. General Film Distribution. *Director and producer:* Gabriel Pascal; *Screenplay:* Anatole de Grunwald, Gabriel Pascal, based on the play by George Bernard Shaw. *Cast:* Wendy Hiller (Major Barbara Undershaft), Rex Harrison (Adolphus Cusins), Robert Morley (Andrew Undershaft), Robert Newton (Bill Walker), Deborah Kerr (Jenny Hill), David Tree (Charles Lomax), Sybil Thorndike (The General), Emlyn Williams (Snobby Price), Marie Lohr (Lady Brittomart), Penelope Dudley-Ward (Sarah Undershaft).

Love on the Dole

1941. British National. *Director and producer:* John Baxter; *Screenplay:* Walter Greenwood, based on his novel and on a play by Ronald Gow. *Cast:* Deborah Kerr (Sally), Clifford Evans (Larry), George Carney (Mr. Hardcastle), Mary Merrall (Mrs. Hardcastle), Geoffrey Hibbert (Harry Hardcastle), Joyce Howard (Helen Hawkins), Frank Cellier (Sam Grundy), Martin Walker (Ned Narkey), Iris Vandeleur (Mrs. Nattle), Marie Ault (Mrs. Jike).

Penn of Pennsylvania
(a.k.a. Courageous Mr. Penn)

1942. British National. *Director:* Lance Comfort; *Producer:* Richard Vernon; *Screenplay:* Anatole de Grunwald, based on the book *William Penn* by C.E. Vulliamy. *Cast:* Clifford Evans (William Penn), Deborah Kerr (Gulielma Maria Springett), Dennis Arundell (Charles II), Aubrey Mallalieu (King's Chaplain), D.J. Williams (Lord Arlington), O.B. Clarence (Lord Cecil), James Harcourt (George Fox), Charles Carson (Admiral Penn), Henry Oscar (Samuel Pepys), Max Adrian (Elton), John Stuart (Bindle), Joss Ambler (Mayor of London).

Hatter's Castle

1942. Paramount-British. *Director:* Lance Comfort; *Producer:* Isadore Goldsmith; *Screenplay:* Paul Merzbach, Rudolph Bernauer and Rodney Ackland, based on the novel by A.J. Cronin. *Cast:* Robert Newton (James Brodie), James Mason (Dr. Renwick), Deborah Kerr (Mary Brodie), Emlyn Williams (Dennis), Enid Stamp-Taylor (Nancy), Henry Oscar (Grierson), Beatrice Varley (Mrs. Brodie), Anthony Bateman (Angus Brodie), June Holden (Janet), Ian Fleming (Sir John Latta).

The Day Will Dawn (a.k.a. The Avengers)

1942. General Film Distributors. *Director:* Harold French; *Producer:* Paul Soskin; *Screenplay:* Anatole de Grunwald, Patrick Kirwan and Frank Owen. *Cast:* Hugh Williams (Colin Metcalfe), Griffith Jones (Police Inspector Gunter), Deborah Kerr (Kari Alstad), Ralph Richardson (Frank Lockwood), Francis L. Sullivan (Kommandant Ulrich Wettau), Roland Culver (Cmdr. Pittwaters), Finlay Curie (Capt. Alstad).

The Life and Death of Colonel Blimp

1943. A Production of the Arches. *Directors, Producers and Screenplay:* Michael Powell and Emeric Pressburger. *Cast:* Roger Livesey (Clive Candy), Anton Walbrook (Theo Kretschmar-Schuldoroff), Deborah Kerr (Edith Hunter/Barbara Wynne/Johnny Cannon), John Laurie (Murdoch), James McKechnie (Spud Wilson), Roland Culver (Colonel Betteridge), Spencer Trevor (Period Blimp), Albert Lieven (Von Ritter), Carl Jaffe (Von Roeumann), Valentine Dyall (Von Schönborn).

Perfect Strangers (a.k.a. Vacation from Marriage)

1945. MGM/London Film. *Director:* Alexander Korda; *Producers:* Ian Dalrymple, Alexander Korda; *Screenplay:* Clemence Dane, Anthony Pellissier. *Cast:* Deborah Kerr (Catherine Wilson), Robert Donat (Robert Wilson), Glynis Johns (Dizzy

Clayton), Ann Todd (Elena), Roland Culver (Richard), Roger Moore (Soldier), Peter Lawford (Introduction — U.S.A. version uncredited).

I See a Dark Stranger (a.k.a. *The Adventuress*)

1946. General Film Distributors. *Director and Producer:* Frank Launder; *Screenplay:* Sidney Gilliat, Frank Launder, Wolfgang Wilhelm. *Cast:* Deborah Kerr (Bridie Quilty), Trevor Howard (Lt. David Baynes), Raymond Huntley (J. Miller), Liam Redmond (Uncle Timothy), William G. O'Gorman (Danny Quilty), Harry Webster (Uncle Joe), Eddie Golden (Terence Delaney), Marie Ault (Mrs. O'Mara), Tony Quinn (Guide), Brefni O'Rorke (Michael O'Callaghan), Michael Howard (Hawkins).

Black Narcissus

1947. General Film Distributors/Archers. *Directors and Producers:* Michael Powell and Emeric Pressburger; *Screenplay:* Michael Powell and Emeric Pressburger, based on the novel by Rumer Godden. *Cast:* Deborah Kerr (Sister Clodagh) David Farrar (Mr. Dean), Jean Simmons (Kanchi), Kathleen Byron (Sister Ruth), Sabu (Dilip Rai), Flora Robson (Sister Philippa) Esmond Knight (General Toda Rai), Jenney Laird (Sister Honey), Judith Furse (Sister Briony), Nancy Roberts (Mother Dorothea).

The Hucksters

1947. MGM. *Director:* Jack Conway; *Producer:* Arthur Hornblow, Jr.; *Screenplay:* Luther Davis, based on a novel by Frederic Wakeman. *Cast:* Clark Gable (Victor Albee Norman), Deborah Kerr (Kay Dorrence), Ava Gardner (Jean Ogilvie), Sydney Greenstreet (Evan Llewellyn Evans), Adolphe Menjou (Mr. Kimberly), Keenan Wynn (Buddy Hare), Edward Arnold (Dave Lash), Gloria Holden (Mrs. Kimberly).

If Winter Comes

1947. MGM. *Director:* Victor Saville; *Producer:* Pandro S. Berman; *Screenplay:* Marguerite Roberts, Arthur Wimperis, based on a novel by A.S.M. Hutchinson. *Cast:* Walter Pidgeon (Mark Sabre), Deborah Kerr (Nona Tybar), Angela Lansbury (Mabel Sabre), Binnie Barnes (Natalie Bagshaw), Janet Leigh (Effie Bright), Dame May Whitty (Mrs. Perch), Rhys Williams (Mr. Bright), Reginald Owen (Mr. Fortune), John Abbott (Mr. Twyning).

Edward, My Son

1948. MGM. *Director:* George Cukor; *Producer:* Edwin H. Knopf; *Screenplay:* Donald Ogden Stewart, based on a play by Robert Morley and Noel Langley. *Cast:* Spencer Tracy (Arnold Boult), Deborah Kerr (Evelyn Boult), Ian Hunter (Dr. Larry Woodhope), James Donald (Bronton), Leueen MacGrath (Eileen Perrin), Mervyn Johns (Harry Sempkin), Tilsa Page (Betty Foxley), Harriette Johns (Phyllis Mayden).

Please Believe Me

1950. MGM. *Director:* Norman Taurog; *Producer:* Val Lewton; *Screenplay:* Nathaniel Curtis. *Cast:* Deborah Kerr (Alison Kirbe), Robert Walker (Terence Keath), Mark Stevens (Matthew Kinston), Peter Lawford (Jeremy Taylor), James Whitimore (Vincent Marran), J. Carrol Naish ("Lucky" Reilly), Spring Byington (Mrs. Milwright), Carol Savage (Sylvia Rumley).

King Solomon's Mines

1951. MGM. *Directors:* Compton Bennet and Andrew Marton; *Producer:* Sam Zimbalist; *Screenplay:* Helen Deutsch, based on the novel by H. Rider Haggard. *Cast:* Deborah Kerr (Elizabeth Curtis), Stewart Granger (Allan Quatermain), Hugo Haas (Van Brun a.k.a. Smith), Richard Carlson (John Goode), Siriaque (Umbopa, Tall Prince in Exile), Lowell Gilmore (Eric Masters).

Quo Vadis

1952. MGM. *Director:* Mervyn LeRoy; *Producer:* Sam Zimbalist; *Screenplay:* S.N. Behrman, Sonya Levien, John Lee Mahin, based on the novel by Henryk Sienkiewicz. *Cast:* Robert Taylor (Marcus Vinicius), Peter Ustinov (Nero), Deborah Kerr (Lygia), Leo Genn (Petronius), Patricia Laffan (Poppaea), Buddy Baer (Ursus), Finlay Currie (Peter), Marina Berti (Eunice), Abraham Sofaer (Paul), Nora Swimburne (Pomponia), Felix Aylmer (Plautius), Elspeth March (Miriam), Sophia Loren (Lygia's slave, uncredited), Walter Pidgeon (Narrator), Bud Spencer (Imperial Guard, uncredited), Elizabeth Taylor (Christian Prisoner in arena, uncredited).

Thunder in the East

1952. Paramount. *Director:* Charles Vidor; *Producer:* Everett Riskin; *Screenplay:* Jo Swerling, George Tabori, Frederick Hazlitt Brennan and Lewis Meltzer, based on the novel *The Rage of the Vulture* by Alan Moorehead. *Cast:* Alan Ladd (Steve

Gibbs), Deborah Kerr (Joan Willoughby), Charles Boyer (Prime Minister Singh), Corinne Calvet (Lizette Damon), John Williams (General Henry Harrison), Cecil Kellaway (Dr. Willoughby), Mark Calvell (Moti Lal), John Abbott (Nitra Putra), Leonard Carey (Dr. Paling).

Prisoner of Zenda

1952. MGM. *Director:* Richard Thorpe; *Producer:* Pandro S. Berman; *Screenplay:* John L. Balderston, Noel Langley and Wells Root, from the novel by Anthony Hope. *Cast:* James Mason (Rupert of Hentzau), Stewart Granger (Rudolf Rassendyll/King Rudolf V), Deborah Kerr (Princess Flavia), Jane Greer (Antoinette de Mauban), Louis Calhern (Colonel Zapt), Lewis Stone (The Cardinal), Robert Douglas (Michael, Duke of Strelsau), Robert Coote (Fritz von Tarlenheim), Francis Pierlot (Josef), Peter Brocco (Jonan).

Young Bess

1953. MGM. *Director:* George Sidney; *Producer:* Sidney Franklin; *Screenplay:* Jan Lusting, Arthur Wimperis, from a novel by Margaret Irwin. *Cast:* Jean Simmons (Young Bess/Queen Elizabeth I), Stewart Granger (Thoams Seymour) , Charles Laughton (King Henry VIII), Deborah Kerr (Catherine Parr), Cecil Kellaway (Mr. Parry), Kay Walsh (Mrs Ashley), Leo G. Carroll (Mr. Mums), Guy Rolfe (Ned Seymour), Kathleen Byron (Ann Seymour), Rex Thompson (Prince Edward/King Edward VI), Elaine Stewart (Anne Boleyn).

Dream Wife

1953. MGM. *Director:* Sidney Sheldon; *Producer:* Dore Schary; *Screenplay:* Sidney Sheldon, Herbert Baker and Alfred Lewis Levitt. *Cast:* Cary Grant (Clemenson Reade), Deborah Kerr (Effie), Walter Pidgeon (Walter McBride), Betta St. John (Tarjii), Eduard Franz (Khan), Richard Anderson (Henry Malvine), Buddy Baer (Vizier), Les Tremayne (Ken Ladwell), Bruce Bennett (Charlie Elkwood), Donald Randolph (Ali).

Julius Caesar

1953.MGM. *Director:* Joseph L. Mankiewicz; *Producer:* John Houseman; *Screenplay:* Joseph L. Mankiewicz, from the play by William Shakespeare. *Cast:* John Gielgud (Cassius), James Mason (Brutus), Marlon Brando (Mark Antony), Greer Garson (Calpurnia), Louis Calhern (Julius Caesar), Edmond O'Brien (Casca), Deborah Kerr (Portia), George Macready (Marullus), Edmund Purdom (Strato),

Alan Napier (Cicero), Ian Wolfe (Ligarius), John Hardy (Lucius), Michael Pate (Flavius), William Cottrell (Cinna).

From Here to Eternity

1953. Columbia. *Director:* Fred Zinnemann; *Producer:* Buddy Adler; *Screenplay:* Daniel Taradash, from a novel by James Jones. *Cast:* Burt Lancaster (Sgt. Milton Warden), Deborah Kerr (Karen Holmes), Montgomery Clift (Pvt. Rober Prewitt), Frank Sinatra (Pvt. Angelo Maggio), Donna Reed (Lorene), Ernest Borgnine (Sgt. Fatso Judson), Philip Ober (Capt. Dana Holmes), Jack Warden (Cpl. Buckley), Mickey Shaughnessy (Sgt. Leva), Harry Bellaver (Mazzioli), George Reeves (Sgt. Maylon Stark), John Dennis (Sgt. Ike Galovitch), Tim Rayan (Sgt. Pete Karelsen), Barbara Morrison (Mrs. Kipfer), Kristine Miller (Georgette), Jean Willes (Annette), Arthur Keegan (Treadwell), Claude Akins (Sgt. Baldy Dhom), George Reeves (Sgt. Maylon Stark).

The End of the Affair

1955. Columbia. *Director:* Edward Dmytryk; *Producer:* David Lewis; *Screenplay:* Leonore J. Coffee from a novel by Graham Greene. *Cast:* Deborah Kerr (Sarah Miles), Van Johnson (Maurice Bendrix), John Mills (Albert Parkins), Peter Cushing (Henry Miles), Michael Goodlife (Smythe), Stephen Murray (Father Crompton), Nora Swinburne (Mrs. Bertram).

The Proud and Profane

1956. Paramount. *Director:* George Seaton; *Producer:* William Perlberg; *Screenplay:* George Seaton, based on the novel *The Magnificent Bastards* by Lucy Herndon Crockett. *Cast:* William Holden (Lt. Col. Colin Black), Deborah Kerr (Lee Ashley), Thelma Ritter (Kate Connors), Dewey Martin (Eddie Wodcik), William Redfield (Chaplain Holmes), Ward Wood (Sgt. Peckinpaugh), Ray Stricklyn (First Casualty).

The King and I

1956. 20th Century–Fox. *Director:* Walter Lang; *Producer:* Charles Brackett; *Screenplay:* Ernest Lehman, based on the novel *Anna and the King of Siam* by Margaret Landon and on the musical by Richard Rodgers and Oscar Hammerstein II. *Cast:* Deborah Kerr (Anna Leonowens), Yul Brynner (King Mongkut of Siam), Rita Moreno (Tuptim), Martin Benson (Kralahome), Alan Mowbray (Sir John Hay), Geoffrey Toone (Edward Ramsay), Rex Thompson (Louis Leonowens), Leonard Strong (Interpreter), Carlos Rivas (Lu Tha).

Tea and Sympathy

1957. MGM. *Director:* Vincente Minnelli; *Producer:* Pandro S. Berman; *Screenplay:* Robert Anderson based on his play. *Cast:* Deborah Kerr (Laura Reynolds), John Kerr (Tom Robinson Lee), Leif Erickson (Bill Reynolds), Edward Andrews (Herbert Lee), Dean Jones (Ollie), Darryl Hickman (Al), Norma Crane (Ellie Martin), Jacqueline deWit (Lilly Sears), Tom Lauglin (Ralph).

Heaven Knows, Mr. Allison

1957. 20th Century–Fox. *Director:* John Huston; *Producers:* Buddy Adler, Eugene Frenke; *Screenplay:* John Huston and John Lee Mahin, from a book by Charles Shaw. *Cast:* Deborah Kerr (Sister Angela), Robert Mitchum (Cpl. Allison, USMC).

An Affair to Remember

1957. 20th Century–Fox. *Director:* Leo McCarey; *Producer:* Jerry Wald; *Screenplay:* Delmer Daves, Leo McCarey, based on an unpublished original story by Leo McCarey and Mildred Cram. *Cast:* Cary Grant (Nickie Ferrante), Deborah Kerr (Terry McKay), Cathleen Nesbitt (Grandmother Janou), Richard Denning (Kenneth Bradley), Louis Mercier (Mario), Charles Watts (Ned Hathaway) Fortunio Bovanova (Courbet), Matt Moore (Father McGrath).

Bonjour Tristesse

1958. Columbia. *Director:* Otto Preminger; *Producer:* Otto Preminger, John Palmer; *Screenplay:* Arthur Laurents, from a novel by Françoise Sagan. *Cast:* Deborah Kerr (Anne Larson), David Niven (Raymond), Jean Seberg (Cecile), Mylène Demongeot (Elsa), Juliette Gréco (Herself), Walter Chiari (Pablo), Martitia Hunt (Philippe's Mother), Geoffrey Horne (Philippe), Roland Culver (Mr. Lombard), Jean Kent (Helen Lombard).

Separate Tables

1959. United Artists. *Director:* Delbert Mann; *Producer:* Harold Hecht; *Screenplay:* Terence Rattigan and John Gay, from a play by Terence Rattigan. *Cast:* Rita Hayworth (Ann Shankland), Deborah Kerr (Sibyl Railton-Bell), David Niven (Major Angus Pollock), Gladys Cooper (Mrs. Railton-Bell), Burt Lancaster (John Malcom), Wendy Hiller (Pat Cooper), Rod Taylor (Charles), Cathleen Nesbitt (Lady Matheson), Felix Aylmer (Mr. Fowler), Audrey Dalton (Jean), Priscilla Morgan (Doreen), May Hallatt (Miss Meacham).

The Journey

1959. MGM. *Director* and *Producer:* Anatole Litvak; *Screenplay:* George Tabori. *Cast:* Yul Brynner (Major Surov), Deborah Kerr (Lady Diana Ashmore), Jason Robards, Jr. (Paul Kedes), Anouk Aimée (Eva), Robert Morley (Hugh Deverill), E.G. Marshall (Harold Rhinelander), Ron Howard (Billy Rhinelander), Anne Jackson (Margie Rhinelander), David Kossoff (Simon Avron), Marie Daëms (Françoise Hafouli).

Count Your Blessings

1959. MGM. *Director:* Jean Negulesco; *Producer:* Karl Tunberg; *Screenplay:* Karl Tunberg, based on the novel *The Blessing* by Nancy Mitford. *Cast:* Rossano Brazzi (Charles-Edouard de Valhubert), Deborah Kerr (Grace Allingham), Maurice Chevalier (Duc de St. Cloud), Martin Stephens (Sigismond), Tom Helmore (Hugh Palagrave), Patricia Medina (Albertine), Mona Washbourne (Nanny), Ronals Squire (Sir Conrad Allingham), Steven Geray (Guide), Lumsden Hare (John), Kim Parker (Secretary), Frank Kreig (Tourist).

Beloved Infidel

1959. 20th Century–Fox. *Director:* Henry King; *Producer:* Jerry Wald; *Screenplay:* Sy Bartlett, based on a book by Sheilah Graham and Gerold Frank. *Cast:* Gregory Peck (Francis Scott Fitzgerald), Deborah Kerr (Sheilah Graham), Eddie Albert (Carter), Philip Ober (John Wheeler), Herbert Rudley (Stan Harris), John Sutton (Lord Donegall), Karin Booth (Janet Pierce), Ken Scott (Robinson) Buck Class (Dion), Cindy Armes (Miss Bull).

The Sundowners

1960. Warner Bros. *Director:* Fred Zinnemann; *Producer:* Gerry Blattner; *Screenplay:* Isobel Lennart, from a novel by Jon Cleary. *Cast:* Deborah Kerr (Ida Carmody), Robert Mitchum (Paddy Carmody), Peter Ustinov (Rupertr Venneker), Glynis Johns (Mrs. Firth), Dina Merrill (Jean Halstead), Wylie Watson (Herb Johnson), Chips Rafferty (Quinlan), Michael Anderson, Jr. (Sean Carmody), Lola Brooks (Liz Brown), Ronald Fraser (Ocker), Ewen Solon (Halstead), Mervyn Johns (Jack Patchogue).

The Grass Is Greener

1961. Universal-International. *Director* and *Producer:* Stanley Donen; *Screenplay:* Hugh Williams and Margareth Vyner, from their original play. *Cast:* Cary Grant

(Victor Rhyall, Earl), Deborah Kerr (Lady Hilary Rhyall), Robert Mitchum (Charles Delacro), Jean Simmons (Hattie Durant), Moray Watson (Trevor Sellers, the Butler).

Naked Edge

1961. Warner Bros. *Director:* Michael Anderson; *Producers:* Walter Seltzer, George Glass; *Screenplay:* Joseph Stefano, from the novel *First Train to Babylon* by Max Ehrlich. *Cast:* Gary Cooper (George Radcliffe), Deborah Kerr (Martha Radcliffe), Eric Portman (Jeremy Clay), Diane Cilento (Mrs. Heath), Hermione Gingold (Lilly Harris), Peter Cushing (Mr. Wrack) Michael Wilding (Morris Brooke), Ronald Howard (Mr. Claridge), Ray McAnally (Donald Heath).

The Innocents

1961. 20th Century–Fox. *Director* and *Producer:* Jack Clayton; *Screenplay:* William Archibald, Truman Capote, from the novel *The Turn of the Screw* by Henry James. *Cast:* Deborah Kerr (Miss Giddens), Megs Jenkins (Mrs. Grose), Pamela Franklin (Flora), Martin Stephens (Miles), Michael Redgrave (The Uncle), Peter Wyngarde (Peter Quint), Clytie Jessop (Miss Jessel), Isla Cameron (Anna), Eric Woodburn (Coachman).

The Chalk Garden

1964. Universal-International. *Director:* Ronald Neame; *Producer:* Ross Hunter; *Screenplay:* John Michael Hayes, based on a play by Enid Bagnold. *Cast:* Edith Evans (Mrs. St. Maugham), Deborah Kerr (Miss Madrigal), Hayley Mills (Laurel), John Mills (Mailand), Felix Aylmer (Judge McWhirrey), Elizabeth Sellars (Olivia), Lally Bowers (Anna), Tonie MacMillan (Mrs.Williams).

The Night of the Iguana

1964. MGM. *Director:* John Huston; *Producers:* Ray Stark, John Huston; *Screenplay:* John Huston and Anthony Veiller, from a play by Tennessee Williams. *Cast:* Richard Burton (Rev. Dr. Lawrence Shannon), Ava Gardner (Maxine Faulk), Deborah Kerr (Hannah Jelkes), Sue Lyon (Charlotte Goodall), James "Skip" Ward (Hank Prosner), Grayson Hall (Judith Fellowes), Cyril Delevanti (Nonno), Mary Boylan (Miss Peebles).

Marriage on the Rocks

1965. Warner/Pathé/Sinatra Enterprise. *Director:* Jack Dohuane; *Producer:* William H. Daniels; *Screenplay:* Cy Howard. *Cast:* Frank Sinatra (Dan Edwards), Deborah

Kerr (Valerie Edwards), Dean Martin (Ernie Brewer), Cesar Romero (Miguel Santos), Hermione Baddeley (Jeannie MacPherson), Nancy Sinatra (Tracy Edwards), John McGiver (Shad Nathan), Tony Bill (Jim Blake), Davey Davison (Lisa Sterling).

Eye of the Devil (a.k.a. 13)

1966. MGM-Filmways. *Director:* J. Lee Thompson; *Producers:* John Calley, Martin Rosohoff; *Screenplay:* Dennis Murphy and Robin Estridge, from the novel *Day of the Arrow* by Philip Loraine. *Cast:* Deborah Kerr (Catherine de Montfaucon), David Niven (Philippe de Montfaucon), Donald Pleasence (Père Dominic), Edward Mulhare (Jean-Claude Ibert), Sharon Tate (Odile de Caray), David Hemmings (Christian de Caray), Flora Robson (Countess Estelle), Emlyn Williams (Alain de Montfaucon), Donald Bisset (Rennard), Suky Appleby (Antoinette de Montfaucon), John le Mesurier (Dr. Monnet).

Casino Royale

1967. Columbia. *Directors:* John Huston, Ken Hughes, Robert Parrish, Joseph McGrath, Val Guest; *Producers:* Charles K. Feldman, Jerry Bresler; *Screenplay:* Wolf Mankovitz, John Law, Michael Sayers, loosely based on the novel by Ian Fleming. *Cast:* David Niven (Sir James Bond), Peter Sellers (Evelyn Tremble), Deborah Kerr (Agent Mimi/ Lady Fiona McTarry), Ursula Andress (Vesper Lynd), Orson Welles (Le Chiffre), Joanna Pettet (Mata Bond), Woody Allen (Jimmy Bond), William Holden (Ransome), Charles Boyer (Le Grand), John Huston (McTarry), Jean-Paul Belmondo (French Legionnaire), Jacqueline Bisset (Miss Goodthings), Barbara Bouchet (Miss Moneypenny).

Prudence and the Pill

1968. 20th Century–Fox. *Directors:* Fielder Cook, Ronald Neame; *Producers:* Kenneth Harper, Ronald J. Kahn; *Screenplay:* Hugh Mills, from his novel. *Cast:* Deborah Kerr (Prudence Hardcastle), David Niven (Gerald Hardcastle), Irina Demick (Elizabeth Brett), Robert Coote (Henry Hardcastle), Joyce Redman (Grace Hardcastle), Judy Geeson (Geraldine Hardcastle), Keith Michell (Dr. Alan Hewitt), Edith Evans (Lady Roberta Bates), David Dundas (Tony Bates), Vickery Turner (Rose), Hugh Armstring (Ted), Peter Butterworth (Chemist).

The Gypsy Moths

1969. MGM. *Director:* John Frankenheimer; *Producers:* Hal Landers, Bobby Roberts; *Screenplay:* William Hanley, from a novel by James Drought. *Cast:* Burt

Lancaster (Mike Rettig), Deborah Kerr (Elizabeth Brandon), Gene Hackman (Joe Browdy), Scott Wilson (Malcom Webson), Bonnie Bedelia (Annie Burke), William Windom (V. John Brandon), John Napier (Dick Donford), Ford Rainey (Stand Owner), Carl Reindel (Pilot), Sheere North (Waitress).

The Arrangement

1969. Warner Bros. *Director, Producer* and *Screenplay:* Elia Kazan, based on his novel. *Cast:* Kirk Douglas (Eddie Anderson), Faye Dunaway (Gwen), Deborah Kerr (Florence Anderson), Hume Cronyn (Arthur), Richard Boone (Sam Anderson), Hume Cronyn (Arthur), Michael Higgins (Michael), John Randolph Jones (Charles), Carol Eve Rossen (Gloria), Harold Gould (Dr. Leibman).

The Assam Garden

1986. A Moving Picture Company Film. *Director:* Mary McMurray; *Producer:* Nigel Stafford-Clark; *Screenplay:* Elisabeth Bond. *Cast:* Deborah Kerr (Helen), Madhur Jaffrey (Ruxmani), Alec McCowen (Mr. Philpott), Anton Lesser (Mr. Sutton), Zia Mohyeddin (Mr. Lal), Ian Cuthbertson (Arthur), Tara Shaw (Sushi).

Television Appearances

TELEVISION PROGRAMS

1963. *Three Roads to Rome*, ITV Play of the Week, December 30, 1963 (Season 9, Episode 19). *Director:* Ronald Marriott; *Screenplay:* Tad Mosel. ITV. *Cast:* Deborah Kerr (Moira/Grace Ansley/Miranda), Andrew Lawrence (Robert), Geoffrey Chater (Hugh), Judy Stephens (Miranda), Janet Thompson (Jill).

1982. *A Song at Twilight*, BBC2 Playhouse, July 9, 1982 (Season 8, Episode 30). *Director:* Cedric Messina; *Screenplay:* Noël Coward. BBC2. *Cast:* Deborah Kerr (Carlotta Gray), Bruce Lidington (Felix), Paul Scofield (Hugo Latimer), June Tobin (Hilde).

TELEVISION FILMS

Witness for the Prosecution

1982. CBS Entertaining Production. *Director:* Alan Gibson; *Producer:* Norman Rosemont; *Screenplay:* John Gay, from a short story by Agatha Christie and from a script by Billy Wilder. *Cast:* Ralph Richardson (Sir Wilfred Robarts), Deborah Kerr (Nurse Plimsoll), Diana Rigg (Christine Vole), Beau Bridges (Leonard Vole), Wendy Hiller (Janet Mackenzie), Donald Pleasence (Mr. Mayhew), Michael Gough (Judge), Peter Sallis (Carter).

A Woman of Substance

1984. Portman Artemis Production. *Director:* Don Sharp; *Producer:* Diane Baker; *Screenplay:* Barbara Taylor Bradford. *Cast:* Deborah Kerr (Emma Harte), Jenny Seagrove (Young Emma Harte), Barry Bostwick (Major Paul McGill), Peter Chelsom (Edwin Fairley), John Mills (Henry Rossiter), Liam Neeson (Blackie O'Neill), Miranda Richardson (Paula McGill Armory), Mick Ford (Frank Harte).

Hold the Dream

1986. Bradford Enterprises. *Director:* Don Sharp; *Producer:* Harry R. Sherman; *Screenplay:* Tom Blomquist and Lee Langley, from a novel by Barbara Taylor Bradford. *Cast:* Deborah Kerr (Emma Harte), Jenny Seagrove (Paula Fairley), John Mills (Henry Rossiter), Liam Neeson (Blackie O'Neill), Claire Bloom (Edwina, Lady Dunvale), Stephen Collins (Shane O'Neill), James Brolin (Ross Nelson), Nigel Havers (Jim Fairley), Paul Daneman (David Amory).

Reunion at Fairborough

1985. Columbia Pictures TV/HBO. *Director:* Herbert Wise; *Producer:* William Hill; *Screenplay:* Arthur Ruben. *Cast:* Robert Mitchum (Carl Hostrup), Deborah Kerr (Sally Wells Grant), Red Buttons (Jiggs Quealy), Judi Trott (Sheila), Barry Morse (Nathan Barsky), Shane Rimmer (Joe Szyluk), Don Fellows (Duffy), Manning Redwood (Col. Bigard).

Ann and Debbie

1986. Granada Television, March 29, 1986. *Director* and *Producer:* June Howson; *Screenplay:* Lionel Goldstein. *Cast:* Deborah Kerr (Ann), Claire Bloom (Debbie), Donald Eccles (Arthur), Angus Mackay (Frank).

Stage Appearances

Harlequin and Columbine

1937 Knightstone Pavilion, Weston-Super-Mare, U.K., *Director:* Phyllis Jane Smale.

Prometheus

March 29, 1938. Ballet with music by Ludwig van Beethoven. *Directors:* Ninette de Valois (ballet), Constant Lambert (music). Open Air Theatre, Regent's Park, London. Deborah Kerr (Member of the corps-de ballet).

Much Ado About Nothing

June 3, 1938. Comedy by William Shakespeare. *Director:* Robert Atkins. Open Air Theatre, Regent's Park, London. Deborah Kerr (One of the ladies).

Pericles

June 20, 1939. Comedy by William Shakespeare. *Director:* Robert Atkins. Open Air Theatre, Regent's Park, London. Deborah Kerr (Page to Pericles).

A Midsummer Night's Dream

July 4, 1939. Comedy by William Shakespeare. *Director:* Robert Atkins. Open Air Theatre, Regent's Park, London. Deborah Kerr (Attendant to Hyppolyta).

Twelfth Night

July 31, 1939. Comedy by William Shakespeare. *Director:* Robert Atkins. Open Air Theatre, Regent's Park, London. Deborah Kerr (Attendant to Olivia).

Tobias and the Angel

August 7, 1939. Comedy by James Bridie. *Director:* Robert Atkins. Open Air Theatre, Regent's Park, London. Deborah Kerr (Attendant to Sara).

Dear Brutus

April 29, 1940. Comedy by Sir James Barrie. *Director:* Leslie French. Playhouse Theatre, Oxford. Deborah Kerr (extra).

The Two Bouquet

May 6, 1940. Comedy by Eleanor and Herbert Farjeon. *Director:* Leslie French. Playhouse Theatre, Oxford. Deborah Kerr (Patty Moss).

The Playhouse Revue

May 20, 1940. Presented by the Oxford Rerpertory Players. *Director:* Leslie French. Playhouse Theatre, Oxford. Deborah Kerr (Soubrette).

Heartbreak House

March 19, 1943. Comedy by George Bernard Shaw. *Director:* John Burrell. Cambridge Theatre, London. Deborah Kerr (Ellie Dunn).

Gaslight

March 31, 1945. Drama by Patrick Hamilton. *Director:* John Fernald. Theatre Royal, Drury Lane, London. Deborah Kerr (Bella Manningham).

Tea and Sympathy

September 30, 1953. Drama by Robert Anderson. *Director:* Elia Kazan. Barrymore Theatre, New York. Deborah Kerr (Laura Anderson).

Separate Tables

January 10, 1972. Drama by Terence Rattigan. *Director:* Nigel Patrick. Haymarket Theatre, London. Deborah Kerr (Sybil Railton-Bell).

The Day After the Fair

October 4, 1972. Play by Frank Harvey. *Director:* Frith Banbury. Shubert Theatre, Los Angeles Deborah Kerr (Letty Harnham).

Seascape

January 26, 1975. Comedy by Edward Albee. *Director:* Edward Albee. Shubert Theatre, New York. Deborah Kerr (Nancy).

Souvenir

October 29, 1975. Comedy by Peter Viertel and George Axelrod. *Director:* Gerald Freedman. Shubert Theatre, Los Angeles. Deborah Kerr (Julie Stevens).

Long Day's Journey into Night

February 18, 1977. Drama by Eugene O'Neill. *Director:* Peter Wood. Ahmanson Theatre, Los Angeles. Deborah Kerr (Mary Tyrone).

Candida

June 23, 1977. Comedy by George Bernard Shaw. *Director:* Michael Blakemore, Albery Theatre, London. Deborah Kerr (Candida).

The Last of Mrs. Cheyney

August 26, 1978. Drama by Frederick Lonsdale. *Director:* Frank Dunlop, Eisenhower Theatre, Kennedy Center, Washington, D.C., Deborah Kerr (Mrs. Cheyney).

Overheard

May 7, 1981. Comedy by Peter Ustinov. *Director:* Clifford Williams. Theatre Royal, London. Deborah Kerr (Iris Caulker).

The Corn Is Green

May 22, **1985**. Drama by Emlyn Williams. Director: Frith Banbury. Old Vic Theatre, London Deborah Kerr (Lilly Moffat).

Radio Programs

"Vacation from Marriage," *Lux Radio Theatre*, CBS, May 26, 1947.
"Jane Eyre," *University Theatre*, NBC, April 3, 1949.
The Big Show, NBC, December 17, 1950.
The Jack Benny Show, CBS, January 7, 1951.
The Jack Benny Show, CBS, January 14, 1951.
"Good-bye Mr. Chips," *Hallmark*, CBS, February 1, 1951.
"Edward, My Son," *Lux Radio Theatre*, CBS, June 18, 1951.
"That Forsyte Woman," *Lux Radio Theatre*, CBS, November 5, 1951.
"Persuasion," *Hallmark*, CBS, February 7, 1952.
"This Pleasant Leave," *Hallmark*, CBS, March 13, 1952.
"Lady Pamela," *Suspense*, CBS, March 31, 1952.
"King Solomon's Mines," *Lux Radio Theatre*, CBS, December 1, 1952.

Chapter Notes

Chapter 1

1. Paul Spicer, *Herbert Howells* (Bridgend, Wales: Seren Books, 1999), pp. 84–85.
2. Sheilah Graham, "Deborah," *Photoplay*, November 1947, p. 68.
3. Jim Meyer, "Deborah Kerr," *Screen Facts*, N. 19, Vol. 4, 1968, p. 2.
4. Ken Doeckel, "Deborah Kerr," *Films in Review*, January 1978, p. 2.
5. Kyle Crichton, "The Huckster's Lady," *Collier's*, October 4, 1947, p. 54.
6. Eric Braun, *Deborah Kerr* (London: W. H. Allen, 1977), p. 32.
7. Harvey Breit, "Deborah Kerr, Minus the Icicles," *New York Times Magazine*, October 11, 1953.
8. Ken Doeckel, "Deborah Kerr," *Films in Review*, p. 2.
9. Jim Meyer, "Deborah Kerr," *Screen Facts*, p. 4.
10. Harvey Breit, "Deborah Kerr, Minus the Icicles," *New York Times Magazine*, October 11, 1953.
11. Kyle Crichton, "The Huckster's Lady," *Collier's*, October 4, 1947, p. 54.
12. Joyce Haber, "Deborah Kerr — She Really Isn't a Prude," *Los Angeles Times*, June 15, 1969, p. 15.
13. Ken Doeckel, "Deborah Kerr," *Films in Review*, p. 3.
14. Braun, *ibid.*, p. 46.
15. Valerie Pascal, *The Discipline and His Devil* (London: Michael Joseph, 1971), pp. 96–97.
16. Kevin Brownlow, *David Lean* (London: Richard Cohen Books, 1996), p. 135.
17. Joyce Haber, "Deborah Kerr — She Really Isn't a Prude," *Los Angeles Times*, June 15, 1969, p. 15.

Chapter 2

1. Jerry Vermilye, *The Great British Films* (Secaucus, NJ: The Citadel Press, 1978), p. 9.
2. Jonathan Croall, *Sybil Thorndike: A Star of Life* (London: House Books, 2008), p. 306.
3. Brownlow, *ibid.*, p. 135.
4. Gene D. Phillips, *Beyond the Epic: The Life & Films of David Lean* (Lexington, KY: The University Press of Kentucky, 2006), p. 40.
5. Allen Eyes, *Rex Harrison* (London: W. H. Allen, 1985), p. 3.
6. Croall, *ibid.*, p. 307.
7. Vermilye, *Great British Films*, p. 10.
8. Bernard F. Dukore, *Bernard Shaw and Gabriel Pascal* (Toronto: University of Toronto Press, 1996), p. 133.
9. Geoff Brown, *The Common Touch: The Films of John Baxter* (London: NTF Dossier 5, 1989), p. 77.
10. Michael Thornton, *Jessie Matthews* (London: Hart-Davis, MacGibbon, 1974), p. 156.

11. Brown, *The Common Touch*, p. 80.

12. Jim Meyer, "Deborah Kerr," *Screen Facts*, p. 6.

13. T.M.P. "At the 55th Street," *New York Times*, December 23, 1945, p. 26.

14. James Mason, *Before I Forget* (London: Hamish Hamilton, 1985), pp. 128–129.

15. Lilli Palmer, *Change Lobsters — and Dance* (London: W. H. Allen, 1976), p. 112.

16. C. A. Lejeune, "The Films," *The Observer*, May 10, 1942, p. 3.

Chapter 3

1. Michael Powell, *A Life in Movies* (London: Faber and Faber, 2000), p. 409.

2. *Ibid.*, p. 410.

3. *Ibid.*

4. Peter Waymark, "Ruffling the PM's Feathers," *The Times*, July 22, 1989, p. 14.

5. James Chapman, *The British at War* (London: I. B. Tauris Publication, 1998), pp. 194–195.

6. T.M.P., "Colonel Blimp, Technicolor Film from Britain at the Gotham," *New York Times*, March 30, 1945, p. 18.

7. Archer Winsten, "British Colonel Blimp Great Despite Handicaps," *New York Post*, March 30, 1945.

8. Powell, *A Live in Movies*, p. 436.

9. Kenneth Barrow, *Mr. Chips: The Life of Robert Donat* (London: Methuen 1985), pp. 130–131.

10. *Ibid.*, p. 133.

11. J. C. Trewin, *Robert Donat: A Biography* (London: Heinemann, 1968), p. 143.

12. Louise Sweeney, "Deborah Kerr: A Face the Camera Loves," *The Christian Science Monitor*, October 17, 1978, p. B6.

13. Harry Alan Towers and Leslie Mitchell, *The March of the Movies* (London: Sampson Low, Marston, 1947), pp. 43–44.

14. Charles Drazin, *Korda: Britain's Only Movie Mogul* (London: Sidgwick & Jackson, 2002), p. 263.

15. Roland Culver, *Not Quite a Gentleman* (London: William Kimber, 1979), p. 106.

16. Roger Moore, *My World Is My Bond* (London: Michael O'Mara Books, 2008), p. 40.

17. Barrow, *Mr. Chips*, p. 149.

18. Michelangelo Capua, *Vivien Leigh* (Jefferson, NC: McFarland, 2003), p. 91.

19. Stewart Granger, *Sparks Fly Upward* (London: Granada, 1981), pp. 87–88.

20. Anthony Bartley, *Smoke Trails in the Sky* (London: William Kimber, 1984), p. 193.

21. *Ibid.*

22. Hedda Hopper, "Debut for Deborah," *Chicago Sunday Tribune*, May 4, 1947, p. 7.

23. Bartley, *Smoke Trails*, p. 193.

24. *Ibid.*, p. 198.

25. Lee Mortimer, "It Could Only Happen on Broadway," *New York Mirror*, May 4, 1947.

26. "Movie of the Week: The Adventuress," *Life Magazine*, April 7, 1947, p. 60.

27. Peter Hay, *Movie Anecdotes* (New York: Oxford University Press, 1990), p. 18.

28. Geoff Brown, *Launder and Gilliat* (London: BFI, 1977), p. 118.

29. Braun, *Deborah Kerr*, p. 94.

30. Bartley, *Smoke Trails*, p. 201.

31. *Ibid.*, p. 202.

32. Powell, *A Life in Movies*, p. 576.

33. *Ibid.* p. 577.

34. Kenneth Barrow, *Flora: An Appreciation of the Life and Work of Dame Flora Robson* (London: Heinemann, 1981), p. 159.

35. Harry Alan Towers and Leslie Mitchell, *The March of the Movies*, p. 46.

36. Steven Smith, *Getting to Know Deborah* (Documentary), Prometheus Entertainment, A&E Network, 2000.

37. Barrow, *Flora*, p. 160.

38. Roddy McDowall, *Double Exposure: Take Four* (New York: Morrow, 1993), p. 130.

39. David Lemon, *A Profile on Black Narcissus* (Documentary), Carlton International Media 2000.

40. James Howard, *Michael Powell* (London: BT Batsford, 1996), p. 56.

41. Scott Salwolke, *The Films of Michael Powell and the Archers* (Lanham, MD: The Scarecrow Press, 1997), p. 143.

42. Powell, *A Life in Movies*, p. 584.

Chapter 4

1. "A Star Is Born," *Time*, February 10, 1947, p. 98.

2. Deborah Kerr, "Erskine Johnson," *Los Angeles Daily News*, August 9, 1947.

3. Bertrand Tavernier, *Amis Américains* (Paris: Institut Lumière/Actes Sud, 1993), pp. 492–493.

4. "A Star Is Born," *Time*, February 10, 1947, p. 99.

5. Deborah Kerr, "Erskine Johnson," *Los Angeles Daily News*, August 9, 1947.

6 . Sheilah Graham, "Deborah," *Photoplay*, November 1947, p. 118.

7. Ron Moseley, *Evergreen: Victor Saville in His Own Words* (Carbondale: Southern Illinois University Press, 2000), pp. 171–172.

8. Janet Leigh, *There Really Was a Hollywood* (New York: Doubleday, 1984), p. 68.

9. "A Star Is Born," *Time*, February 10, 1947, p. 100.

10. Robert W. Marks, "The Woman All Women Want to Be: Deborah Kerr," *Collier's*, December 7, 1956, p. 35.

11. Donald Spoto, "Deborah Kerr. Six-Time Nominee in Pacific Palisades," *Architectural Digest*, April 1992, p. 220.

12. Emanuel Levy, *George Cukor, Master of Elegance* (New York: Morrow, 1994), p. 170.

13. Spencer Tracy, "I Looked as If I'd Been Picked by the Property-Man," *The Film Fan's Bedside Book*, n. 2, 1949, p. 29.

14. Deborah Kerr, "The Role I Liked Best...," *The Saturday Evening Post*, November 5, 1949, p. 106.

15. Levy, *George Cukor*, p. 171.

16. Peter S. Haig, "Deborah Likes the Type of Role That Shocked Her Mother," *Film Review*, October 1957, p. 5.

17. Rudy Behlmer, "King Solomon's Mines: Part I," *American Cinematographer*, May 1989, pp. 40–41.

18. Deborah Kerr, "My Jungle Adventure," *The Star*, January 1, 1951, p. 9.

19. Rudy Behlmer, "King Solomon's Mines: Part I," *American Cinematographer*, May 1989, pp. 39–40.

20. Granger, *Sparks Fly Upward*, p. 156.

21. Joanne D'Antonio, *Andrew Marton* (Metuchen, NJ: The Scarecrow Press, 1991), pp. 162–163.

22. Deborah Kerr, "My Jungle Adventure," *The Star*, January 1, 1951, p. 9.

23. Pete Martin, "The Movies' Beautiful Brute," *Saturday Evening Post*, December 22, 1951, p. 52.

24. *Ibid.*

25. Rudy Behlmer, "King Solomon's Mines: Part I," *American Cinematographer*, May 1989, p. 43.

26. Peter Noble, "King Solomon's Mines," *ABC Film Review*, February 1951.

27. Rudy Behlmer, "King Solomon's Mines: Part I," *American Cinematographer*, May 1989, p. 44.

28. D'Antonio, *Andrew Marton*, p. 176.

Chapter 5

1. Charles Hingham, *Merchant of Dreams. Louis B. Mayer, MGM, and the Secret Hollywood* (New York: Donald I. Fine, 1993), pp. 393–394.

2. Mervyn LeRoy, *Mervyn LeRoy: Take One* (New York: Hawthorn Books, 1974), p. 170.

3. Jane Wayne Allen, *Robert Taylor* (London: Robson Books, 1991), pp. 147–148.

4. John Kobal, *Romance & the Cinema* (London: Studio Vista, 1973), p. 8.

5. Stefan Kanfer, *The Life and Times of Julius Henry Marx* (London: Penguin Books, 2001), p. 341.

6. Sidney Sheldon, *The Other Side of Me* (New York: Warner Books, 2005), p. 235.

7. Dore Schary, *Heyday: An Autobiography* (Boston, MA: Little, Brown & Co., 1979), pp. 258–259.

8. Lionel Godfrey, *Cary Grant: The Light Touch* (New York: St. Martin Press, 1981), p. 142.

9. John Houseman, *Front and Center* (New York: Simon & Schuster, 1979), pp. 388–389.

10. Darwin Porter, *Brando Unzipped* (New York: Bloom Moon Productions, 2006), p. 380.

11. James Robert Parish and Don E. Stanke, *The Swash Bucklers* (New Rochelle, NY: Arlington Press, 1976), pp. 382–384.

12. Beverly Linet, "The Films of Deborah Kerr," *Screen Stories*, May 1971, p. 56.

Chapter 6

1. Jay Fultz, *In Search of Donna Reed* (Iowa City: University of Iowa Press, 1998), p. 88.

2. Darwin Porter, *Merv Griffin: A Life in the Closet* (New York: Blood Moon Productions, 2009), p. 178.

3. Fred Zinnemann, *A Life in the Movies* (New York: Scribner's, 1992), pp. 122–123.

4. Gabriel Miller, *Fred Zinnemann* (Jackson: University Press of Mississippi, 2004), p. 91.

5. Bob Thomas, *King Cohn. The Life and Times of Harry Cohn* (New York: Putnam, 1967), pp. 310–311.

6. Zinnemann, *A Life in the Movies*, p. 122.

7. Gary Fishgall, *Against Type: A Biography of Burt Lancaster* (New York: Simon & Schuster, 1995), p. 114.

8. *Ibid.*, p. 115.

9. Ronald Hayman, "Deborah Kerr," *The Times*, September 2, 1972, p. 11.

10. Zinnemann, *A Life in the Movies*, p. 123.

11. Miller, *Fred Zinnemann Interviews*, p. 60.

12. Angela Fox Dunn, "An Intimate Chat with Deborah Kerr," *Star*, April 8, 1986, p. 44.

13. Porter, *Merv Griffin*, pp. 178–179.

14. Fultz, *In Search of Donna Reed*, p. 90.

15. Linet, *Ladd*, p. 58.

16. John L. Scott, "Deborah to Embark on Broadway Debut," *Los Angeles Times*, August 9 1953.

17. *Ibid.*

18. Richard L. Coe, "Miss Kerr Displays Anxiety," *New York Times*, September 27, 1953.

19. Braun, *Deborah Kerr*, p. 143.

20. Elia Kazan, *A Life* (New York: Knopf, 1988), p. 504.

21. Howard Kissel, "Deborah Kerr," *Central Stage*, November 1978, p. 15.

22. Brooks Atkinson, "First Night at the Theatre," *New York Times*, October 1, 1953, p. 35.

23. "Tea and Sympathy," *Life Magazine*, October 19, 1953, p. 121.

24. Richard Lee, "Deborah Kerr Still Rhymes with Star," *New York Post*, January 25, 1975, p. 13.

25. Jim Meyer, "Deborah Kerr," *Screen Facts*, p. 6.

26. Peter Hay, *Broadway Anecdotes* (New York: Oxford University Press, 1989), p. 348.

27. William Baer, *Elia Kazan: Interviews* (Jackson: University Press of Mississippi, 2004), p. 33.

28. Barbara L. Goldsmith, "Tony Perkins — Hollywood's Wonder Boy," *McCall's*, October 1957, p. 128.

29. Paul Holt, "My 7 Lean Years in Hollywood," *Picturegoer*, July 17, 1954, p. 13.

30. Harold Conway, "Goody-goody Deborah Clinches It," *Daily Sketch*, July 15, 1954.

31. Paul Holt, "My 7 Lean Years in Hollywood," *Picturegoer*, July 17, 1954, p. 13.

32. Edward Dmytryk, *It's a Hell of a Life but Not a Bad Living* (New York: Times Books, 1978), p. 188.

33. Robert Tanitch, *John Mills* (London: Collins & Brown, 1993), p. 84.

34. John McCallum, *Life with Googie* (London: Heinemann, 1979), p. 80.

Chapter 7

1. David Chierichetti, *George Seaton* (Beverly Hills: Louis B. Mayer/American Film Institute, 1975), p. 163.

2. *Ibid.*, pp. 165–166.

3. Liza Wilson, "First Lady of Hollywood," *The American Weekly*, April 14, 1957, p. 10.

4. Dick Richards, "Love, Marriage and Me: Part II," *Picturegoer*, Sept. 29, 1956.

5. Roderick Mann, *Sunday Express*, November 27, 1977.

6. Wanda Hale, "Rates Governess Role as Her Career's Best," *New York Daily News*, April 15, 1956.

7. Richard Rodgers, *Musical Stages: An Autobiography* (New York: Random House, 1975), p. 270.

8. Hugh Fordin, *Getting to Know Him: A Biography of Oscar Hammerstein* II (New York: Ungar, 1977), p. 296.

9. Patrick Garland, *The Incomparable Rex: A Memoir of Rex Harrison in the 1980s*

(New York: Macmillan, 1998), p. 15.

10. Richard Rodgers, *Musical Stages*, pp. 271–272.

11. Mary Martin, *My Heart Belongs* (New York: Morrow, 1976), p. 122.

12. Otis L. Guernsey Jr., "The King and I," *Herald Tribune*, March 30, 1950.

13. Wanda Hale, "Rates Governess Role as Her Career's Best," *New York Daily News*, April 15, 1956.

14. Braun, *Deborah Kerr*, p. 153.

15. "Yul Brynner — Golden Egged," *Newsweek*, May 19, 1958, p. 103.

16. Gene Feldman, *Yul Brynner. The Man Who Was King*, 1995 videocassette.

17. Herbert Whittaker, "Deborah Kerr's Mind Is Made Up — Broadway Is Out," *Globe and Mail*, December 17, 1973.

18. Marni Nixon, *I Could Have Sung All Night* (New York: Billboard Books, 2006), p. 86.

19. *Ibid.*, pp. 88–89.

20. Braun, *Deborah Kerr*, p. 154.

21. Joel Sayre, "Yul Brynner: Why Do Women Find Him Irresistible," *Collier's*, July 6, 1956, p. 33.

22. Marni Nixon, *I Could Have Sung All Night*, pp. 95–96.

23. Geoffrey Block, *The Richard Rodgers Reader* (New York: Oxford University Press, 2002), p. 102.

24. Edwin Schallert, "Deborah Sets Pace," *Los Angeles Times*, July 15, 1956, p. 12.

25. Dick Richards, "Love, Marriage and Me: Part II," *Picturegoer*, Sept. 29, 1956, p. 16.

26. Bosley Crowther, *New York Times*, June 29, 1956, sec. 6, p. 15.

27. Ronald L. Davis, *Yul Brynner: Oral History Project N. 85* (Dallas: Southern Methodist University, 1978), pp. 31–32.

28. Robert Cushman and Stacey Endress, *Hollywood at Your Feet* (Los Angeles: Pomegranate Press, 1992), p. 257.

29. Jhan Robbins, *Yul Brynner: The Inscrutable King* (New York: Dodd, Mead, 1987), p. 67.

Chapter 8

1. Vincente Minnelli, *I Remember It Well* (New York: Doubleday 1974), p. 299.

2. Schary, *Heyday*, p. 311.

3. Augusto Torress, *Vincente Minnelli* (Madrid: Cátedra, 1995), p. 264.

4. Edwin Schallert, "Deborah Sets Place," *L.A. Times*, July 15, 1956, p. 12.

5. Minnelli, *I Remember It Well*, p. 301.

6. Nan Robertson, "On the Tumult in Tobago for 'Mr. Allison,'" *New York Times*, November 18, 1956.

7. "Heaven Knows, and So Does Mr. Mitchum," *Photoplay*, February 1985, pp. 12–13.

8. Roddy McDowall, *Double Exposure. Take Three* (New York: Morrow, 1994), p. 232.

9. Nan Robertson, "On the Tumult in Tobago for 'Mr. Allison,'" *New York Times*, November 18, 1956.

10. Lawrence Grobel, *The Hustons* (New York: Avon Books, 1990), p. 439.

11. John Huston, *An Open Book* (London: Macmillan, 1980), p. 262.

12. David Downing, *Robert Mitchum* (London: W. H. Allen, 1985), p. 123.

13. Roddy McDowall, *Double Exposure. Take Three*, p. 232.

14. Mike Tomkies, *The Robert Mitchum Story* (Chicago: Henry Regnery, 1972), p. 159.

15. Geoffrey Wansell, *Haunted Idol: The Story of the Real Cary Grant* (New York: Morrow, 1984), p. 231.

16. Gary Morecambe and Martin Sterling, *Cary Grant: In Name Only* (London: Robson Books, 2001), pp. 211–212.

17. Jerry Vermilye, *Cary Grant* (New York: Pyramid, 1973), p. 124.

18. Nixon, *I Could Have Sung All Night*, p. 97.

19. Lionel Godfrey, *Cary Grant: The Light Touch* (New York: St. Martin's, 1981), p. 136.

20. Thomas M. Pryor, "New Film Offered to Deborah Kerr," *New York Times*, February 18, 1957, p. 22.

21. David Richards, *Played Out: The Jean Seberg Story* (New York: Random House, 1981), p. 62.

22. Foster Hirsch, *Otto Preminger: The Man Who Would Be King* (New York: Knopf, 2007), p. 268.

23. Richards, *Played Out*, p. 63.

24. Graham Lord, *Niv: The Authorized Biography of David Niven* (New York: St. Martin's, 2003), p. 195.

25. Hirsch, *Otto Preminger*, p. 270.

26. Logan Gouday, "Miss Kerr's Puzzle," *Daily Express*, July 14, 1957.

27. Barbara Leming, *If This Was Happiness* (New York: Viking, 1989), p. 328.

28. Sidney Skolsky, "Tintyped: Deborah Kerr," New York Post, November 8, 1959.

29. Barry Norman, *The Film Greats* (London : Hodder and Stoughton 1985), p. 42.

30. Peter Haining, *Last Gentleman. Tribute to David Niven* (London: W. H. Allen, 1984), p. 80.

31. Sheridan Morley, *The Other Side of the Moon. The Biography of David Niven* (New York: Harper & Row, 1985), p. 205.

32. Fishgall, *Against Type*, p. 181.

Chapter 9

1. Steven Smith, *Getting to Know Deborah.*

2. Russ Bradley, "It's Never Dull with Yul," *Sunday News*, August 10, 1958, p. 77.

3. *Ibid.*

4. Elizabeth Hardie, "Spot on Yul Brynner," *Film Review*, July 1959, p. 31.

5. "Yul Brynner — Golden Egghead," *Newsweek*, May 19, 1958, pp. 100–103.

6. Peter Viertel, *Dangerous Friends* (New York: Doubleday, 1992), p. 346.

7. *Ibid.*

8. *Ibid.*, p. 347.

9. "Actress Deborah Kerr Estranged from Mate," *Los Angeles Times*, June 1, 1958.

10. Jim Meyer, "Deborah Kerr," *Screen Facts*, N. 19, Vol. 4, 1968, p. 29.

11. David Bret, *Up on Top of a Rainbow* (London: Robson Books: 1992), p. 180.

12. Sheilah Graham, *The Rest of the Story* (New York: Coward-McCann, 1964), p. 253.

13. Gary Fishgall, *Gregory Peck. A Biography* (New York: Scribner, 2002), p. 215.

14. Michael Freedland, *Gregory Peck* (New York: Morrow, 1980), p. 162.

15. Joe Hyams, "Deborah Kerr's Holly-Word Games," *Herald Tribune*, September 9, 1959.

16. Bosley Crowther, "Beloved Infidel," *New York Times*, November 18, 1959, p. 46.

17. Lynn Haney, *Gregory Peck, a Charmed Life* (New York: Carroll & Graff, 2004), p. 287.

18. Sheilah Graham, "The Reel Me Is Deborah," *New York Mirror*, October 11, 1959, p. 46.

Chapter 10

1. Miller, *Fred Zinnemann Interviews*, p. 131.

2. John Mitchum, *Them Ornery Mitchum Boys* (Pacifica: CA: Creatures at Large Press, 1988), p. 191.

3. John Miller, *Peter Ustinov: The Gift of Laughter* (London: Weidenfeld & Nicholson, 2002), p. 104.

4. Christopher Warwick, *The Universal Ustinov* (London: Sidgwick & Jackson 1990), p. 131.

5. Bart Mills, "Deborah Kerr: Late and Early," *Los Angeles Times*, November 28, 1982, p. 26.

6. Alvin H. Marill, *Robert Mitchum on the Screen* (Lancaster, UK: Gazelle Book Services, 1978), p. 10.

7. "Down-to-Earth Deborah," *ABC Film Review*, May 1960, p. 24.

8. Marill, *Robert Mitchum on the Screen*, p. 166.

9. Kitty Kelley, *Elizabeth Taylor: The Last Star.* (London: Michael Joseph, 1981), p. 138.

10. Ken Doeckel, "Deborah Kerr," *Films in Review*, p. 10.

11. Stephen H. Silverman, *Dancing on the Ceiling. Stanley Donen and His Movies* (New York: Knopf, 1996), pp. 280–282.

12. Charles Higham, *Cary Grant: The Lonely Heart* (New York: Harcourt, 1989), pp. 259–260.

13. Silverman, *Dancing on the Ceiling*, p. 282.

14. Silverman, *ibid.*, pp. 282–283.

15. Roddy McDowall, *Double Exposure. Take Three*, p. 232.

16. Noël Coward and Graham Payn, *The Noël Coward Diaries* (New York: Da Capo Press, 2000), p. 441.

17. "Hope by Snow Bride Deborah," *Daily Mail*, July 25, 1960.

18. Jon Whitcomb, "The Ladylike Sexpot," *Cosmopolitan*, March 1961, p. 20.

19. Stuart M. Kaminsky, *Coop: The Life and Legend of Gary Cooper* (New York: St. Martin's, 1980), p. 211.

20. *Ibid.*

21. Hermione Gingold, *How to Grow Old Disgracefully* (London: Gollancz, 1989), p. 158.

22. Stephen Rebello, "Jack Clayton's The Innocents," *Cinefantastique*, June 1983, p. 52.

23. *Ibid.*, p. 53.

Chapter 11

1. C.R., "Deborah's TV Debut," *Daily Mail*, December 30, 1963.

2. Val Adams, "Star to Make Video Trilogy by Tad," *New York Times*, December 17, 1961, p. 25.

3. Roderick Mann, *Sunday Express*, March 17, 1963.

4. William Hall, "That's the New Deborah," *Evening News*, April 20 1963.

5. Ronald Neame, *Straight from the Horse's Mouth* (Lanham, MD: The Scarecrow Press, 2003), p. 196.

6. Anne Sebba, *Enid Bagnold: A Biography* (London: Weidenfeld and Nicolson, 1986), p. 236.

7. Lydia Lane, "Deborah, the Willowy One," *Los Angeles Times*, August 11, 1963, p. 11.

8. Deborah Kerr," The Days and Nights of the Iguana," *Esquire*, May 1964, p. 132.

9. Ava Gardner, *Ava: My Story* (New York: Bantam Books, 1990), p. 249.

10. Deborah Kerr, "The Days and Nights of the Iguana," *Esquire*, May 1964, p. 140.

11. *Ibid.*, p. 132.

12. Ross Lowell, *On the Trail with the Iguana*, Warner Bros., 1964.

13. Tavernier, *Amis Américains*, p. 406.

Chapter 12

1. Wes Herschensohn, *Resurrection in Cannes: The Making of the Picasso Summer* (London: A. S. Barnes, 1979), p. 70.

2. Jim Meyer, "Deborah Kerr," *Screen Facts*, N. 19, Vol. 4, 1968, p. 37.

3. David Hemmings, *Blow-Up and Other Exaggerations* (London: Robson Books, 2004), p. 125.

4. Steve Chibnall, *J. Lee Thompson* (Manchester: Manchester University Press, 2000), p. 308.

5. Sheilah Graham, "Deborah Doing One Film a Year," *New York Post*, September 21, 1967, p. 36.

6. Hemmings, *Blow-Up and Other Exaggerations*, pp. 218–219.

7. Fishgall, *Against Type*, p. 259.

8. *Ibid.*, p. 267.

9. Kelvin Thomas, "Deborah Kerr and the Lady Image," *Los Angeles Times*, January 15, 1969.

10. "Remarkable Miss Kerr," *West Style*, April 27, 1969, p. 17.

11. Tom Burke, "That's Why the Lady Is a Lady," *New York Times*, June 22, 1969.

12. Richard Schickel, *Elia Kazan: A Biography* (New York: HarperCollins, 2005), p. 426.

13. Michel Ciment, *Kazan on Kazan* (London: Secker & Warburg, 1973), p. 158.

14. Braun, *Deborah Kerr*, p. 208.

Chapter 13

1. "Miss Kerr, in an Absolute Funk," *The Evening Standard*, December 31, 1971.

2. Dorothy Manners, "Deborah Kerr Gets Eerie Gift," *Los Angeles Herald-Examiner*, September 19, 1973.

3. Mel Gussow, *Edward Albee: A Singular Journey* (London: Oberon Books, 1999), p. 291.

4. *Ibid.*, p. 293.

5. Florence Fletcher, "Deborah Kerr: A Figure in an Enigmatic 'Seascape,'" *Cue*, January 27, 1975, p. 64.

6. Ron Pennington, "Curtain Calls," *Hollywood Reporter*, February 17, 1977.

7. Charlton Heston, *In the Arena* (New York: HarperCollins, 1995), p. 487.

8. Ron Pennington, "Curtain Calls," *Hollywood Reporter*, February 17, 1977.

9. Sheridan Morley, "Deborah Kerr on Her Return to the Theatre," *The Times*, May 5, 1981.

10. *Ibid.*

11. Miller, *Peter Ustinov*, p. 176.

12. David Lazar, *Michael Powell Interviews* (Jackson: University Press of Mississippi, 2003), p. 103.

Chapter 14

1. Bart Mills, "Deborah Kerr: Late and Early," *Los Angeles Times*, November 28, 1982, p. 24.

2. Kay Gardella, "'Witness' Puts Kerr in Drive," *Daily News*, December 1, 1982.

3. Brian Baxter, Deborah Kerr, *Film & Filming*, December 1984, p. 16.

4. *Ibid.*

5. Marybeth Kerrigan, "Deborah Kerr: A Rose in the Garden," *Women's Wear Daily*, August 11, 1986, p. 12.

6. Nick Roddick, "On Location: The Assam Garden," *Still*, n.13, October 1984, p. 40.

7. Walter Goodman, "Displaced Persons," *New York Times*, July 30, 1986, p. 18.

8. "Heaven Knows, and So Does Mr. Mitchum," *Photoplay*, February 1985, pp. 11–13.

9. Douglas Thompson, "Mitch and Kerr: Back with the Magic Match," *TV Times*, March 22, 1986, p. 5.

10. "Shame of Forgetful Deborah," *Daily Express*, April 11, 1985.

11. Lynda Lee-Potter, "We Love You," *Daily Mail*, May 5, 1985.

12. Barry Wigmore, "Nightmare of Deborah Kerr...," *Sunday People*, April 14, 1986.

13. Lynda Lee-Potter, "We Love You," *Daily Mail*, May 5, 1985.

14. Martin Hoyle, "The Corn Is Green," *Play & Players*, July 1985, p. 22.

15. Victor Davis, "For Those Brief Moments Cary and I Loved Each Other...," *Mail on Sunday*, August 8, 1993, p. 31.

Bibliography

Andersen, Christopher. *An Affair to Remember.* New York: Morrow 1997.

Andreychuck, Ed. *Burt Lancaster. A Filmography and Biography.* Jefferson, NC: McFarland, 2000.

Ashman, Chuck, and Pamela Trescott, *Cary Grant.* London: W. H. Allen, 1987.

Babington, Bruce, *British Stars and Stardom.* Manchester: Manchester University Press, 2001.

_____. *Launder and Gilliat.* Manchester: Manchester University Press, 2000.

Barrow, Kenneth. *Flora: An Appreciation of the Life and Work of Dame Flora Robson.* London: Heinemann, 1981.

_____. *Mr. Chips: The Life of Robert Donat.* London: Methuen, 1985.

Bartley, Anthony. *Smoke Trails in the Sky.* London: William Kimber, 1984.

Base, Ron. *Starring Roles.* London: Little, Brown, 1994.

Borgnine, Ernest. *Ernie. The Autobiography.* New York: Citadel Press, 2008.

Brady, John. *The Craft of the Screenwriter.* New York: Touchstone, 1981.

Braun, Eric. *Deborah Kerr.* New York: St. Martin's, 1978.

Bret, David. *Clark Gable. Tormented Star.* New York: Carroll & Graf, 2007.

_____. *Up on Top of a Rainbow.* London: Robson Books, 1992.

Brode, Douglas. *The Films of the Fifties.* Secaucus, NJ: Citadel Press, 1976.

Brown, Geoff. *The Common Touch: The Films of John Baxter.* London: NTF Dossier N°5, 1989.

_____. *Launder and Gilliat.* London: BFI, 1977.

Brownlow, Kevin. *David Lean.* London: Richard Cohen Books, 1996.

Brynner, Rock. *Yul, the Man Who Would Be King.* New York: Simon & Schuster, 1989.

Brynner, Victoria. *Yul Brynner: Photographer.* New York: Abrams, 1996.

Buehrer, Beverley Bare. *Cary Grant: A Bio-Bibliography.* Westport, CT: Greenwood, 1990.

Burkart, Jeff, and Stuart Bruce. *Hollywood's First Choices.* New York: Crown Trade, 1994.

Callow, Simon. *Charles Laughton: A Difficult Actor.* London: Methuen, 1987.

Capua, Michelangelo. *Anthony Perkins. Prigioniero della paura.* Turin: Lindau, 2003.

_____. *Montgomery Clift: A Biography.* Jefferson, NC: McFarland, 2002.

_____. *Yul Brynner: A Biography.* Jefferson, NC: McFarland, 2005.

Carey, Gary. *Cukor & Co. The Films of George Cukor and His Collaborators.* New York: MOMA, 1971.

Casper, Joseph Andrew. *Stanley Donen.* Metuchen, NJ: The Scarecrow Press, 1983.

Chapman, James. *The British at War.* London: I. B. Tauris, 1998.

Chassagnard, Guy. *Charles Boyer.* Paris: Segnat Editions, 1999.

Chibnall, Steve. *J. Lee Thompson.* Manchester: Manchester University Press, 2000.

Christie, Ian, and Andrew Moor. *The Cinema of Michael Powell.* London: BFI, 2005.

Ciment, Michel. *Kazan on Kazan.* London: Secker & Warburg, 1973.

Clinch, Minty. *Burt Lancaster.* New York: Stein and Day, 1985.

Coppedge, Walter. *Henry King's America.* Metuchen, NJ: The Scarecrow Press, 1986.

Coursodon, Jean Pierre. *American Directors II.* New York: McGraw-Hill, 1983.

Croall, Jonathan. *Sybil Thorndike: A Star of Life.* London: Haus Books, 2008.

Crowther, Bruce. *Mitchum: The Film Career of Robert Mitchum.* London: Robert Hale, 1991.

Culver, Roland. *Not Quite a Gentleman.* London: William Kimber, 1979.

Cushing, Peter. *Past Forgetting.* London: Weidenfeld and Nicolson, 1988.

Cushman, Robert, and Endress Stacey. *Hollywood at Your Feet.* Los Angeles: Pomegrate Press, 1992.

D'Antonio, Joanne. *Andrew Marton.* Metuchen, NJ: The Directors Guild of America & The Scarecrow Press, 1991.

Daniell, John. *Ava Gardner.* London: W. H. Allen, 1982.

Darlow, Michael. *Terence Rattigan: The Man and His Work.* London: Quartet Books, 2000.

Davis, Ronald L. *Van Johnson: MGM's Golden Boy.* Jackson, MS: University Press of Mississippi, 2001.

Demongeot, Mylène. *Tiroirs secrets.* Paris: Le Pré aux Clercs, 2001.

Deschner, Donald. *The Films of Cary Grant.* Secaucus, NJ: Citadel Press, 1973.

_____. *The Films of Spencer Tracy.* Secaucus, NJ: Citadel Press, 1968.

Dick, Bernard F. *Joseph L. Mankiewicz.* Boston: Twayne, 1983.

_____. *The Merchant Prince of Poverty Row: Harry Cohn of Columbia Pictures.* Lexington: University of Kentucky Press, 1993.

Dickens, Homer. *The Films of Gary Cooper.* Secaucus, NJ: Citadel Press, 1974.

Dmytryk, Edward. *It's a Hell of a Life but Not a Bad Living.* New York: Times Books, 1978.

Douglas, Kirk. *The Ragman's Son: An Autobiography.* New York: Simon & Schuster, 1998.

Downing, David. *Robert Mitchum.* London: W. H. Allen, 1985.

Drazin, Charles. *The Finest Years: British Cinema of the 1940s.* London: I. B. Tauris, 2007.

_____. *Korda. Britain's Only Movie Mogul.* London: Sidgwick & Jackson, 2002.

Dukore, Bernard F. *Bernard Shaw and Gabriel Pascal.* Toronto: University of Toronto Press, 1996.

Dunaway, Faye. *Looking for Gatsby.* New York: Simon & Schuster, 1995.

Dunbar, Janet. *Flora Robson.* London: George G. Harrap & Co., 1960.

Edelman, Rob, and Audrey E. Kupferberg. *Angela Lansbury: A Life on Stage and Screen.* New York: Birch Lane Press, 1996.

Eliot, Marc. *Cary Grant.* New York: Harmony Books, 2004.

Epstein, Edward Z. *Portrait of Jennifer: A Biography of Jennifer Jones.* New York: Simon & Schuster, 1995.

Essoe, Gabe. *The Films of Clark Gable.* Secaucus, NJ: Citadel Press, 1970.

Eyles, Allen. *Rex Harrison.* London: W. H. Allen, 1985.

Farrar, David. *No Royal Road.* London: Mortimer Publication, 1947.

Fisher, James *Spencer Tracy. A Bio-Bibliography.* Westport, CT: Greenwood Press, 1994.

Fishgall, Gary. *Against Type: The Biography of Burt Lancaster.* New York: Scribner, 1995.

Flamini, Roland. *Ava Gardner.* New York: Coward, McCann, 1983.

Forbes, Bryan. *Ned's Girl. The Authorized Biography of Dame Edith Evans*. London: Elm Tree Books, 1977.

Fowler, Karin J. *Ava Gardner: A Bio-Bibliography*. Westport, CT: Greenwood Press, 1990.

_____. *David Niven: A Bio-Bibliography*. Westport, CT: Greenwood Press, 1995.

Freedland, Michael. *Gregory Peck*. New York: Morrow, 1980.

Friedman, Lenemaja. *Enid Bagnold*. Boston: Twayne, 1986.

Frischauer, Willi. *Behind the Scenes of Otto Preminger*. NY: Morrow, 1974.

Fultz, Jay. *In Search of Donna Reed*. Iowa City: University of Iowa Press, 1998.

Garceau, Jean, and Inez Cocke. *Dear Mr. G-. The Biography of Clark Gable*. Boston: Little, Brown, 1961.

Gardner, Ava. *Ava: My Story*. New York: Bantam Books, 1990.

Garrett, Gerald. *The Films of David Niven*. London: LSP Books, 1975.

Gaston, George. *Jack Clayton. A Guide to References and Resources*. Boston: G. K. Hall, 1981.

Gehring, Wes D. *Leo McCarey*. Lanham, MD: The Scarecrow Press, 2005.

Geist, Kenneth L. *Pictures Will Talk. The Life and Films of Joseph L. Mankiewicz*. New York: Scribner's, 1978.

Giles, James. *James Jones*, Boston: Twayne, 1981.

Gingold, Hermione. *How to Grow Old Disgracefully*. London Victor Gollancz, 1989.

Godfrey, Lionel. *Cary Grant: The Light Touch*. New York: St. Martin's, 1981.

Gott, Mark. *Balancing Act: The Authorized Biography of Angela Lansbury*. New York: Little Brown, 1999.

Graham, Sheilah. *My Hollywood: A Celebration and a Lament*. London: Michael Joseph, 1984.

_____. *The Garden of Allah*. New York: Crown, 1970.

_____. *The Rest of the Story*. New York: Coward-McCann, 1964.

Granger, Stewart. *Sparks Fly Upward*. London: Granada, 1981.

Gray, Beverly. *Ron Howard: From Mayberry to the Moon ... and Beyond*. Nashville, TN: Rutledge Hill Press, 2003.

Griffin, Mark. *A Hundred or More Hidden Things. The Life and Films of Vincente Minnelli*. New York: Da Capo Press, 2010.

Griggs, John. *The Films of Gregory Peck*. Secaucus, NJ: Citadel Press, 1984.

Grobel Lawrence. *The Hustons*. New York: Avon Books, 1990.

Guerif, François. *Vincente Minnelli,* Paris: Edilig, 1984.

Gussow, Mel. *Edward Albee: A Singular Journey*. London: Oberon books, 1999.

Hadleigh, Boze. *Leading Ladies*. London: Robson Books, 1992.

Haining, Peter. *The Last Gentleman: A Tribute to David Niven*. London: W. H. Allen, 1984.

Haney, Lynn. *Gregory Peck: A Charmed Life*. New York: Carroll & Graf, 2004.

Harding, James. *Emlyn Williams: A Life*. London: Weidenfeld & Nicolson, 1993.

_____. *Maurice Chevalier*. London: Secker & Warburg, 1992.

Harrison, Rex. *A Damned Serious Business*. London: Bantam Press, 1991.

_____. *Rex: The Autobiography of Rex Harrison*. New York: Morrow, 1975.

Harvey, Stephen. *Directed by Vincente Minnelli*. New York: The Museum of Modern Art/ Harper & Row, 1989.

Hay, Peter. *Broadway Anecdotes*. New York: Oxford University Press, 1989.

_____. *Movie Anecdotes*. New York: Oxford University Press, 1991.

Hemmings, David. *Blow-Up and Other Exaggerations*. London: Robson Books, 2004.

Henry, Marilyn, and Ron DeSourdis. *The Films of Alan Ladd*. Secaucus, NJ: Citadel Press, 1981.

Herschensohn, Wes. *Resurrection in Cannes. The Making of the Picasso Summer*. Cranbury, NJ: A. S. Barnes, 1979.

Heston, Charlton. *The Actor's Life Journals: 1956–1976*. New York: Dutton, 1978.

_____. *In the Arena: An Autobiography.* New York: Simon & Schuster, 1995.

Higham, Charles. *Charles Laughton: An Intimate Biography.* London: W. H. Allen, 1976.

_____. *Merchant of Dreams. Louis B. Mayer, M.G.M., and the Secret Hollywood.* New York: Donald I. Fine, 1993.

_____. *Sisters: The Story of Olivia de Havilland and Joan Fontaine.* New York: Coward-McCann, 1984.

_____, and Roy Moseley. *Cary Grant: The Lonely Heart.* New York: Harcourt Brace Jovanovich, 1989.

Hill, James. *Rita Hayworth: A Memoir.* New York: Simon & Schuster, 1983.

Hirsch, Foster. *Otto Preminger: The Man Who Would Be King.* New York: Knopf, 2007.

Hirschhorn, Clive. *The Films of James Mason.* London: LSP Books, 1975.

Holtzman, Will. *William Holden.* New York: Pyramid Publication, 1976.

Houseman, John. *Front and Center.* New York: Simon & Schuster, 1979.

Howard, James. *Michael Powell.* London: B. T. Batsford, 1976.

Hunter Allan. *Burt Lancaster: The Man and His Movies.* Edinburgh: Paul Harris, 1984.

_____. *Faye Dunaway.* New York: St. Martin's, 1986.

_____. *Gene Hackman.* London: W. H. Allen, 1987.

Huston, John. *An Open Book.* New York: Knopf, 1980.

Jamison, R. J. *Grayson Hall: A Hard Act to Follow.* New York: iUniverse 2006.

Kalfatovic, Mary C. *Montgomery Clift: A Bio-Bibliography.* Westport, CT: Greenwood Press, 1994.

Kaminsky, Stuart M. *Coop: The Life and Legend of Gary Cooper.* New York: St. Martin's, 1980.

Kanfer, Stefan. *Groucho: The Life and Times of Julius Henry Marx.* London: Penguin Books, 2001.

Kashner, Sam, and Jennifer MacNair. *The Bad & the Beautiful. Hollywood in the Fifties.* London: Little Brown, 2002.

Kazan, Elia. *A Life.* New York: Knopf, 1988.

Kelley, Kitty. *Elizabeth Taylor: The Last Star.* London: Michael Joseph, 1981.

_____. *His Way: The Unauthorized Biography of Frank Sinatra.* New York: Bantam Books, 1985.

Kennedy, A. L. *The Life and Death of Colonel Blimp.* London: BFI, 1997.

Knight, Vivienne. *Trevor Howard: A Gentleman and a Player.* New York: Beaufort Books, 1987.

Kobal, John. *Romance & the Cinema.* London: Studio Vista, 1973.

Kolin, Philip C. *Conversations with Edward Albee.* Jackson: University Press of Mississippi, 1988.

Korda, Michael, *Charmed Lives.* New York: Perennial, 2002.

Kulik, Karol. *Alexander Korda.* London: W. H. Allen, 1975.

Lacourbe, Roland. *Burt Lancaster.* Paris: Edilig, 1987.

LaGuardia, Robert. *Monty: A Biography of Montgomery Clift.* New York: Arbor House, 1977.

Landstone, Charles. *I Gate-Crashed.* London: Stainer & Bell, 1976.

Lazar, David. *Michael Powell Interviews.* Jackson: University of Mississippi Press, 2001.

Leaming, Barbara. *If This Was Happiness: A Biography of Rita Hayworth.* New York: Viking Press, 1989.

Leff, Leonard J., and Jerold L. Simmons. *The Dame in the Kimono.* New York: Grove Weidenfeld, 1991.

Leigh, Janet. *There Really Was a Hollywood.* Garden City, NY: Doubleday, 1984.

LeRoy, Mervyn, and Dick Kleiner, *Mervyn LeRoy: Take One.* New York: Hawthorne Book, 1974.

Levitt, Alfred Lewis. *Tender Comrades.* New York: St. Martin's, 1977.

Levy, Emanuel. *George Cukor, Master of Elegance.* New York: Morrow, 1994.

Levy, Shawn. *Rat Pack Confidential.* London: Fourth Estate, 1998.

Lew, Peter. *Transforming the Screen.* Berkeley: University of California Press, 2003.

Leyda, Jay. *Voice of Film Experience.* New York: Macmillan, 1977.

Linet, Beverly. *Ladd: The Life, the Legend, the Legacy of Alan Ladd.* New York: Arbor House, 1979.

_____. *Star-Crossed. The Story of Robert Walker and Jennifer Jones.* New York: Putnam, 1986.

Lord, Graham. *Niv: The Authorized Biography of David Niven.* London: Orion, 2003.

Love, Damien. *Robert Mitchum: Solid Dad Crazy.* London: B. T. Batsford, 2002.

MacFarlane, Brian. *Lance Comfort.* Manchester: Manchester University Press, 1999.

MacShane, Frank. *Into the Eternity: In the Life of James Jones, American Writer.* Boston: Houghton Mifflin, 1985.

Madsen, Axel. *John Huston.* New York: Doubleday, 1978.

Marill, Alvin H. *Robert Mitchum on the Screen.* London: Barnes, 1978.

Martin, Mart. *Did He or Didn't He?* New York: Citadel Press, 2000.

Mason, James. *Before I Forget.* London: Hamish Hamilton, 1985.

McBride, Joseph. *Kirk Douglas.* New York: Pyramid Publication, 1976.

McCallum, John. *Life with Googie.* London: Heinemann 1979.

McCarthy, John. *The Films of John Huston.* Secaucus, NJ: Citadel Press, 1987.

McDougal, Dennis. *The Last Mogul.* New York: Crown, 1998.

McDowall, Roddy. *Double Exposure: Take Three.* New York: Morrow, 1992.

_____. *Double Exposure: Take Four.* New York: Morrow, 1993.

McGilligan, Patrick. *Backstory 2: Interviews with Screenwriters of the 1940s and 1950s.* Berkeley: University of California Press, 1991.

Mellen, Joan. *Big Bad Wolves: Masculinity in the American Films.* New York: Pantheon Books, 1977.

Menjou, Adolphe, and M. M. Mussel-

man. *It Took Nine Taylors.* New York: McGraw-Hill, 1948.

Meyer, William. *Warner Brothers Directors: The Hard Boiled, the Comic, and the Weepers.* New Rochelle, NY: Arlington House, 1978.

Meyers, Jeffrey. *Gary Cooper: An American Hero.* London: Robert Hale, 2001.

Miller, Gabriel. *Fred Zinnemann Interviews.* Jackson: University Press of Mississippi, 2004.

Miller, John. *Peter Ustinov: The Gift of Laughter.* London: Orion, 2003.

Minnelli, Vincente. *I Remember It Well.* New York: Doubleday, 1974.

Mitchum, John. *Them Ornery Mitchum Boys.* Pacifica, CA: Creatures at Large Press, 1989.

Moix, Terenci. *Mis inmortales del cine Hollywood. años 50.* Barcelona: Planeta, 2001.

Molt, Cynthia. *Vivien Leigh: A Bio-Bibliography.* Westport, CT: Greenwood Press, 1992.

Molyneaux, Gerard. *Gregory Peck: A Bio-Bibliography.* Westport, CT: Greenwood Press, 1995.

Morecambe, Gary, and Martin Sterling. *Cary Grant: In Name Only.* London: Robson Books, 2001.

Morgan, Thomas B. *Self-Creations 13 Impersonalities.* London: Michael Joseph, 1966.

Morley, Margaret. *Larger Than Life. A Biography of Robert Morley.* London: Robson Books, 1979.

Morley, Sheridan. *Gladys Cooper: A Biography,* New York: McGraw-Hill, 1979.

_____. *James Mason: Odd Man Out.* New York: Harper & Row, 1989.

_____. *The Other Side of the Moon.* New York: Harper & Row, 1985.

_____. *Our Theatres in the Eighties.* London: Hodder & Stoughton, 1991.

_____. *Robert: My Father.* London: Weidenfeld and Nicolson, 1993.

_____. *Tales from the Hollywood Raj.* New York: The Viking Press, 1983.

Moseley, Roy. *Evergreen. Victor Saville in*

His Own Words. Carbondale: Southern
Illinois University Press, 2000.

_____. *Rex Harrison: The First Biography.*
London: New English Library, 1987.

_____. *Roger Moore: A Biography.* London:
New English Library, 1985.

Munn, Michael. *Charlton Heston.* New
York: St. Martin's 1986.

_____. *The Films of Kirk Douglas.* Secau-
cus, NJ: Citadel Press, 1972.

_____. *Gene Hackman.* London: Robert
Hale, 1997.

_____. *Trevor Howard: The Man and His
Films.* Chelsea, MI: Scarborough
House, 1990.

Murdoch, Helen. *Travelling Hopefully. The
Story of Molly Urquart.* Edinburgh: Paul
Harris, 1981.

Neame, Ronald. *Straight from the Horse's
Mouth.* Lanham, MD: The Scarecrow
Press, 2003.

Negulesco, Jean. *Things I Did ... and
Things I Think I Did.* New York: Lin-
den Press, 1984.

Nelson, Nancy. *Evenings with Cary Grant.*
New York: Morrow, 1991.

Nesbitt, Cathleen. *A Little Love & Good
Company.* London: Faber & Faber, 1975.

Niven, David. *The Moon's a Balloon.* New
York: Putnam, 1972.

Nixon, Marni. *I Could Have Sung All
Night.* New York: Billboard Books,
2006.

Nolan, William F. *John Huston: King
Rebel,* Los Angeles: Sherbourne Press,
1965.

Norman, Barry. *The Film Greats.* London:
Hodder and Stoughton, 1995.

Palmer, Lilli. *Change Lobster — and Dance:
An Autobiography.* New York: Macmillan, 1975.

Palmer, Scott. *The Films of Agatha
Christie.* London: B. T. Batsford 1993.

Paris, Barry. *Audrey Hepburn.* New York:
Putnam, 1996.

_____. *Garbo: A Biography.* New York:
Knopf, 1995.

Parish, James Robert. *Hollywood's Great
Love Teams.* Carlstadt, NJ: Rainbow
Books, 1974.

_____, and Don E. Stanke. *The
Debonairs.* New Rochelle, NY: Arlington House, 1975.

_____, and _____. *The Swashbucklers.*
New Rochelle, NY: Arlington House,
1976.

Parish, James Robert, and Mark Gregory.
The Hollywood Reliables. Westport, CT:
Arlington House, 1980.

Parish, James Robert, and Ronald L. Bowers. *The MGM Stock Company.* New
Rochelle, NY: Arlington House, 1973.

Pascal, Valerie. *The Discipline and His
Devil.* London: Michael Joseph, 1971.

Pettigrew, Terence. *Trevor Howard: A Personal Biography.* London: Peter Owen,
2001.

Phillips, Gene. *Beyond the Epic: The Life
and Films of Davis Lean.* Lexington:
The University Press of Kentucky,
2006.

_____. *The Films of Tennessee Williams.*
East Brunswick, NJ: Associated University Press, 1980.

_____. *George Cukor.* Boston: Twayne,
1982.

Pickard, Roy. *Frank Sinatra at the Movies.*
London: Robert Hale, 1994.

Porter, Darwin. *Brando Unzipped.* New
York: Blue Moon Productions, 2006.

_____. *Merv Griffin: A Life in the Closet.*
New York: Blue Moon Productions,
2009.

Powell, Michael. *A Life in Movies.* London
Faber & Faber, 2000.

Pratley, Gerald. *The Cinema of Otto Preminger.* New York: Castle Books, 1971.

_____. *The Films of John Frankenheimer.*
London: Cygnus Art, 1998.

_____. *The Films of John Huston.* London:
Barnes, 1977.

Quirk, Lawrence J. *The Complete Films of
William Holden.* Secaucus, NJ: Citadel
Press, 1986.

Read, Piers Paul. *Alec Guinness: The Authorized Biography.* New York: Simon
& Schuster, 2003.

Richards, David. *Played Out. The Jean Seberg Story.* New York: Random House,
1981.

Ringgold, Gene. *The Films of Rita Hayworth.* Secaucus, NJ: Citadel Press, 1974.

Ringgold, Gene, and Clifford McCarty. *The Films of Frank Sinatra.* Secaucus, NJ: Citadel Press, 1971.

Ringgold, Gene, and Dewitt Bodeen. *Chevalier: The Films and Career of Maurice Chevalier.* Secaucus, NJ: Citadel Press, 1973.

Robbins, Jhan. *Yul Brynner: The Inscrutable King.* New York: Dodd, Mead, 1987.

Roberts, Jerry. *Mitchum in His Own Words.* New York: Limelight Editions, 2000.

Robertson, James. *The British Board of Film Censors.* London: Croom Helm, 1985.

Salter, Elizabeth. *Helpmann: The Authorized Biography of Sir Robert Helpmann, CBE.* Brighton: Angus & Robertson, 1978.

Salwolke, Scott. *The Films of Michael Powell and the Archers.* Lanham, MD: The Scarecrow Press, 2005.

Sanders, Dennis. *The Agatha Christie Companion.* London: W. H. Allen, 1985.

Schary, Dore. *Heyday: An Autobiography.* Boston: Little, Brown, 1979.

Schickel, Richard. *Elia Kazan: A Biography.* New York: HarperCollins, 2005.

Schoell, William. *Martini Man: The Life of Dean Martin.* New York: Cooper Square Press, 2003.

Schumach, Murray: *The Face on the Cutting Room Floor.* New York: Morrow, 1964.

Sebba, Anne. *Enid Bagnol: A Biography.* London: Weidenfeld and Nicholson, 1986.

Sennett, Ted. *Master of Menace: Greenstreet and Lorre.* New York: Dutton, 1979.

Server, Lee. *Ava Gardner: Love is Nothing.* New York: St. Martin's, 2006.

_____. *Robert Mitchum: Baby, I Don't Care.* New York: St. Martin's, 2001.

Sheldon, Sidney. *The Other Side of Me.* New York: Warner Books, 2005.

Shiach, Don. *Stewart Granger: The Last of the Swashbucklers.* London: Aurum, 2005.

Shipman, David. *The Great Movie Stars: The International Years.* London: Angus & Robertson, 1972.

Shnayerson, Michael. *Irwin Shaw: A Biography.* New York: Putnam, 1989.

Silverman, Stephen M. *Dancing on the Ceiling.* New York: Knopf, 1996.

Sinatra, Nancy. *Frank Sinatra, My Father.* London: Hodder and Stoughton, 1995.

Singer, Kurt. *The Charles Laughton Story.* London: Robert Hale, 1954.

Sklar, Robert. *Resisting Images: Essays on Cinema and History.* Philadelphia: Temple University Press, 1990.

Spada, James. *Peter Lawford: The Man Who Kept the Secrets.* London: Bantam Press, 1991.

Spicer, Paul. *Herbert Howells.* Wales: Seren Books, 1999.

Strachan, Alan. *Secret Dreams: The Biography of Michael Redgrave.* London: Weidenfeld & Nicholson, 2004.

Street, Sarah. *Black Narcissus.* London: I. B. Tauris, 2005.

Stricklyn, Ray. *Angels & Demons.* Los Angeles: Belle Publishing, 1999.

Suntree, Susan. *Rita Moreno.* New York: Chelsea House Publishers, 1993.

Swenson, Karen. *Greta Garbo: A Life Apart.* New York: Scribners, 1997.

Swindell, Larry. *Charles Boyer: The Reluctant Lover,* New York: Doubleday, 1983.

_____. *Spencer Tracy: A Biography.* New York: The World Publishing Company, 1969.

Tabori, Paul. *Alexander Korda.* London: Oldbourne, 1959.

Tanitch, Robert. *John Mills.* London: Collins & Brown, 1993.

Taraborrelli, J. Randy. *Sinatra. Behind the Legend.* New York: Birch Lane Press, 1997.

Tavernier, Bertrand. *Amis Américains.* Paris: Actes Sud, 1993.

Thomas, Bob. *Golden Boy: The Untold Story of William Holden.* New York: St. Martin's, 1983.

Thomas, Bob. *King Cohn*. New York: Putnam's Son, 1967.

Thomas, Tony. *Ustinov on Focus*. New York: A. J. Barnes, 1971.

Thornton, Michael. *Jessie Matthews. A Biography*. London: Hart-Davis, MacGibbon, 1974.

Tims, Hilton. *Once a Wicked Lady: A Biography of Margaret Lockwood*. London: Virgin Books, 1989.

Todd, Ann. *The Eighth Veil*. London: William Kimber, 1980.

Tomkies, Mike. *The Robert Mitchum Story*. Chicago: Henry Regnery, 1972.

Toress, Augusto. *Vincente Minnelli*. Madrid: Cátedra, 1995.

Tornabene, Lyn. *Long Live the King: A Biography of Clark Gable*. New York: Putnam's, 1976.

Towers, Harry Alan, and Leslie Mitchell. *The March of the Movies*. London: Sampson Low, Marston, 1947.

Trewin, J. C. *Robert Donat: A Biography*, London: Heinemann, 1968.

Troyan, Michael. *A Rose for Mrs. Miniver: The Life of Greer Garson*. Lexington: The University Press of Kentucky, 1999.

Ustinov, Peter. *Dear Me*. London: Heinemann, 1977.

Vermilye, Jerry. *Cary Grant*. New York: Pyramid Publication, 1973.

_____. *The Great British Films*. Secaucus, NJ: Citadel Press, 1978.

Vickers, Hugo. *Cecil Beaton: The Authorized Biography*. London: Weidenfeld and Nicolson, 1985.

_____. *Vivien Leigh: A Biography*, Boston: Little Brown, 1988.

Walker, Alexander. *Elizabeth*. London: Weidenfeld & Nicolson, 1990.

Wallace, David. *Exiles in Hollywood*. New York: Limelight Editions, 2006.

Wander Bonanno, Margaret. *Angela Lansbury: A Biography*. New York: St. Martin's, 1987.

Wansell, Goeffrey. *Cary Grant: Dark Angel*. New York: Arcade Publishing, 1996.

_____. *Haunted Idol: The Real Story of Cary Grant*. New York: Morrow, 1984.

Warwick, Christopher. *The Universal Ustinov*. London: Sidgwick & Jackson, 1990.

Wayne, Jane Ellen. *Gable's Women*. New York: Prentice Hall, 1987.

_____. *The Golden Guys of MGM*. London: Robson Books, 2004.

_____. *The Leading Men of MGM*. New York: Da Capo Press, 2005

_____. *Robert Taylor*. London: Robson Books, 1991.

Williams, Esther. *The Million Dollar Mermaid*. New York: Simon & Schuster, 1999.

Williams, Tony. *Structures of Desire*. New York: State University of New York, 2002.

Windeler, Robert. *Burt Lancaster*. New York: St. Martin's, 1984.

Zinnemann, Fred. *A Life in the Movies: An Autobiography*. New York: Scribner's, 1992.

Index